CLEAN UP YOUR CREDIT

CLEAN UP YOUR CREDIT

A Black Ops Guide to
Credit Repair and Restoration

RJ Mansfield

Guilford, Connecticut

An imprint of Globe Pequot, the trade division of The Rowman & Littlefield Publishing Group, Inc.
4501 Forbes Blvd., Ste. 200
Lanham, MD 20706
www.rowman.com

Distributed by NATIONAL BOOK NETWORK

British Library Cataloguing in Publication Information available

Library of Congress Cataloging-in-Publication Data available

ISBN 978-1-4930-6401-4 (paperback)
ISBN 978-1-4930-6697-1 (e-book)

♾️™ The paper used in this publication meets the minimum requirements of American National Standard for Information Sciences—Permanence of Paper for Printed Library Materials, ANSI/NISO Z39.48-1992.

Legal Disclaimer
The information contained in this book is not intended to be legal advice or a substitute for legal advice.

This book is not intended to be a full, comprehensive explanation of law in any area nor should it be used as a replacement for the advice of legal counsel.

The book is a summary of what I have personally done, experienced, and what worked for me. If you need legal advice, contact a licensed attorney. I am not an attorney, and this is not legal advice. If you need advice on tax law or financial matters, contact an accountant or a licensed financial advisor.

While this book describes applicable laws on the subjects covered at the time of its writing, laws continue to develop with the passage of time. Revisions of state and federal consumer protection laws occur rarely and slowly. Even so, before relying exclusively upon this book, care should be taken to verify that the laws described herein have not changed. This can be accomplished by Googling the law you're researching.

Without having a conversation with everyone who reads this book and without knowing the specifics of your particular circumstances, I covered everything I possibly could. For most people, the information in the book will be enough. If you have a particularly difficult situation that's not covered, I offer FREE consultations. I also conduct private, personalized coaching. My coaching includes, among other services, speaking to collectors, creditors, and the credit bureaus on your behalf along with composing letters as needed.

For complete details on coaching and for a FREE consultation, go to my website at www.rickmansfield.com/credit-repair-coaching. You can email me using the form at the bottom of the website page.

If you decide to contact me, let me know you bought the book. I'm happy to answer one or two questions, no strings attached, for people who have purchased my book.

CONTENTS

PREFACE

Bad things happen to good people. Events not always under our control can often result in our credit scores going down—and sometimes way, way down. But there are consumer protection laws you can use to remove negative items from your credit report. Because of a quirk in the law, you can (as I did) remove items that really are yours. The Fair Credit Reporting Act (FCRA) says they must remove unverifiable items. Meaning, if you dispute anything the bureaus are required to contact the information furnisher, who has thirty days to reply. If the credit bureaus don't reply within that thirty-day window, they're required to remove the disputed item from your credit report.

If you go it alone, the credit repair and restoration journey can be a nightmare. I devised a step-by-step guide to clean up your credit that anyone can use. Using the credit restoration tools outlined here, instead of being penalized for years, you can delete every negative item from your credit report.

If you follow the procedures here, you won't need to sue anyone to get the negative listings removed from your credit report. But just in case you want to make some cash, I outlined the procedure for suing on your own in chapter 19. I sued creditors, collection agencies, and the three major credit bureaus: Equifax, Experian, and TransUnion. As a result, I've won or settled lawsuits for over $127,000.

Figure 1 shows a listing of just a few of my suits against collection agencies and credit bureaus. These are only the ones that were in federal court; they don't include suits pursued in state courts or Small Claims Court. This information comes from an internet record called PACER, an acronym for Public Access to Court Electronic Records. Anyone can register to use PACER. It provides the public with online access to more than one billion documents filed in federal courts. If you have ever been part of a lawsuit as a plaintiff or defendant that was filed in a federal court, including bankruptcy, it's recorded here.

I raised my credit score 281 points, from 461 to 742, in less than five months. I didn't pay anyone a dime, not a single cent to the creditors or collection agencies, and I didn't waste time or money on a credit repair company. It's not rocket science or brain surgery. It's being aware of what creditors, credit bureaus, and collection agencies legally can do, can't do, and must do. Once you know your rights and know what to do when those rights are violated, your credit scores and financial future will change dramatically.

I included copies of a few of the checks for some of the suits I've won in this book and on my Twitter page, @DebtAssassin15. I also included dispute letters I wrote to the collection agencies and credit bureaus. I show their response letters to my disputes, telling me that the negative items I disputed were deleted or in some cases that they were "verified, will remain as reported." It's extremely important that you know what to do if you get one

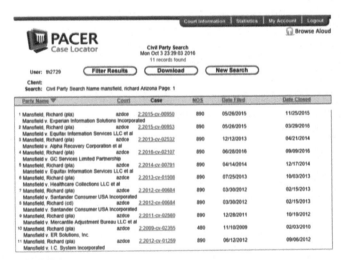

FIGURE 1

of those letters from a credit bureau that says they aren't removing what you disputed.

I've personally done everything I say that you can do. I purposely let my credit go down the crapper, to prove what I claim can be done can actually be done. I had a car repossessed, a foreclosure, tax liens by the state and IRS, civil judgments, and I filed for bankruptcy. Every single item reported is gone, removed from my credit report without paying anyone. I'm not just someone saying, "Hey, you know what you should do?" I put my money where my mouth is. I did it and you can do it too.

If your dispute letter claims an account isn't yours, the creditor may respond saying that the account has been verified. A "not my account" letter will absolutely work if you filed a police report and include it with your letter.

That said, any dispute reason can work! If the information reporter, original creditor, or collection agency fails to respond to the credit bureau in thirty days, the law requires that the disputed account be removed. As I'll point out later, according to the Fair Credit Reporting Act and the Fair Debt Collection Practices Act, it isn't your obligation to file a police report. I never filed a police report regarding any collection account or credit report dispute. It isn't your job to do anything except dispute what they report. It's their job to prove the debt is yours, not your job to prove it isn't.

The only reason I suggest in the book that your first dispute be "not my account" is that sometimes this boils down to a numbers game. The more disputes you send, the more likely that errors will occur on the furnisher's part or the credit bureau's part. The more shots you fire, the more likely you are to hit your target. A "not my account" letter is another bullet in the chamber. The more letters you send for a dispute, the more likely that the information furnisher doesn't respond, and the item is removed. Don't despair. If a dispute letter doesn't work, I outline numerous other weapons to use in your credit restoration arsenal later in the book.

Just in case you're feeling guilty about not paying what they claim you owe, there are two things to keep in mind. First, when lenders set ridiculously high interest rates, their reasoning is that not everyone is going to repay the loans. So, in effect, you're helping them justify their excessive interest rates. Second, if they weren't breaking the law, we wouldn't be winning these lawsuits. The only way that these financial vampires will stop abusing consumers is to make it financially painful for them to

continue their illegal and destructive violations of the law.

To say that the credit reporting and scoring systems are bewildering is an understatement. They are a nightmare. Navigating your way through the maze of laws that were passed to protect consumers is virtually impossible. Even lawyers and judges struggle to interpret consumer protection laws. Consumers all have questions. How do I know when my consumer protection rights are violated? What do I do when they are? This book is based on my forty-nine-plus years of experience in the banking, credit reporting, credit scoring, and collection industries.

I wrote *Clean Up Your Credit* so it can be easily read and understood. I converted the mumbo-jumbo legalese of the important sections of the Fair Debt Collection Practices Act (FDCPA) and Fair Credit Reporting Act (FCRA) into plain English.

Because I wanted to prove everything I did was totally legitimate, I referenced legal cases to show where I found the information I cited and used in my disputes.

I received or made calls to collectors, the credit bureaus, the IRS, bankruptcy courts, and county recorders' offices. I went the extra mile to prove that this isn't some fairy tale, theory, or myth. This book wasn't written by a "credit expert" telling you what you should do that they never did themselves. I did it. This works!

In books like this, most people are interested in information specific to their circumstances. Most people don't read the entire book; they skim. Heck, I do it myself. So, what I did was repeat what I considered the most important ideas in several places, making sure the "skimmers" like me would read the essential concepts.

When I read "how-to" books, all the filler annoys the heck out of me. I don't want to read the history of the automobile to learn how to fix my brakes. Pick out what you need, skip the rest, and come back to the sections you passed over if and when you need them. The single exception to this advice is the section on medical bills in chapter 13. You'll want to know most of the information there before you're aware that you needed it!

In the appendix there are copies of letters I've sent that you can modify to fit your needs. There are also letters I've received, along with copies of some of the checks I cashed for the suits I won. I document everything I did and never recommend you do anything I haven't successfully done myself.

COMMON WORDS, ACRONYMS, AND ABBREVIATIONS

Here are some common words, phrases, acronyms, and abbreviations that I figured the average person might not be familiar with. For instance, a collection agency is noted as CA. The law that governs what, when, and how a CA can communicate with a borrower is called the Fair Debt Collection Practices Act (FDCPA). The law that governs credit reporting agencies is the Fair Credit Reporting Act (FCRA).

AU = Authorized user
BK = Bankruptcy
CA = Collection agency
CRA(s) = Credit reporting agency (usually Experian, Equifax, or TransUnion)
Creditor = Anyone who holds your debt: original creditor, debt buyer, judgment holder, collection agency, attorney, etc.
DVL = Debt validation letter
FACTA = Fair and Accurate Credit Transaction Act (an update of the FCRA)
FCBA = Fair Credit Billing Act
FCRA = Fair Credit Reporting Act
FDCPA = Fair Debt Collection Practices Act
FICO = Widely used credit score from the Fair Isaac Corporation
GLBA = Gramm-Leach-Bliley Act
INF = information furnisher
OC = original creditor
PACER = Public Access to Court Electronic Records
SOL = statute of limitations

Chapter 1
WHO IS "THE DEBT ASSASSIN"?

In 1973, I started out as a collector at Vanguard Bank in New York, later known as Guardian Bank. My job was to call borrowers two payments or more past due to find out why they hadn't paid. The goal was to make arrangements to bring their accounts up to date.

Once the account was six payments past due, the bank wrote off the loan as a loss. It didn't mean that the money was no longer owed. It's simply an accounting procedure that says the bank can no longer consider the loan an asset. It also says the loan's ultimate repayment is in doubt.

Back in the day, banks simply wrote off and held onto charged-off, unsecured loans, with little or no attempt to collect them. If a bank was aware of any easily attachable assets, for instance, a paycheck that could be garnished, the bank's attorney sued. Charged-off accounts usually laid dormant without any attempt to recover the unpaid loan. This was before collection agencies became commonplace and the advent of debt buyers.

Being an ambitious new employee and wanting to move up the corporate ladder, I started pulling charged-off loan documents and making calls. To me it was beyond comprehension that nobody was trying to collect these things. I was told that they were "dead files" and uncollectable. My contention was people's life circumstances change. Just because they couldn't pay a year or two years ago doesn't mean they couldn't or didn't want to pay today.

I made four calls and spoke with four people. This was before caller ID . . . you remember those days when people actually answered the phone. All four said they were unaware balances were owed and paid them off. The balances were small but all four paid in full. After bringing this to my boss's attention, he authorized the start of an internal "bad debt recovery" unit. It consisted of a single individual . . . me. It was so successful we started a full-blown bad debt recovery department. They gave me a raise and the title of assistant vice president.

Along with setting up the collection division at Vanguard Bank, I was also "on loan" to other banks. I was helping them set up debt recovery departments. Remember, this was all new uncharted territory. This was also during the time when consumer protection laws were just being enacted. I was one of the few that had any experience in this new area of "bad debt recovery." Because collection law and consumers' rights were such a new and specific area of expertise, even most attorneys were in the dark regarding a consumer's legal rights. Having become well known in the debt collection industry, and having hands-on experience, attorneys were calling me for collection advice. I was educating them!

Back in the day, outsourcing the task of debt recovery to third-party collectors was almost unheard of. The collection industry was in its infancy. No one was prepared for the deceptive tactics collection agencies would employ.

Years after leaving the bank I started a collection agency. I taught collectors to treat consumers like human beings. Apparently, that's a novel idea for bill collectors. Collectors back then all had the same aggressive mentality. They thought they knew better than anyone how to effectively, but not always legally, collect money. In their minds threats and harassment motivated people to pay. No matter how much I stressed being empathetic and adhering to the law, collectors always seemed to want to do it their way. They kept harassing and badgering people, violating the FDCPA. Consequently, I wound up firing about a quarter of my collection staff every month. I was frustrated with how collectors were abusing people on the phone. With no resolution in sight, other than constantly firing people, I decided to get out of the business. I

1

became a consumer advocate. I did tons of in-depth personal research. I wanted to see what it was like on the other side of those nasty unsympathetic collection calls. I didn't want to be that so-called expert telling you to do something I had never done. I stopped paying every bill I had. I let them repo my car, foreclose on my house—judgments, federal and state tax liens. You name it, I stopped paying it! I was no longer the "hunter"; I became the "hunted." I even went so far as to file bankruptcy just to experience what that was like. I took the experiences from both sides of that dreaded collection call, cleaned up my horrible credit, and wrote this book.

Just to prove I could do it, I later disputed the bankruptcy, which was subsequently removed from my credit report. But, as I'll explain later, I strongly recommend against removing a discharged bankruptcy from your credit report. If you were discharged in bankruptcy I recommend that you leave it alone.

Being in the collection industry most of my life, I've always kept on top of the new and constantly changing consumer protection laws like the Fair Debt Collection Practices Act, the Fair and Accurate Collection Transactions Act, Fair Credit Reporting Act, and Telephone Consumer Protection Act.

What I knew from years in the industry was that when people are dealing with credit and collection problems, they're totally unaware of their rights. The FDCPA and FCRA were enacted by Congress specifically to eliminate abusive collection tactics and inaccuracies in our credit files.

None of the people who claim to be experts in this field did what I did to prove what I've proven! You can clear up your credit, on your own, simply by using the tools the law provides. The other alleged experts' advice is theory; mine is fact. I've been the "predator" and the "prey." Who could possibly know more than I do about the inner workings and illegal practices the collection industry employs? This book is about establishing credit for the first time, cleaning up damaged credit reports, and reestablishing credit even after a bankruptcy. I'll walk you through your credit lifetime from the cradle to the grave.

It's amazing how much misinformation is out there about what to do with collectors and how to clean up your credit report. The so-called experts are giving advice that's totally inaccurate. One of my favorite tidbits of misguided information is, "Tell collectors to stop calling." Well of course you can, but you really don't want them to stop calling. You don't even have to answer the phone when collectors call to clean up your report and make money. I sued collectors settling the suits for $127,000, $31,000 of that just based on the wording of messages collectors left that violated the FDCPA. I'd love it if they called me every day. After reading this book and knowing your rights instead of being annoyed by collection calls, you'll look forward to them!

A collection agency called my cellphone looking for someone who allegedly owed them money. I wasn't the person they were looking for. They didn't have authorization to call me. Apparently, my cell number was this person's old number. He or she may have given them permission to call, but the collector didn't have my permission. Without my permission, and having called using an automated dialer, their call was in violation of the Telephone Consumer Protection Act.

Here's a copy of the check I received because of the TCPA violation:

As a result of decades of experience, successful lawsuits, and run-ins with collectors, creditors, and credit bureaus, I developed a step-by-step procedure that everyone can easily follow to clean up their credit reports. The method I outline throughout the book raised my credit score from 461 in March 2016 to 742 in August 2016. That's an increase of 281 points in six months. Everyone in the industry will tell you that's impossible. I've proven it's not. If you know what you're doing, it's not only possible—it isn't difficult. Your score's improvement will be different than mine because of numerous variables, but your score will go up substantially if you meticulously follow this book. You didn't destroy your credit overnight and it won't be corrected overnight. Getting a score increase that was thought to be impossible well on its way in four months isn't bad!

I know right now a few months seems like forever but, if you conscientiously follow what I outline, your score will usually start to recover in forty-five days. Once you see your score climbing, it's a great feeling and well worth the wait. Keep in mind, if you used a credit repair service, they would charge anywhere from $89 to $129 a month or more: They charge monthly and have zero incentive to do anything quickly.

When I started research for this book, using myself as the guinea pig, my only intention was to prove I could clean up my credit without paying the creditors. I had no intention of suing anyone until I realized how many laws were being violated by these bloodsucking collection agencies and the three major credit bureaus. The agencies and bureaus assume that nobody knows their rights. Unfortunately, most people don't!

Just in case somebody does know their rights, collection agencies and credit bureaus set aside large sums of money to pay lawsuits. They look at it as the cost of doing business. For them, breaking the law and settling a few lawsuits is more profitable than obeying the law.

The basis for the dispute process and lawsuits against the credit bureaus is the one-hundred-plus-page Fair Credit Reporting Act (FCRA), legally known as 15USC §1681. The relevant section that's the basis for most of the credit bureau disputes is §611 (5)(a). It states that if the consumer reporting agency investigates a dispute, and finds that it's inaccurate, incomplete, or cannot be verified, it must be promptly deleted. Usually, the key is "cannot be verified," and they have thirty days to prove it or remove it. The basis for lawsuits against collectors and collection agencies is the Fair Debt Collection Practices Act (FDCPA I explain the relevant parts in chapter 6).

I know more about the legal system regarding consumers' rights than most judges and attorneys. And thanks to a judge in Arizona, I have it in writing. Following are three documents. Exhibit A is a letter from a judge, telling me that my FDCPA lawsuit can't be heard in his court. He challenges me to prove it can. Exhibit B is the letter where I cited the legal authority as to why it could be heard. Finally, Exhibit C is the letter from the judge saying that I was right. He agreed that based on the legal citation I outlined my case was allowed to be filed.

This is Exhibit A: the letter from Justice of the Peace Mark Anderson:

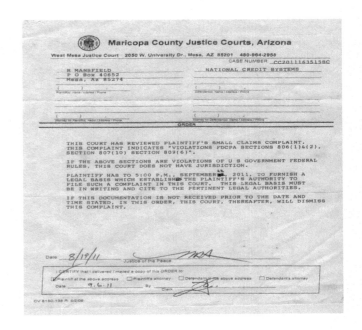

Here's Exhibit B—my letter pointing out the legal authority that allows this case, and all FCRA and FDCPA cases, to be heard in Justice / Small Claims Court:

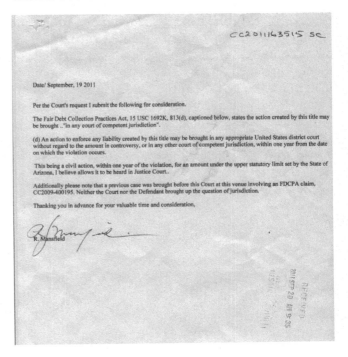

And finally Exhibit C—the letter from the judge agreeing that based on my letter and legal citations, I was right, and the case can proceed in Justice / Small Claims Court:

these suits rarely do. Here is a copy of the "Notice of Mediation" and settlement check:

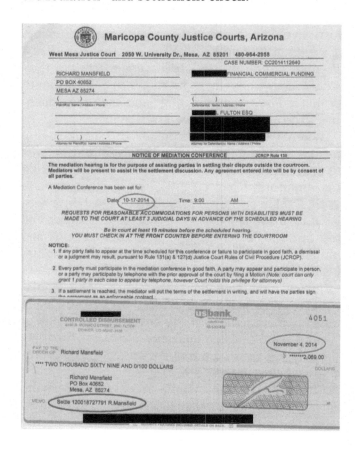

Prior to going to court in this case against National Credit Systems, I withdrew the suit. The negative notation was removed from my credit report. In a second case, I sued another collection agency. As part of the settlement, I agreed not to disclose its terms. In conjunction with that agreement, I redacted (blacked-out) any identifying information for the agency in the following figure where I show the check and mediation document. I settled.

I can't disclose the particulars of the settlement but let's say I received between $2,000 and $2,100. Along with the money, they removed the negative item from my credit report. This case was settled in mediation and never went in front of a judge;

Now, you may be saying to yourself, "Heck, I don't know what I'm doing, and I sure don't want to go to court."

Unless you want to, or a specific case isn't profitable enough for an attorney, you're never going to sue on your own. I did it for the book to show how easy it is. If you sue on your own, you will want to do it in Small Claims Court. Attorneys are barred from representing either side unless it's agreed to by both sides. And of course, you'd never allow their attorney to be present. I can virtually guarantee you won't see the inside of a courtroom. The details of any settlement will usually be resolved by phone, regular mail, or email, prior to any court date or pre-trial mediation. A pre-trial mediation is a discussion between you, the defendant's representative, and a third-party mediator at the courthouse. When I sued on my own, only once did it even get as far as mediation. The mediator was a law student at Arizona State University who was just there to move the discussion along and record any settlement agreement. During the mediation, you'll usually agree to a settlement, the terms of which will be finalized by filing paperwork with the court. If a settlement can't be worked out, then, and only then, might you go in front of a judge or possibly a jury. These consumers' rights cases are always tilted in our favor because collectors and credit bureaus NEVER want to go in front of a jury. Whose side do you think the jury is going to be on?

In consumer litigation suits, where you are the plaintiff, the judgment or settlement will normally wind up with:

- Legal fees being paid by the defendant
- Cash for you
- Removal of the item from your credit report
- A commitment from the collection agency not to sell the account
- The company you sue will not admit any wrongdoing
- You agree not to reveal the terms of the settlement.

Chapter 2

DIY CREDIT REHABILITATION AND RESTORATION

1. Open a Secured Credit Card That Reports to All Three Major Credit Bureaus

Apply for a secured credit card that reports to all three bureaus: Equifax, Experian, and TransUnion.

I opened a secured card at Capital One. The minimum required deposit was $200. Remember, one of the many things that separates me from other so-called credit experts is that I did whatever I say you can do.

I recommend you open and start using a secured card now. It will immediately go to work raising your credit score. In addition to the card, if you have the cash, get a secured loan from a bank or credit union too. Having both the card and the loan will improve your credit score drastically. If you don't have the money to do both, open the secured card first. Opening a secured credit card is more significant. Since credit cards don't have an end date, they have an ongoing credit score benefit. Also, if the card is handled properly for six months, the lender will usually invite you to apply for an unsecured line of credit. Once you have the unsecured line, close the secured line, and have the lender refund your deposit.

Now, back to the secured bank loan. The secured bank loan would be a great scoring asset too, but they usually require a larger security deposit. Having both a secured card and a secured loan will put your credit score on steroids. A secured loan at a bank ties up the money you pledge as security, but you do get cash in hand, equal to the security deposit. Put the cash you receive from the bank aside and use it to make payments on the loan. You're looking to establish credit, not go into debt! For consumers who are reestablishing credit, secured cards and loans help raise your credit score while you work on removing the negative items from your reports. If the money to open secured credit isn't available, go ahead and start working on the negative items and open the secured

accounts as soon as possible. Opening and properly handling secured borrowings is extremely important to rapidly reestablishing credit and increasing your credit score.

If you're reestablishing credit or just starting out, use the secured card to pay for purchases or bills you would normally pay in cash like food, gas, and your cellphone. Set up the card so that you get your monthly billing online. Pay it as soon as any new charge appears. That's what I did, and after six months, my deposit was refunded, and I had an unsecured line of $1,000. It took six months to get that unsecured line, but my credit score was on an upward swing immediately after the card's first billing cycle. Capital One has given me unsecured increases, varying from $1,000 to as high as $3,000, every six months since opening the account. I was up to having an unsecured line of $10,000 in two years.

2. Keep a Notebook

There's no other way to keep your sanity except by maintaining great records. You've got to be able to access documents when you need them.

If you receive a collection letter, or if you record a conversation or have a recorded message from a collector, immediately contact a consumer affairs attorney to have them review those documents.

The FDCPA 15USC § 692g(a) says a debt collector's first communication with you, whether by a call, text, or letter, must include the following:

1. the amount of the debt;

2. the name of the creditor to whom the debt is owed;

3. a statement that unless the consumer, within thirty days after receipt of the notice, disputes the validity of the debt, or any portion

thereof, the debt will be assumed to be valid by the debt collector;

4. a statement that if the consumer notifies the debt collector in writing within the thirty-day period that the debt, or any portion thereof, is disputed, the debt collector will obtain verification of the debt or a copy of a judgment against the consumer and a copy of such verification or judgment will be mailed to the consumer by the debt collector;

5. and a statement that, upon the consumer's written request within the thirty-day period, the debt collector will provide the consumer with the name and address of the original creditor, if different from the current creditor.

If the first communication is a call and the required information is not included during that call, they must send you a letter with the required information within five days of the date of the call.

If you receive a call from a collector, and you aren't prepared to record the conversation, get a direct number for the collector, and hang up. Prepare to record the conversation and call back.

There are a few things a collector must do and some things they can't. I give a detailed outline of what a collector can and can't do toward the middle of chapter 18, under the heading, "What Collectors Can't Say, and What They Must Say."

When you call back, don't be afraid to identify yourself as the person they're trying to reach. But never admit you owe the bill.

If they ask directly, "Is this your account?" tell them you don't recall the account. Just acknowledging the debt is yours could restart or extend the statute of limitations (SOL). The time frame for the SOL is important because once it expires, they can no longer win a suit against you. The statute of limitations is not something you want to restart or extend.

Let the collector ramble on. The more you talk to a collector, the more likely they are to violate the FDCPA. Then you can use the violation as leverage to wipe out the debt, have the item removed from your credit report, and make some cash for yourself. Ask the collector the following questions and feel free to make up some of your own.

- Who is the original creditor?
- What was the date of last payment?

- How were payments made: check, money order, online?
- Are you collecting for the original creditor or do you own the account?
- Do you report to the credit bureau?
- Has this account been reported to a credit bureau?
- Has the statute of limitations expired?
- If I eventually recognize that this account is in fact mine, is there a settlement available?
- How much is the settlement?
- Is that the best you can do on a settlement?
- Can the settlement be done in payments?
- If they say it can't or can only be in a specific number of payments, ask if that's a creditor requirement or the agency's internal guidelines.
- Are you guys licensed to collect in (whatever state you live in)?
- Send me a copy of the contract I signed. (If you opened the account online, they won't have a signed contract. Online transactions are covered under an "account stated" doctrine. There's an explanation of what that is at the end of chapter 20.)
- Ask for the contract anyway and see what they say.
- Ask, "What will happen if I don't pay; will you sue me?"

None of the questions you ask need to be relevant to what you ultimately do. You're asking questions to put the collector on the defensive and have them potentially violate the Fair Debt Collection Practices Act.

Call a consumer affairs attorney and have them listen to any recording you make. Lawyers, just like doctors, specialize. Make sure you're calling a lawyer that represents consumers, not a real estate, criminal defense, or any attorney not specializing in consumers' rights. Also make sure you're calling a lawyer who represents consumers, not creditors.

If the attorney starts talking about any out-of-pocket expenses, call a different lawyer. In consumers' rights litigation, the fees and court costs should be paid by the attorney and reimbursed from the defendant after you win the case. Win or lose, nothing should ever come out of your pocket. And when I say nothing, I mean zero, including but not limited to filing fees, court costs, case review, or consultation.

After an attorney reviews your recordings or other documents, if the attorney says there aren't any violations, that doesn't mean you give up or stop the dispute process. If the possible violation was by a credit bureau regarding a credit reporting dispute, then dispute the listing again using a different reason for the dispute. Sometimes this is a marathon, not a sprint.

If you have an attorney review a letter for a possible Fair Debt Collection Practices Act violation, make sure the thirty days for sending a debt validation letter (DVL) doesn't expire. During your first contact with the attorney, ask if you should send a DVL. If the lawyer takes your case, they'll take care of everything. If not, send the DVL yourself. There's a sample DVL in the appendix. As with every letter you send, send it certified mail, return receipt requested. Once the collector signs for the letter, the thirty-day clock starts ticking for them to reply if they intend to try to keep collecting the debt. They're required to stop all collection activity until they comply with the validation request. But unlike the thirty-day window for a credit bureau to respond to a dispute, collection agencies are not required to respond at all. They can simply stop all collection activity, including calls, letters, and reporting to the credit bureau. If after they sign for your letter, they continue any kind of collection activity before they reply, call an attorney: That's a violation of the FDCPA.

If they stop collections and they own the account, they can sell it to another agency. If they're collecting the account for the original creditor or any third party, they'll return it to whoever owns the debt, who can then place it with another agency. If you receive a letter or call from a different agency, about the same account, go through the same procedure just outlined. Get the new documents to a consumers' rights attorney, send another DVL, etc. Like it says on the shampoo bottle, "Repeat as needed."

Keep a record of all correspondence. When I say all I mean *all*: every letter and call you make or receive. Keep track of all scheduled follow-up dates, the dates you had conversations with anyone, who the conversation was with, and what the conversation was about. Keep all the return receipts from your certified mail. If you ever have to go to court, the party with the most documents usually wins.

The courts will treat anything that can't be documented like it didn't happen. If you ever need a consumers' rights attorney, the attorney will ask you for every document you have. They'll sort through them and decide what's important and what isn't. Better to have it and not need it, then need it and not have it.

Most things you'll do on the way to restoring your credit will be time-sensitive. If there's a deadline for something to happen, make sure you know the date and act accordingly. Disregarding the time frame for action or follow-up will doom you to failure.

Momentum is very important. This isn't something to take casually. It's not something you want to start and stop and get back to when you have time. Make the time! Once you start seeing that the system works, and your credit score starts climbing, it gets exciting. Collection agencies and credit bureaus rely on people getting discouraged and giving up. Don't be one of those people who gives up.

Every debt-related letter should be treated as if it were money, because it might very well be. I've won lawsuits based solely on letters from collectors and numerous others based entirely on messages on my phone where the wording of the message they left violated the Fair Debt Collection Practices Act (FDCPA).

I've also won suits against the credit bureaus either because they didn't reply to my disputes or didn't follow the legally mandated procedure for verifying the disputed items, both violations of the Fair Credit Reporting Act (FCRA).

3. Pull Free Credit Reports

There are free scores and reports available all over the place. Not all are reliable sources for gauging what you look like to lenders as a credit risk. For example, CreditWise from Capital One gives you a VantageScore 3.0 based on your TransUnion credit report. Discover generates a FICO score also based on your TransUnion report. Vantage and FICO scores based on the same credit data will be different. The truth is VantageScores might as well be a score provided by your next door neighbor. I don't know of any financial institution that relies on Vantage to make a credit decision. Capital One, who gives you your VantageScore, doesn't use it to make credit decisions. They use FICO!

When you're comparing scores to track your credit score progress, make sure you're comparing apples to apples. For example, don't compare the score from Discover to one you looked at from Capital One. They will almost always be different.

Another thing you should be aware of is that FICO has industry-specific scores. When you apply for a mortgage, the lender will pull a different FICO than if you apply for a car loan and a different one for an application for a credit card or personal loan. You can go directly to FICO and pay for all the industry-specific scores bundled together. The scores directly from FICO will cost from $19.95 to $39.95.

Prior to the COVID-19 pandemic, you could get free credit reports (no scores) directly from Equifax, Experian, and TransUnion once every 365 days at www.AnnualCreditReport.com. As of the writing of this book, at the end of 2021, when you go to www.AnnualCreditReport.com it says, "During the COVID-19 pandemic, accessing your credit is important. That's why Equifax, Experian and TransUnion are continuing to offer free weekly online credit reports."

Credit reports may still be free on a weekly basis.

Before we go any further, I'll explain the difference between a credit score and a credit report. Too many people use the terms interchangeably. They're very different.

Your credit score is a numeric grade used by creditors to evaluate the risk of lending you money. It's established based on what your credit report says about your credit history. Credit reports are pages long; a score is simply a three-digit number. Reports outline all your borrowings and repayment history for the last seven to ten years. They basically show who you owe, how much you owe, and how you've repaid them. It's used to calculate the score. If you never had credit, or don't have any credit, good or bad, for the last seven to ten years, you may not have a score. When you get your report, if you don't have any credit or any recent credit, it'll indicate something like, "No Record Found." Don't get confused when I say seven to ten years. Good credit, for instance paid as agreed, stays on your credit report for ten years. The bad stuff, in most cases, should only appear for seven.

To raise your score, you've got to remove the negatives on your report, keep paying anything that you have that's up to date, and/or add some positive tradelines. The quickest way to add positive tradelines is to become an authorized user (AU). Later I explain the advantages of being an AU, and I detail more specific ways to raise your score: but first things first. Let's work on getting rid of the garbage.

4. Review Your Credit Reports and Take Notes

Once you have the reports, make notations about each item you intend to dispute. Include specifics in your notes, detailing exactly what the creditor listed, and specifically what you're disputing and how you'll be disputing it. Go ahead, dispute the paid and settled accounts that were delinquent. Dispute all the settled accounts, but only dispute paid accounts if they show you were past due before paying them off. Dispute paid and settled accounts using the "Not my account" letter supplied in the appendix. In the vast majority of cases, when you dispute an account when there's no balance due, they're not going to waste the time and manpower to respond. As usual, if the information furnisher doesn't respond within thirty days, the disputed item is removed.

To collectors, it's a numbers game. You're one out of millions of accounts. They're looking for the easy prey: people who are unaware of their rights. They don't want to put much effort into collecting accounts. Sooner or later they give up, and it's usually sooner rather than later. Make sure they give up before you do.

Don't get me wrong. You may run into overly aggressive, desperate collectors and agencies who seem like they'll never give up; but that's a good thing. They're the ones that screw up, violate the FDCPA, and you wind up being able to sue. Don't be afraid to record every collection-related conversation. If you call a collector, bank, or credit bureau they will tell you that your call is or may be recorded. That notification allows you to record the conversation too. Once they make that announcement, you are under no obligation to tell them you're recording and I never do! Record every debt-related conversation and keep asking the collector questions. For instance: Will you sue me if I don't pay? Is my account being reported by your company to a credit bureau? Are you licensed to collect in my state? How did you arrive at the balance you claim I owe? Ask anything you can think of. Feel free to be creative. The longer you're on the phone, the more likely they are to screw up. Collectors hate people who ask questions.

5. Write Letters

Write letters to all the bureaus, disputing everything you want to be removed. Never dispute online. If you dispute online, you'll be waiving your right to sue. If you can't sue, you've lost your most important credit repair leverage.

Here are a couple important terms to understand. "Information furnishers" are the companies like banks, credit card companies, mortgage companies, and collection agencies. They report the "status" of your account, for example, late payments, charge-off, foreclosure, repossession, or the current balances.

When you dispute an item, you're either saying it's not your account, or the status that's being reported is wrong. What's wrong? For instance, date of last payment, account number, balance . . . anything they report you can say is in error. The companies that claim to do "credit repair" are often charging $39 to a $129 a month. This is exactly what they do, and it's the only thing they do.

Here's a partial list of specific disputable items:

- Not my account

- I didn't pay late that month

- Wrong balance

- Wrong payment amount

- Wrong account number

- Wrong date of last payment

- Wrong opening date

- Wrong original creditor

- Wrong credit limit

- I am not financially responsible. I was an authorized user.

Go to this book's appendix for letter templates, most with legal citations, and the "Cheat Sheet" for common collector violations.

For each account you dispute, send a letter to each of the credit bureaus that lists the negative item. On the letters, list the information furnisher, for instance, Wells Fargo, ABC Collection Agency, IRS, XYZ County Court, or County Recorder. Next to the name of the information furnisher, list what they reported that you're disputing: for example, not my account, wrong date of the last payment, wrong balance. There's an example of an initial dispute letter in the appendix. Use it as a generic letter to dispute anything that there isn't another specific letter for in the appendix.

Contrary to what the average consumer would believe, your credit reports may not be identical.

Each report may have slightly different information, and the three reports will often result in different credit scores. Outlining all the reasons why that is would take another entire book. But I'll give you one reason as an example. When you apply for credit, most lenders only look at one credit report. Each inquiry is a slight ding on your credit score, usually 2–4 points. Any score based on the report they pulled will be marginally lower due to the inquiry. More importantly, whether you pay for it or it's free, the score a lender sees is rarely the one you see.

As far as which credit report is more important, the answer is, "It's up to the lender." Some lenders, for instance, credit card companies, pull one, two, or three scores but mortgage lenders will always pull all three. Mortgage lenders, after pulling all three, will usually throw out the high and low scores and use the middle score.

Unless you know that something specific is wrong on your credit report, the reason for your first dispute should always be "Not my account." By law, the information furnisher has thirty days to reply. If the response to your dispute is "deleted," you're done. Here's a copy of one of my many deletion letters. The fact it was removed is noted below, in the middle of the page under the heading "Credit Items Outcome."

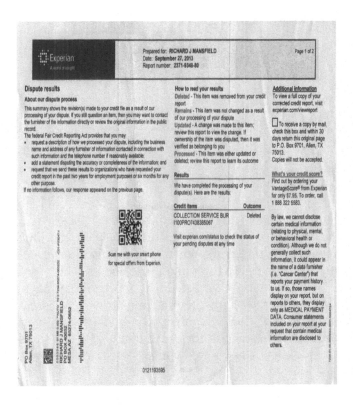

I've also sent disputes directly to collection agencies, but only after I sent a dispute sent to at least one of the bureaus. If you dispute with the information furnisher first, you lose your right to sue. Your ability to file suit is motivation for the information furnisher to delete the disputed item! On the next page is a copy of a deletion letter received from a collection agency. They removed the item from all three bureaus. When you file a dispute with a bureau, and they delete the disputed item, it will only be removed from that single credit bureau. If a disputed item is removed by the information furnisher, they are required to remove it from all the

bureaus where they reported the item.

These are the type of letters that you can look forward to receiving when you follow the procedures enumerated throughout the book.

If an investigation results in a letter that says, "We verified that this item belongs to you" or similar wording, then dispute the item again using a different reason for the next dispute. Never use the identical reason to dispute the same item with

the same bureau. By law, they can refuse to reinvestigate any dispute that they have already investigated. For example, you couldn't say the wrong opening date in two dispute letters, for the same Wells Fargo account, to the same credit reporting agency. An example of a follow-up dispute letter is in the appendix. Re-use the letter as often as needed. Again, like it says on the shampoo bottle, "Repeat as needed."

The credit bureau employee reviewing your dispute is more than likely someone in India, the Philippines, or South America. They're taking four minutes to review your letter and any affiliated documents. English isn't their first language. Yet, they have only four minutes allotted for each dispute and have a quota for the number of disputes they review daily. This works in your favor. They're under stress. Mistakes happen.

Remember, the employee reviewing your dispute isn't there to make a judgment on your dispute reasoning, but they are allowed, by law, to disregard repetitious disputes. The bureau agents are there to assign a numeric dispute code, and forward that code to the information furnisher, or reject identical disputes.

I am going to repeat this because I want to make this crystal clear, since re-disputing is often a key element in the dispute process. You can dispute the identical item forever if you can come up with a new reason for the dispute, but you can't use the same reason, for disputing the same item, with the same bureau. Hopefully, I've said this enough.

On occasion, the bureaus don't answer your letter at all. No answer is a good thing. If they fail to answer your dispute letter, not only are they legally required to remove the disputed item, but you can sue for $1,000 for a violation of the Fair Credit Reporting Act. The FCRA says they must send you a reply within thirty days of the dispute. I sued because they failed to reply, twice, and won both times.

It's not your job to prove an account isn't yours or the information is incorrect. The Fair Credit Reporting Act (FCRA) says the credit reporting agencies (CRAs) must verify that it is your account and that the information reported is correct. Many of the replies, to your first letters to the CRAs, will come back indicating, "Verified." Sometimes this is a marathon, not a sprint. A dispute resolution, in your favor, may take a couple months and a few different disputes. Patience and timely follow-up are important. In every case, your result will be faster, more likely to result in a deletion, and less expensive than any credit repair company.

6. Send the Dispute Letters Immediately

There are two things that will doom your credit restoration: inadequate records and poor follow-up. Do everything as outlined and be timely with your follow-up. Never put off until tomorrow what you should do today. Send the letters using certified mail through the post office. Make sure to get a return receipt. Just in case you've never sent a certified letter, the return receipt is a three-by-five-inch green index-type card. The recipient must sign and date the card, showing when they received your mail. The date they sign for your mailing is the day that starts the thirty-day clock ticking for them to respond.

7. Record All Debt-Related Conversations

The legality of recording phone calls varies from state to state. Google "phone recording requirements by state" and you'll get a list of the legal requirements. In many states, only one party to the conversation needs to know it's being recorded. That person is you and no notification is necessary. In some states, all parties to the call must know. When you call someone, or they call you, for instance, a collection agency, if they advise you that the call is or may be recorded, that takes care of the notification mandate. You don't need to notify them that you're recording the call too.

Recordings enable you to have a permanent record if needed. Better to have it and not need it, then to need it and not have it.

You should have a consumers' rights attorney review every collection call that you record, every collection message left for you, and every collection letter you receive. They'll review them and tell you if you have a case. Remember, it's possibly $1,000 or more, in your pocket, per violation, and removal of the negative item from your credit report.

Attorney reviews are free. If a lawyer decides you have a case, they lay out all the court costs and fees. They'll collect the court costs and any fees from the defendant when you win. Since the lawyer is laying out all the upfront costs in these consumer litigations, they only take cases they're sure to win.

8. If All Else Fails, Take Them to Court!

15USC 1681p says that you can file suit in "any court of competent jurisdiction." I've sued both collection agencies and credit bureaus in Small Claims Court.

One of the first cases I filed without an attorney was in the small claims division of a Justice Court in Mesa, Arizona. The judge sent me a letter indicating that the case couldn't be filed in his court. He indicated that it needed to be litigated in a federal court. I informed him, in writing, that according to law, I could file the case in his court. He replied and said I was correct. Here are those documents.

The first letter (Figure 2) is from the judge indicating I must sue in federal court. The second document (Figure 3) is my reply to the judge citing the FDCPA that says I can sue in any court. And the third letter (Figure 4) is from the judge, agreeing I'm right, and the suit can go forward.

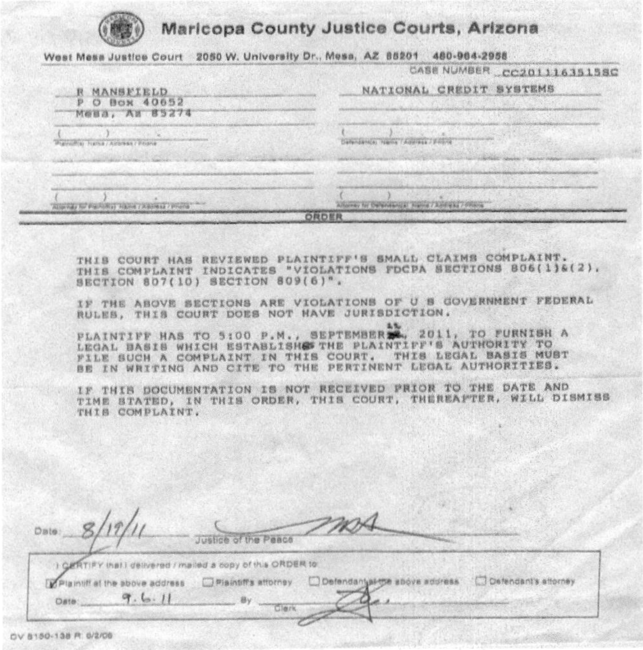

Maricopa County Justice Courts, Arizona

West Mesa Justice Court 2050 W. University Dr., Mesa, AZ 85201 480-964-2958

CASE NUMBER CC2011163515SC

R MANSFIELD
P O Box 40652
Mesa, Az 85274

Plaintiff(s) Name / Address / Phone

NATIONAL CREDIT SYSTEMS

Defendant(s) Name / Address / Phone

ORDER

THIS COURT HAS REVIEWED PLAINTIFF'S SMALL CLAIMS COMPLAINT. THIS COMPLAINT INDICATES "VIOLATIONS FDCPA SECTIONS 806(1)&(2), SECTION 807(10) SECTION 809(6)".

IF THE ABOVE SECTIONS ARE VIOLATIONS OF U S GOVERNMENT FEDERAL RULES, THIS COURT DOES NOT HAVE JURISDICTION.

PLAINTIFF HAS TO 5:00 P.M., SEPTEMBER 12, 2011, TO FURNISH A LEGAL BASIS WHICH ESTABLISHES THE PLAINTIFF'S AUTHORITY TO FILE SUCH A COMPLAINT IN THIS COURT. THIS LEGAL BASIS MUST BE IN WRITING AND CITE TO THE PERTINENT LEGAL AUTHORITIES.

IF THIS DOCUMENTATION IS NOT RECEIVED PRIOR TO THE DATE AND TIME STATED, IN THIS ORDER, THIS COURT, THEREAFTER, WILL DISMISS THIS COMPLAINT.

Date: 8/19/11 Justice of the Peace

I CERTIFY that I delivered / mailed a copy of this ORDER to:
☒ Plaintiff at the above address ☐ Plaintiff's attorney ☐ Defendant at the above address ☐ Defendant's attorney
Date: 9.6.11 By Clerk

DV 8150-138 R: 6/2/09

FIGURE 2

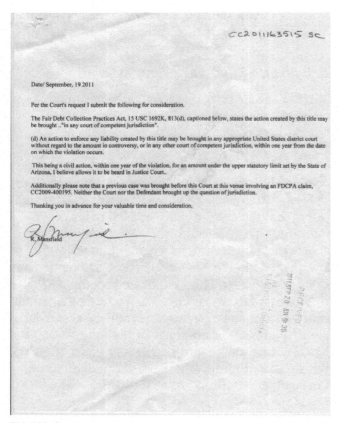

FIGURE 3

FIGURE 4

If you decide to sue on your own, remember, every defendant you will be suing under the Fair Debt Collection Practices Act, or the Fair Credit Reporting Act, is a corporation. All corporations will be represented by an attorney. Attorneys aren't allowed to be a part of Small Claims lawsuits. That being the case, they may file a motion to move the suit out of the small claims division, to a different part of the same court or federal court. Moving the case usually means just a different room in the same building. It's more time consuming and expensive for them to change venue. Let them spend the money it takes to move the proceeding. The more money involved to defend a case, the more likely they are to offer a settlement to limit their expenses. They consider these settlements the cost of doing business.

When you sue on your own, it should always be done in Small Claims. The procedures are less complicated, and the filing fees are a lot less than any other venue. Small Claims Courts are set up so the average person can represent themself.

Although attorneys normally can't appear in Small Claims Court cases, one will usually contact you by phone, letter, or email to discuss a settlement prior to any court date.

In most cases, if you are simply looking to get a negative removed from your credit report, without a monetary settlement, they'll agree to do it and you will settle the case without you leaving home. In most cases, these suits are worked out before you go to a mediation. The details of any settlement will usually be worked out by phone, email, or regular mail and confirmed by an email or regular mail and filed with the court.

9. Pull Those Free Credit Reports and Scores Again

It is very important, when you're measuring the success of your credit repair efforts, that you compare apples to apples. Don't compare a FICO score to a VantageScore. The only way to see that your efforts are successful is to compare FICO to FICO or Vantage to Vantage.

Most people look at being approved for credit as a good sign; oddly, credit scoring algorithms don't. Don't get upset if your scores go down in any given month, especially, the month after you obtain new credit. Your score will usually take a temporary dip. The decrease in your score is due to the inquiry generated by the lender and the decrease of the overall time you've had credit. For example, if you had one credit card for ten years with the addition of another card you have two accounts for ten years. The scoring algorithms now have the average age of your credit at five years. It's not a major ding on your credit score but this is why that happens. In the months following slight decline in your score, it will start going back up . . . assuming you didn't do anything negative like carrying additional debt or missing a payment.

You may not see a credit score increase every month. There will be various reasons for monthly ups and downs on your credit score like interest added onto accounts that are delinquent. DO NOT get discouraged! This is designed to be a comprehensive attack that will end in the results you are looking for. Of course, you want to win individual battles resulting in deletions, but temporarily losing a single battle is meaningless to winning the war. The more you follow the credit restoration tools outlined here and the more closely you adhere to a strict follow-up schedule, the faster this gets done.

Keep track of dates for follow-up. Make sure you stick to them as if your life depended on it. Your financial well-being does. Remember, you could have paid someone else to do this and it would have cost hundreds or thousands of dollars, with no guarantee of results. When you pay a "credit repair" company, they like to take their time since they're charging you by the month! You decided to save the money and speed up the process by tackling this yourself, so be conscientious and do everything in a timely fashion. Strictly follow the credit restoration guidance outlined in this book.

Map out a schedule, keep a calendar for "things to do," and do them! Pay attention to the follow-up dates for everything. Letters, notes, calendar, follow-up. Letters, notes, calendar, follow-up. Letters, notes, calendar, follow-up. Did I say that enough?

Don't try to re-invent the wheel. Take into account that I intentionally let my credit go down the crapper just to prove this works. It works!

Chapter 3
HOW TO ESTABLISH CREDIT

Obtaining Credit for the First Time

We would all like to go through life having plenty of money, never needing to borrow. Unfortunately, for most of us, that's not the way it's going to be. New cars and homes are expensive. Most of us can't simply write a check for major purchases; we need good credit and a lender.

Credit, when used properly, gives us financial freedom. Good credit allows us to have access to traditional forms of credit and to avoid predatory loans that can easily become a financial noose around our necks.

The government broadly defines predatory lending as financing that imposes high-interest rates or overly restrictive loan conditions: for instance, uncommonly short repayment terms and interest rates over 29 percent. Rent-a-Center, payday, and title loans, that traditionally have insane interest rates, from 200 percent to 2,000 percent, and repayment terms that are almost impossible to comply with, are predatory. Credit cards with high yearly fees and that have interest rates of 30 percent or more, also fall into the category of predatory. The Consumer Financial Protection Bureau is currently monitoring these types of lenders. They're attempting to regulate them, so that the borrowers who use them aren't being financially strangled. Be careful of any lender that requires weekly payments!

What Lenders Look For from First-Time Borrowers

Without any credit history at all, you can qualify for services like utilities and cellphones; but having those and paying them on time won't establish a credit score. People ask me about Experian Boost. I'll address that a little later in the section about alternative forms of credit.

At a minimum, you'll need a traditional credit score, like FICO, around 670 or above, to qualify for decent loan and credit card rates. FICOs of 760 and above will have lenders knocking on your door asking if you'd like to borrow money. With a 760 FICO, you could walk into an auto dealership and get a vehicle with no down payment and zero interest.

BANK ACCOUNTS

Since credit isn't a requirement to open a checking or savings account, neither one will help you establish credit. Yet, poorly handled bank accounts can hurt. It doesn't come into play for normal loans, but I've seen poorly handled checking accounts create problems on mortgage applications. Checking accounts that are habitually overdrawn or closed by a financial institution may be reported to a specialty bureau like ChexSystems.

ChexSystems only records derogatory transactions and it's normally only pulled when you apply to open a bank account; but it could become a problem on a mortgage application, especially if you're self-employed.

If a checking account is closed with a negative balance, it may be sent to a collection agency. Collection agencies report to credit bureaus. When that happens, poorly handled bank accounts can have a negative effect on your credit score. A positive banking history is only relevant if you try to borrow from either the institution you have the account with or a lender that considers "alternative forms of credit." Lenders that consider alternative forms of credit may want to see that you don't bounce checks. All this having been said, unpaid overdrafts and miscellaneous bank charges are easily removed from your credit report, even after being sent to a collection agency.

EMPLOYMENT HISTORY AND INCOME

It may seem counterintuitive and contrary to everything you now believe, but when you apply for a credit card online, they're not verifying your employment or income. The fact is you can tell them anything you want. Their credit decision will be made solely based on your credit score and stated income.

Mortgages, auto, and personal loans are a different story. When you're talking about big-ticket items, they want to see pay stubs and tax returns.

IF YOU HAVE A BANK ALREADY

Establishing a relationship with a financial institution may improve your chances of obtaining a loan or credit card directly with that lender. If you already do business with a bank or credit union, it should be the first place you consider applying. But before you fill out an application, ask them if they lend to first-time borrowers. If they tell you that they don't, then don't apply. Their credit inquiry itself would have a negative effect when you apply elsewhere. There are other ways to establish credit and other lenders that are friendly to first-time borrowers. Here are a few.

GET A SECURED LOAN FROM A BANK OR CREDIT UNION

Another a good source for your first loan is a called a "secured installment loan." This isn't a credit card. You don't get a piece of plastic. This is a loan with a specific amount due each month on a specific date. It is unlike a credit card where you may or may not owe money every month and the payments vary. Unlike a credit card, you can pay this type of loan months in advance. Unlike a credit card, you have the same payment due each month for a specific number of months. Credit cards are often referred to as "open-ended" or "revolving credit" because they can be used over and over without a specific date for a final payment. Installment loans, for example, auto or personal loans, are referred to as "close-ended" and have a specific end date.

A secured loan is similar to a secured credit card, since the lender requires collateral. The lender holds onto the collateral until you pay off the loan. Most banks will only take collateral that is on deposit with their institution, but some may also take stocks, bonds, or funds held by another institution. Ask your bank or credit union what their policy is about taking out a secured loan.

CREDIT CARDS

TRY A DEPARTMENT STORE CREDIT CARD

You've probably been shopping and been asked if you'd like to sign up for a store credit card and save $25 on your purchase, and you politely declined. Maybe you thought that you wouldn't qualify. On the contrary, these cards are a very good idea for establishing credit.

You may want to consider going into one of the major stores like Home Depot or Best Buy to see what type of cards they offer. You can either go to the store and ask the employee at the customer service desk or go online. Apply at any store that offers a credit card. You're not limited to the stores I mention.

If you apply and are unable to obtain a department store card, wait four weeks and then apply for one of the cards listed below.

between most credit applications. The exception is a secured card. You can apply for those immediately. Because it's secured, there is no risk to the lender, regardless of what your credit report does or doesn't say about you.

TRY A GAS CARD

Another good source for your first credit card is a gas card. When you're at a gas station, they usually have credit card applications either at the pump or inside. If they don't, just ask the cashier or go online.

GET A SECURED CREDIT CARD

Whether your credit applications for store and/or oil cards are declined or approved, as soon as you're able to come up with the required deposit ($200 is usually the minimum), apply for a secured card that reports to the credit bureaus. If your credit requests were previously declined, this is a surefire approval and will start your credit history. If you were previously approved for credit, this will supercharge your newly established credit score. Since secure card lenders require a deposit, equal to your credit line, they don't have any risk. You can ignore the Four-Week Rule and apply immediately before or after any credit application.

When a credit card or loan is secured, it means that you deposited money with the lender, equal to your line of credit. By paying the card on time, you'll be establishing yourself as a good credit risk. Remember, if you don't make payments when they're due, that's reported too, hurting future attempts to get credit.

One of the nice things about most secured cards—in addition to being reported to all three major bureaus—is that you can use it like a credit card. As an example, if you try to rent a car with a debit card, only a few car rental companies will allow it, and there are restrictions. Using a secured card that can be used as a credit card and reports to the credit bureaus has major advantages over debit cards.

When I used my $200 secured card, I charged everything on that card: food, gas, cellphone bill, everything I would have normally paid in cash. Every time I used it, I paid it online as soon as the charges appeared. After six months, they refunded my deposit and gave me an unsecured card with a $1,000 credit limit. I almost maxed it out every month but made sure I didn't go over my credit limit and that it was paid at least a week before it was due. After another six months went by, they raised my limit again to $3,500 and six months after that to $5,500. The key to that rapid rise in available credit was using the card to the max, without going over the limit, and paying the balance every month ten days before it was due. Keep in mind the date the credit card company reports to the credit bureau is often before or after the due date. Call your credit card company to find out the reporting date. Pay the balance in full two or three days prior to the reporting date and don't use it again until after the report date. This is a major step in establishing or reestablishing credit.

IF YOU DON'T HAVE THE MONEY TO SECURE A LOAN OR CREDIT CARD, TRY A CO-SIGNER

If you can't qualify for a credit card on your own, because you don't have sufficient income, you have no credit, or don't have the money for a secured card, you can ask a friend or family member to co-sign. The co-signer must meet the lender's criteria for approval. When you ask someone to help you establish credit, realize that the person is taking a risk by co-signing. If you don't repay the loan, the co-signer will be responsible.

Any positives or negatives reported on the account will be reported on both your credit report and the person who co-signed. Be careful. You can destroy both of your credit ratings and lose a friend. PAY ON TIME!

There's another strategy for hooking up with co-signers, always overlooked by the credit "experts." I've never seen it suggested by anyone but me.

Let's say someone you trust and trusts you, your mother, brother, friend, significant other, you get the idea, is making a purchase. And instead of putting it on a credit card they already have, they're applying for new credit, specifically for this purchase. For demonstration purposes, we'll use Best Buy. Ask your "friend," the borrower, if you can be a co-applicant. They're already taking out the loan. They're going to be responsible for paying it. As far as your friend is concerned, you're just along for the ride. The good news is that the credit scoring modules will not consider it as just a tag along. If the loan is paid on time, that "ride" will establish or improve your credit drastically. This won't work if they are using a card they already have. It only works if they are applying for new credit, for a specific purchase.

Don't confuse the terms authorized user and co-signer. There's an enormous difference between the two. FICO and every other scoring system likes to see that you have skin in the game. If you're the co-signer, on a credit card or loan, and it's paid on time that's great. It absolutely helps your credit. On the other hand, once you co-sign, if the loan goes bad the lender will come after everyone, signers and co-signers, for payments. As an authorized user on a credit card or line of credit, you are never responsible for repayment. The following section explains this concept in more detail.

The Advantage of Being an Authorized User (AU)

Most credit scores include AUs in their calculations. As an AU, you're never financially responsible for payments, but you will be penalized for any delinquencies associated with the account. If the primary borrower becomes delinquent, notify the bureaus that you want to be removed from the account. The bureaus will wipe out the entire payment history from your credit report. There's a letter to request removal in the appendix.

If you're looking to establish or reestablish credit, or even just to bump up a good score you already have, try the authorized user route. The great news about being an AU is that the entire history of the card you are added onto is reflected on your credit report. For instance, if the card has been around for five years, paid on-time, and has a $10,000 dollar credit limit that all becomes part of your history.

ESTABLISHING CREDIT IS A MAJOR STEP BUT ONLY THE FIRST STEP

When you're approved for any credit card, you need to be disciplined; use it properly. Don't treat it like free money: It's not. Credit cards are a way to establish good credit, but they can also be a way to get into big trouble.

Once you get your first card, you won't be in the financial shadows anymore. This new piece of plastic will establish a credit score. When used properly, it will have an ongoing positive impact on your credit score and your life. When you're first starting out, if you want to maximize the effect of the card, don't use it for anything except purchases that you would normally make with cash. Use it for items like food, rent, utility bills, your cellphone, gas. You're looking to establish credit, not go into debt.

Once you've become financially established, a whole new world will open up. It's a major step that will help you finance a home, vehicles, send your kids to college, or even help you borrow money to start a business. What you are doing by establishing good credit is laying the foundation for your future. It's a financial life plan. New extensions of credit should begin to be reported within thirty days after the approval or thirty days after you initially use the card.

Paying on time, and not carrying any balances from month to month, is the goal and will optimize your score. Higher credit scores lead to better interest rates. Pay the balance in full before your billing date. Be careful: Don't wait until the day the payment is due to pay the bill. If you pay online, which I absolutely recommend, it sometimes will take a day and even up to three days before your payment is processed.

Establishing a great credit history takes time. The credit restoration guidance outlined here will shorten that time from years to months. Your credit score is calculated based on several things such as payment history, balances in use as compared to the credit that's available, the length of time you have had credit, and types of credit. While it's important to initially establish or reestablish credit, it's equally important to do the right thing to maintain good credit.

DO YOU NEED A JOB TO QUALIFY FOR CREDIT?

The legal age to qualify for a credit card on your own is eighteen. If you are under twenty-one, lenders may require proof that you have the capability to repay the debt. You may be asked to scan and forward recent pay stubs and/or W-2s to the lender. Often, they will require a co-signer.

Before a ruling by the Consumer Financial Protection Bureau in 2013, borrowers were required to have their own source of income, at any age, before they could be approved for a credit card. Otherwise, you would have needed a co-signer.

In 2013 the 2009 Credit Card Accountability Responsibility and Disclosure (CARD) Act was amended to say that credit card issuers could consider income that an applicant shares with a spouse or partner. The lender is permitted to consider income and assets "to which the applicants have a reasonable expectation of access."

CREDIT CARDS ARE NOT ALL THE SAME

Even though credit cards have the same shape and size, they don't have the same terms and conditions, and they're not all meant for the same type of credit card user. You'll be more likely to choose the right credit card if you know the types of credit cards on the market.

Credit cards fall into three general categories:

- Secured cards are for people that are looking to establish or reestablish credit.

- Standard cards are unsecured but usually have higher interest rates than reward cards.

- Reward cards are for the consumers with good credit and the rewards vary. Reward variations are drastic, from money based on a percentage of your spending to travel-related awards.

CREDIT CARD FEATURES WILL HELP YOU CHOOSE THE ONE THAT'S RIGHT FOR YOU

Interest rates, annual fees, and credit limits are just a few important credit card features. For each credit card you consider, make sure you read the credit card disclosure. It's always lengthy, always very boring, and always very important. If there is something you don't understand, don't ask a friend or relative; they're probably just as lost as you are. Call the credit card company. The disclosure notice will spell out the credit card features both positive and negative. Comparing different credit cards will help you see which card features are best for you. In general, low-interest rates and no annual fees are ideal but sometimes hard to get when you're just starting out or reestablishing credit.

EXPECT A MONTHLY STATEMENT

A credit card billing cycle is the number of days between your credit card statements. Billing cycles are typically twenty-five to thirty days. Your credit card issuer should send a monthly statement by email or regular mail. The statement details your transactions for the most recently completed billing cycle. If you have an outstanding balance, you're required to make at least the minimum payment. You might not get a bill; it could happen. Maybe you moved. Maybe it got lost in the mail. Maybe you haven't used your credit card or simply have a zero balance. Make sure you get a bill for the months you know you have charges. Don't think you are beating the system because you didn't get a bill. Not getting a bill is not an excuse for late payment. It will be costly and could hurt your credit score. If you don't get a bill and you know you have a payment due, call your credit card company. Keep track of your finances. It's easy to destroy that good credit score that you've worked so hard to establish.

MANY CREDIT CARDS HAVE UNAVOIDABLE YEARLY FEES, BUT YOU CAN AVOID INTEREST AND LATE CHARGES

You can avoid interest by paying the balance in full prior to your due date. You can avoid late charges by making your credit card payments on time.

Always pay online if possible. If you mail a payment, you have no way of knowing when the credit card company received it. You can avoid a finance charge by paying your full balance every month. If your credit card has an annual fee, you may not be able to avoid it. Shop around and see if there's anything out there you qualify for without an annual fee. Keep in mind that if you don't carry balances and you pay the card in full every month the interest rate doesn't matter. If it's 1 percent or 50 percent, you avoid paying any interest by paying the balance monthly.

REMEMBER

Getting a department store or an oil company credit card is easier than a major credit card like Discover or American Express. While the department store and oil cards are easier to get, they also have higher interest rates and lower credit limits. On the bright side, having a positive history with one of those high-interest rate cards helps. After handling one of those cards properly, you'll qualify for a major credit card with lower interest. Don't forget, if you pay balances in full before the due date, you won't pay any interest.

There's a lot to know about credit. Being unaware of how credit cards work can prove to be costly and severely damage your credit. It helps to know at least the basics before you get your first card. Understanding the positive aspects and the pitfalls of various types of credit cards will help you make the right decisions when choosing and using your cards. Do all you can to pay off your credit cards every month. You are trying to establish great credit, not trying to go into debt.

Chapter 4
REESTABLISHING CREDIT AFTER BANKRUPTCY

Credit reports are often incorrect; that's the reason behind the use of the word *should* instead of *will* in the following bankruptcy descriptions. I can't tell you how your bankruptcy will show up, but I can tell you the way it should show up. If your report doesn't appear the way it should, write a letter to the bureau(s): They'll correct it. If they don't, then contact a consumer rights attorney and sue.

Three Post-Bankruptcy Notations

After a bankruptcy, one of three notations will appear in the public record section of your credit report. Here are the important terms to be familiar with regarding bankruptcy.

DISCHARGED
The court released the debtor from any obligation to pay specific, listed "discharged" debts. You legally owe no one that was discharged. The discharge should show up in the public record section of your credit report. Each discharged account should show up with a zero balance and as "Discharged" in Chapter 7 or "Discharged" upon completion of a Chapter 13.

DISMISSED
The judge turned down your bankruptcy petition. You still owe everyone. The bankruptcy should show up in the public record section of your credit report as dismissed. The status for each account should remain as what they currently are, thirty-sixty-ninety days past due, collection account, etc.

WITHDRAWN
You voluntarily decided not to go bankrupt and withdrew the petition. You still owe everyone. The bankruptcy should show up in the public record section of your credit report as withdrawn. The status

for each account should remain as what they currently are, thirty-sixty-ninety days past due, collection account, etc.

As odd as it may sound, your score will normally go down even more severely due to a dismissal or withdrawal than it will with a discharged bankruptcy. The way creditors look at it, if you actually went bankrupt most or all of your debt was wiped out with the "Discharge." With the dismissed or withdrawn status, scoring algorithms view you as still having financial problems and there's the possibility of you filing bankruptcy in the future.

Don't confuse how long a bankruptcy can be reported with how long each delinquent account can be reported. They're separate issues.

The clock starts ticking for the time a bankruptcy can legally remain on your credit report as of the date it's filed: not the day it was discharged, dismissed, or withdrawn. A chapter 7 bankruptcy can remain on your credit report for ten years from the date it was filed. A chapter 13 can be reported for seven years from the date it was filed.

The discharged accounts themselves, or any accounts still owed, can only be reported for seven years from the date they first became delinquent and were never brought up to date. The bankruptcy date has nothing to do with the allowable length of time a delinquent account can be reported. The time frame for the ability of a delinquency to remain on your credit report is separate and unaffected by the bankruptcy.

What Do You Do?

Bankruptcy is a major wound on your credit report, but one you can heal without it leaving a scar. Reestablishing credit is quicker, easier, and less of a headache than getting the bankruptcy itself removed.

CREDIT CARDS

After your bankruptcy is discharged, within a month or two, most people will start to get credit card and auto loan offers. Unfortunately, these offers come with very high application fees, interest rates, and yearly fees. I received an offer for a card with a $300 limit and a yearly fee of $175.

Ignore all the solicitations you'll get after the bankruptcy. They're all predatory, meaning they have extremely high interest rates and fees. After a bankruptcy, immediately get a secured credit card that reports to the three major bureaus. You can start with as little as a $200 refundable security deposit. Having a secured card that reports will immediately start reestablishing credit. I charged all the items I would have normally paid in cash: food, gas, my cellphone bill—you get the idea. I charged up to my credit limit every month but made sure not to go over the limit. I arranged it so I could make payments online and paid every item as soon as it appeared on my billing. I didn't wait for the month-end billing statement. I paid each item as soon as it appeared. Remember, you're only charging items you'd have normally paid in cash. You're not trying to go into debt; you're reestablishing credit! After six months of using a secured card and paying the balance every month prior to the due date, the lender invited me to apply for an unsecured card. They approved the unsecured card with a $1,000 credit limit. Even after getting the unsecured card, I kept to the same regimen that got me here: only charging items I'd have paid in cash and paying the items as they appeared. The credit card company automatically raised my credit limit every six months. I now have a $10,000 limit on that card.

Though a secured card is good, the best way to reestablish yourself after a bankruptcy is to be added to someone's credit card as an authorized user (AU). When you become an authorized user, your credit report will reflect the entire positive history related to that card. If you have someone who is good enough to add you as an AU you must, and I repeat must, be sure that they have a history of on-time payments. They should never have been late, not even thirty days. They should rarely carry balances from month to month, and the card should be at least five years old. If they can't check all these boxes, you may be doing yourself more harm than good by becoming an AU on their card.

Once you reestablish your credit and qualify for an unsecured line of credit, if absolutely necessary, you can carry a balance. Always pay as much as you are able. Carry as little debt as financially possible from month to month. I strongly recommend, to maximize your creditworthiness, stick with the program that got you here. Even after receiving any new card, unsecured or secured, if possible only charge monthly bills, and only make purchases you would normally pay for in cash. Pay the credit card bill in full before it's due, preferably as soon as you see it appear on your online statement. Pay it daily as charges appear.

To find a secured card that reports, Google "secured credit cards that report to all three credit bureaus."

BANKS AND CREDIT UNIONS

Another way is to go to a bank or credit union. Make sure it's not a lender that was included in the bankruptcy; they're usually not too happy about lending you money right away. Ask the banker if they make secured loans. Find out what the minimum loan is, and if the loans are reported to the credit bureaus. See what kind of an account can be used as security and open one. Ask how soon you can get a loan using it as collateral and do it. Pay it off as fast as you can but not sooner than three months, then do it again. Each time you do this it will have a positive effect on your credit score. Repeat as needed. Or better yet, if you can afford it, do both. Get a secured credit card and a secured loan. Having both will be like putting your credit score on steroids.

TIME HEALS ALL WOUNDS

As more time passes, and as long as you continue to pay all your new bills on time, the negative effects of bankruptcy will fade. To reestablish yourself, you should keep your credit card balances under 10 percent of your available limit. Actually, since all you should be charging is the things you would ordinarily be paying cash for, you shouldn't be carrying any balances at all. Bankruptcies become less significant as you start rebuilding credit. If you adhere to this plan, in six months or so, the effects of the bankruptcy on your credit score will diminish substantially.

The sooner you start the process of reestablishing your credit, the sooner you can put the bankruptcy nightmare behind you. As soon as you charge anything, go online, and pay it as soon as the charge appears. Don't carry any monthly balances. Paying your credit card balance in full, before it's due, will not only maximize your credit score, but it also avoids any interest.

After a few months of properly handling your new credit, you'll start getting pre-screened letters. Unlike the solicitations you were getting immediately after the bankruptcy, these new credit card offerings will usually have better interest rates, higher credit limits, and many will be without yearly fees.

PROPER REPORTING IS IMPORTANT FOR YOUR POST-BANKRUPTCY CREDIT

A judge in California ruled that credit bureaus have two months from your bankruptcy discharge date for it to be properly reflected on your credit report. After your discharge, create a starting point to begin tracking your credit scores. Immediately get your current credit report from www.Annual CreditReport.com. Pull it thirty days after your bankruptcy discharge and again thirty days later. All the accounts included in a bankruptcy should be noted as zero balances, with the wording, "Included in Chapter 7 or Chapter 13" or similar wording. Make sure your bankruptcy is reported properly. If you have additional questions, ask your bankruptcy attorney or contact me. My contact information is included at the beginning and end of the book.

Shortly after your bankruptcy is discharged, you'll get offers from car dealers and other predatory lenders. Within weeks, you'll be able to get approved for a car loan at about 29 percent. The terms and interest rates will be so high, that if you accept one of them, it could easily put you right back in the financial bind you just got out of. Stay away from these types of loans unless you need the money for a kidney transplant. And even then, they'll probably want the kidney as security!

At 29 percent interest, you'll pay approximately $18,000, in interest alone, over five years on a $20,000 car loan.

After you start to rebuild your credit, you should be able to get a car loan at around 6 to 8 percent. Even at the high end of those rates, 8 percent, over five years, you'll pay about $4,000 in interest on a $20,000 car. That's a $14,000 difference compared to a 29 percent interest rate loan. Start reestablishing credit by Googling "Secured credit cards that report." Make sure to read the "Terms and Conditions" for any card you're a for.

People will rarely read a book like this cover to cover. They skim through it looking for specific information. As a result, I repeat important points. If you didn't need them repeated, I apologize for the repetition. If you would have missed it if I didn't repeat it, "You're welcome."

I recommend that you do NOT remove a discharged bankruptcy from your credit report. I did it for the book to prove it could be done. But what I found was it's faster and easier to use the method I just described to reestablish credit after you go bankrupt. If you remove the bankruptcy that's all you remove. The rest of the evidence of your bankruptcy still exists. Every debt that was eliminated is still on your credit report marked as "Dismissed in Chapter 7 or 13."

INVESTIGATIONS AND HOW THEY AFFECT REPORTING

When you dispute public records, like a bankruptcy, judgment, or tax liens, the credit bureaus don't do any part of the investigation. They outsource that to a third party. In most cases it's a company named LexisNexis. The entire scope of the alleged investigation consists of Lexis going online to a publicly viewable site known as PACER (Public Access to Court Electronic Records). With the exception of some bankruptcies, public records are impossible for any of the credit reporting agencies, or third parties they hire, to research effectively enough to comply with the FCRA. For instance, Social Security numbers are fully or partially redacted. Without seeing a complete Social Security number, a consumer can't be definitively identified and can't be absolutely linked to any publicly recorded financial event. Without a complete nine-digit Social Security number, you have a case to remove any public record from your credit report.

The Fair Credit Reporting Act requires bureaus to contact the information furnisher. In the case of public records, they don't even attempt to contact the information furnisher. They, in fact, don't get any updated information from any source of public records information, because the Social Security numbers are entirely or partially redacted (blacked out).

Figure 5 is a copy of the email response from the Maricopa County, Arizona, recorder. It clearly states that the credit reporting agencies don't ever contact them. The administrative manager at the recorder's office emailed me saying, and I quote, "I have never heard that a credit reporting agency uses us during a dispute. The recorder cannot identify personally who a name on a document is."

And another quote from the Recorder's Office email: "There are vendors who purchase our records, daily to disseminate, create lists and sell to others. I have no idea how the credit reporting agencies get our information since they do not buy directly from us."

-----Original Message-----
From: Webmaster - RISCX
Sent: Wednesday, May 29, 2013 10:55 AM
To: datactr New - RISCX
Cc: (Redacted)@msn.com
Subject: Customer Website Comments - Recorder

Department: Recorder
First Name: Rick
Last Name: Mansfield
E-mail Address: (Redacted)@msn.com
Comments: Does the Maricopa County Recorder's office report to credit reporting agencies; for instance, Experian, Transunion, and Equifax? It is my understanding that you do not "report" to them that they, in fact, receive information from a third party.

Secondly, do any of the three named agencies request verification from the recorder's office when a recorded document is disputed?

Below is the Maricopa County Recorder's Office response to my above email.

From: (Redacted)@risc.maricopa.gov
To: (Redacted)@msn.com
Subject: RE: Customer Website Comments - Recorder
Date: Wed, 29 May 2013 22:49:22 +0000

The records in the Recorder's office are public. They review our records for the information they need. I have never heard that a credit reporting agency uses us during a dispute. The Recorder cannot identify personally who a name on a document is.

(Redacted)
Administrative Manager
Maricopa County Recorder
111 S. 3rd Ave.
Phoenix, Az. 85003
(Redacted)@risc.maricopa.gov

Rick Mansfield
(Redacted)@msn.com
RE: Customer Website Comments - Recorder
Rick Mansfield
5/29/13
To: (Redacted) - RISCX
Thank you for your quick response.
Thanks, Rick Mansfield

NEXT MESSAGE:

-----Original Message-----

From: Webmaster - RISCX

Sent: Wednesday, August 27, 2014 3:02 AM

To: datactr New - RISCX

Subject: Customer Website Comments - Recorder

Department: Recorder

First Name: Rick

Last Name: Mansfield

E-mail Address: (Redacted)@msn.com

Comments: How do credit reporting agencies obtain public record information from the Maricopa County Recorder?

From: (Redacted)@risc.maricopa.gov

To: (Redacted)@msn.com

Subject: RE: Customer Website Comments - Recorder

Date: Wed, 27 Aug 2014 16:44:51 +0000

Our records are made available to the public about 3 days after they record. There are vendors who purchase our records, daily to disseminate, create lists and sell to others. I have no idea how the credit reporting agencies get our information since they do not buy directly from us.

(Redacted)

Administrative Manager

Maricopa County Recorder

111 S. 3rd. Ave.

Phoenix, Az. 85003

(Redacted)@risc.maricopa.gov

(End of E-Mail from Recorder)

FIGURE 5

I also contacted the Bankruptcy Courts for the States of Arizona and New York, along with the IRS and the state taxing entity for Arizona known as the Arizona Department of Revenue.They all indicated that they are never contacted by any of the credit bureaus.

The obvious question is, "How do the credit bureaus verify public records without speaking to the only people that would be able to verify information?" The answer is they don't.

The Fair Credit Reporting Act states the information furnisher must be contacted when you dispute any item on your credit report. That includes public records, for example, tax liens, judgments, and bankruptcies. Verification with the "Information Furnisher" of any public record never happens. The bureaus are clearly in violation of the FCRA every time a public record is disputed.

Public records are compiled by recording entities, for example, your local county recorder's office or local and federal courts. They include transactions like bankruptcies, judgments, and tax liens—you know, the legal stuff. These records are never updated to reflect new balances. A new balance could be an increase, due to accrued interest, or a decrease, because you made payments. In both cases, public records are never updated.

Your first thought is probably, "I don't want them to show a higher balance, that can't be good." Normally I would agree, except in this case where you're disputing a balance. The FCRA says the credit bureaus must reflect an "accurate balance" or remove it. Higher or lower, they can't keep it on your credit report unless it's accurate! Whenever I dispute a public record, I always say the balance is incorrect, but never indicate what it should be. Credit reporting agencies must verify the balance. It's not your job to tell them what you know or think your balance is. It's their job to verify and report the correct information.

Judgment creditors never update, state taxing authorities and the IRS never update; those balances will be wrong almost immediately after they're recorded.

State and federal taxing authorities are so overwhelmed by the volume of accounts that they don't even notify the CRAs, the recorders, or the court, even when a balance is paid in full.

TAX LIEN RELEASE INFORMATION]
I copied and pasted the following directly from online tax lien info from the Maricopa County Recorder's Office. Figure 6 is an IRS lien for $32,835.48, and Figure 7 is from the State of Arizona Department of Revenue.

To eliminate the need for notification of a lien being paid and to release the lien, the following or similar wording will appear on the recorded document for tax liens.

"Unless a notice of the lien is refiled by the date given in column 'e,' this notice shall, on the day following such date, operate as a certificate of release as defined in IRC 6325 (a)." It also clearly says, "For each assessment listed, unless this Notice of Lien is extended by the date given in column 2, this notice shall, on the date following such date, operate as a Certificate of Release."

Look at what it says under "Important Release Information" on both. They are automatically released after a specific date unless refiled. I had both removed prior to this "expiration" date, but what that statement means is, if you have tax liens they should no longer appear on your credit report as of the date specified on your lien recordings unless they're refiled. I can't say it never happens, but I've never seen tax liens refiled. My guess is unless you're actively fighting with the taxing entity and therefore on their radar, these don't get refiled.

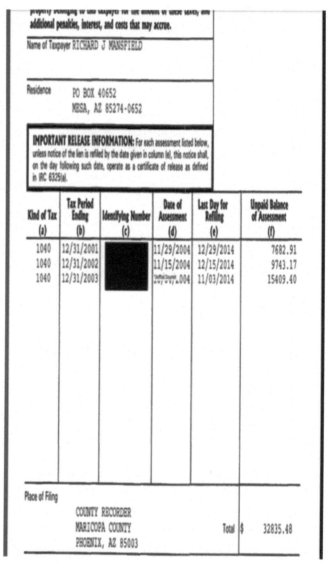

FIGURE 6

MESA   AZ 85202

Pursuant to the Arizona Revised Statutes Section 42-1152, Notice is hereby given that the following named taxpayer owes the Arizona Department of Revenue such unpaid amounts as are herein set forth and that pursuant to Section 42-1151 the Department has a lien against all the property or rights to property belonging to the taxpayer for such unpaid amount, plus accruing interest.

TYPE OF TAX: INCOME

ID NUMBERS: [REDACTED]   PLACE OF FILING: MARICOPA

LIEN NUMBER: 0404284

DATE OF ASSESSMENT	LAST DAY TO EXTEND LIEN	TAX PERIOD	TAX BALANCE	PENALTY	INTEREST THRU 12/31/04	UNPAID BALANCE OF ASSESSMENT
08/19/04	08/19/10	01/03-12/03	2,249.00	562.26	74.22	2,885.48
08/19/04	08/19/10	01/01-12/01	1,628.00	407.00	230.22	2,265.22
08/19/04	08/19/10	01/02-12/02	1,566.00	391.50	124.63	2,082.13

FIGURE 7

DISPUTE THE BALANCE

While the State of Arizona was deducting money from my paycheck due to a lien for unpaid taxes, I received monthly statements. The statements showed my balance going down but the balance at the Maricopa County Recorder's Office never changed.

To see what would happen, I disputed the balance with Equifax, Experian, and TransUnion. In response, they sent me letters saying they had verified the balance as $7,232.83 (the original balance), but my last statement from the Arizona Department of Revenue said it was $.04: yes, four cents. Obviously, there was something wrong.

I called Equifax to find out exactly how they could have possibly verified an incorrect balance. The Equifax rep said they used a third party, who physically went to the recorder's office, verified my balance as $7,232.83, and that it would remain as reported. The rep told me to supply the proof I had showing a corrected balance. My reply was, "It's not my job to prove anything. It's the credit bureau's job to prove what they are reporting is correct; prove it or remove it."

Having been in the credit and collection industry all these years, I know that no one goes anywhere unless they get a summons! Especially, since the advent of the internet, nobody moves from their computer; it's all done online. Trust me when I tell you no one went to the Maricopa County Recorder's Office.

Even if they had gone directly to the Recorder's Office or court, the balances there are rarely or never updated.

My next call and an email went directly to the Maricopa County recorder. I wanted documentation for both this book and a lawsuit against the bureaus. The Recorder's Office confirmed that no one from any of the bureaus ever comes to the Recorder's Office or ever contacts them at all.

Again, the email I posted previously in this chapter, from the Maricopa County (AZ) Recorder's Office, specifically states that they don't have contact with any credit bureau. It also states bureaus don't purchase public record information from the recorder.

Unlike a lender, who will send data directly to a credit bureau, public records aren't reported to any bureau. Every source of public records is a passive entity, meaning, they simply store information; they don't actively report it anywhere or vouch for its accuracy.

The records are stored by the government, namely a court or county recorder, retrieved by a third-party vendor, who then sells the information to the credit bureaus. Recorders don't confirm, nor do they attempt to verify the accuracy of the information they store.

In addition, privacy issues have become so restrictive, I am unaware of any government agency that will verify any personal information without that individuals written approval. I called the IRS, the Maricopa County recorder, and the US Bankruptcy Courts for the districts of Arizona and New York. All three said they do not verify information for anyone, including the credit bureaus. They said the only way information can be obtained is by going online or in person to view documents with redacted Social Security numbers.

LexisNexis, the third-party vendor, claims to verify disputed information when all they're doing is looking online at PACER (Public Access to Court Electronic Records): outdated, never updated, inaccurate, and redacted documentation. The public records they review on PACER were accurate the day they were filed and almost immediately became obsolete.

I called PACER, they clearly stated that they don't verify anything either. And again, as is the case with all viewable public records, at best, only the last four numbers of the Social Security numbers are visible, making it impossible to positively identify anyone.

I sued all three bureaus because they claimed to have researched public record information confirming a balance of $7,232.83. I had documentation to prove it was four cents. Of course, I won. I am not allowed to disclose the specifics of the settlements, but the negative public record items from the IRS and Arizona Department of Revenue were removed from my credit reports and as part of the agreement, I received a cash settlement. And remember, this was after a few disputes were denied. They say in the last paragraph of the following letter from Experian, that they, "will not reinvestigate this information again." Getting that letter from any of the bureaus that says "Verified. Will remain as reported" isn't the end of the dispute process. If you have documentation that what they claim to have verified is in error . . . sue. If you don't have documents, dispute something else: wrong opening date, wrong account number. Dispute everything and anything. Always be conscious of the fact that anything they report can be disputed.

Figures 8 and 9 are a letter from Experian and a copy of the "Settlement and Release Agreement" for the lawsuits I settled with Equifax, TransUnion, and Experian.

In the Experian letter, the last paragraph, they inform me that, "Unless you send relevant information to support your claim, we will not investigate this information again and you will not receive this notice again regarding this particular dispute." I disputed the item again and they didn't reinvestigate. This was a unique situation. Normally, they aren't required to reinvestigate a dispute they already verified. But in this case, I had documentation. It was a tax lien filed with the Maricopa County recorder. I had proof that the balance was four cents, but they kept reporting a $7,000-plus balance. Since I'm not legally required to do it, I never provided them with any proof. It's their job to verify what they're reporting is correct, not my job to

information to determine the accuracy and completeness of any disputed item by contacting the source of the disputed information and informing them of all relevant information regarding the consumer's dispute. If the issue is not resolved, then the consumer credit reporting company must offer to include a consumer statement on the personal credit report. The Consumer Financial Protection Bureau (the government agency charged with enforcement of the FCRA) does not require that the consumer credit reporting company obtain documentation such as the actual signed sales slips, signature cards, contracts, etc.; nor does it require that consumer credit reporting companies act as mediators or negotiators in account disputes.

Unless you send us relevant information to support your claim, we will not investigate this information again and you will not receive this notice again regarding this particular dispute.

MARICOPA COUNTY RECORDER

Sincerely,

Experian
NCAC
P.O. Box 2002
Allen TX 75013

0121193595

FIGURE 8

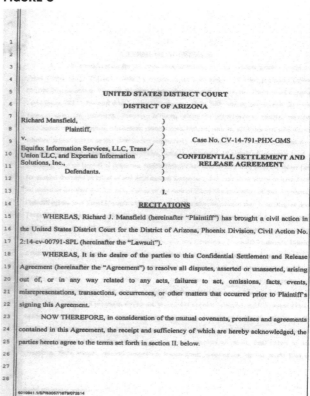

FIGURE 9

supply documents. I sued the bureaus for misreporting and claiming to have verified the balance.

So now your question is, "Why is that important to me?" It's important because the credit bureaus never follow the FCRA rules for validating any public records. It's the legal basis for removing every public record from your credit report.

There is no one who can verify the accuracy of any public records. Since they can't be verified, by law, they must be deleted from your credit report. Banks and credit card companies are information furnishers. They report data directly to the bureaus. If you dispute the information they supply, the bureaus contact them to verify the information they furnished. Information furnishers such as lenders and collectors will research disputes. They will attempt to verify the reported information as correct. If they can't verify it or don't respond at all, the credit bureau will delete the questioned information.

With public records, there is no reliable information furnisher who can or will verify a balance. The government agency, whether it's the recorder, courthouses, or anyone else, they store the information; they do not report, verify, or investigate it.

When a consumer disputes a public record, there is no one that can research and/or correct public information, as required by law. To meet the standards required under the FCRA, most public record information, including the information on PACER, is unreliable. For a public record that includes a balance to be accurate, it must updated to deduct payments or add interest; they rarely are. Judgments may be updated as paid or satisfied. Depending on the judgment creditor, sometimes they aren't even updated when they're paid. Since, in every case of public records, Social Security numbers are redacted, no one can definitively link any public record to any individual. The bureaus cannot link a public record to any individual that meets the legal standard of "beyond a doubt."

Figures 10 and 11 are copies of just two of the judgments I had removed, based on the inability of Equifax and TransUnion to confirm that they were mine.

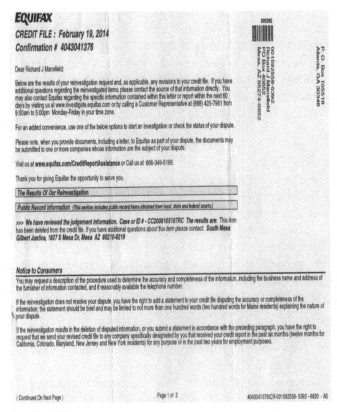

FIGURE 10

FIGURE 11

In the case of *Cushman v. TransUnion Corporation*, it was determined that, quote, "The grave responsibility imposed by §1681i(a) of the FCRA must consist of something more than merely parroting information from other sources." And that's exactly what the credit reporting agencies are doing. They outsource their legal responsibility for the verification of their reporting accuracy. A third party, usually LexisNexis, is saying the reported information is accurate. Lexis is verifying ancient information, from public records that are outdated, never updated, and from unreliable sources. They are "parroting" stale information.

I'll say it again: The best thing to dispute on any public record is the balance. The CRAs may ask you to provide a paid letter or some sort of balance statement, but again, it's not your job to prove anything. It's their job to verify that the disputed item is yours and everything they report is accurate. In the case of a disputed balance, it's impossible for anyone to verify a public record current balance. Since public record balances are never updated, all they can view is the original balance, never the current one which would include interest and/or payments.

The template you should use for disputing public records is in the appendix. You don't need to use it word for word. Keep in mind, with all the templates provided, word it so it works for your situation. Just make sure, in all your letters, that you keep any legal references intact. For example, "in *Cushman v. TransUnion Corporation*" or "*In Hinkle v. Midland Credit Management, Inc.*": anything that references a legal precedent, be sure to include the case.

WHY CREDIT REPORTS ARE RARELY ACCURATE

The Fair Credit Reporting Act mandates credit reporting agencies verify disputed debt with the "Information Furnisher." With any public record, PACER, the court, and/or every county recorder, assembles information from legal proceedings on a daily basis. That data is purchased by a third-party vendor and disseminated to the major credit bureaus. Third-party vendors are not information furnishers.

The data that's collected and uploaded to the recorder, the courts, and PACER came from one or more of the following information furnishers:

- County, state, or federal court
- County clerk or county recorder
- The county, state, or federal government
- State taxing authority
- The IRS
- Bankruptcy court.

Due to very stringent privacy issues, none of the above will verify anything, apart from the IRS and some state taxing authorities, which require specific authorization from the taxpayer, signed and notarized. The credit bureaus never ask for it. As it stands now, public records are unverifiable and if disputed must be deleted.

Here's an example of how strict privacy issues have become. I went to the Mesa, Arizona, police department to get a replacement copy of my police report. Yup, a report where I was the victim; someone had stolen my personal checks and cashed one. My date of birth, address, and Social Security number were all redacted (blacked out) from the police report. I asked for an unredacted copy and I couldn't get it. Here I am, the victim, the reporter of the crime, and I can't get an unredacted copy. They said no one can get an unredacted copy.

When it comes to public information like bankruptcy, tax liens, and judgments, the CRAs don't even claim to try to verify anything themselves with the information furnishers. I called Experian, Equifax, and TransUnion. They all told me they used a third-party vendor to verify my tax liens. The third-party vendor, LexisNexis, isn't going to the information furnisher. They're using PACER, which has the identical records that are at the recorders' offices or courthouse. Public records are never updated to reflect current balances.

I recorded the conversations with the bureaus, sued all three, and settled for in excess of $18,000. They removed my tax liens and the judgments from my reports.

My correspondence with the Maricopa County Recorder's Office proves that there is no contact between the alleged information furnisher and the CRAs. This is absolutely in violation of the FCRA.

As payments are made, on publicly recorded documents, like tax liens or judgments, the only source for a current balance would be the IRS, the state taxing authority, or judgment creditor. Balances on tax liens and judgments cannot be validated since they are never updated and the "information furnishers" are barred by privacy issues. The information reporters, like the IRS, do not speak to anyone without a court order or notarized authority to do so.

This is in direct violation of the FCRA, §611. Procedure in case of disputed accuracy (15 USC § 1681i) which says they must validate the information through the furnisher.

The credit bureaus never get information directly from the recorder or courts. Since the recorder's records are not updated, third-party vendors like LexisNexis who research disputes are repeating stale, inaccurate information. The FCRA says all information must be correct and verifiable or deleted. Correct most certainly includes the balances being accurate.

There are a few ways to dispute all public records and they work. First, remember that credit reporting agencies verify records through a third party that uses a database called PACER. PACER is not an information furnisher as required under the FCRA/FACTA.

Credit reporting agencies (CRAs) will list, for instance, the bankruptcy court as the "furnisher" of the public information. Yet, no one at the credit reporting agency or their third-party agent contacts the bankruptcy court (furnisher) as required under the Fair Credit Reporting Act.

In a call to the Bankruptcy Court for the District of Arizona. I asked if they are ever contacted by any of the CRAs or anyone else regarding record disputes and they said, "No."

The following is the part of the Fair Credit Reporting Act (FCRA) that is the basis for all your credit bureau disputes:

§611. Procedure in case of disputed accuracy {15 USC § 1681i}

(5) Treatment of Inaccurate or Unverifiable Information

(A) In general, if after any reinvestigation... of any information disputed by a consumer, an item of information is found to be inaccurate or incomplete OR CANNOT BE VERIFIED, the consumer reporting agency shall:

(i) promptly delete that item of information from the file of the consumer..."

Pay special attention to these listed areas when disputing the accuracy of your credit report.

Strategies for Removing Public Records (Bankruptcies, Tax Liens, Judgments) from Your Credit Report

INACCURATE REPORTING

Look for an incorrect reporting of facts and dispute that part of the listing. My favorite is always the balance. You don't have to tell them what your records show the balance is, just tell them that the one on your credit report is incorrect. It may get deleted and no further work is necessary. If it's not removed, then there are numerous other ways to proceed.

As always, you can dispute anything they report: dates, account numbers, balances, etc. Sometimes this is a marathon, not a sprint. Bureaus count on you giving up and sadly, most people get so frustrated that they do. Don't be one of those people who give up. This is very important to your financial future.

METHOD OF VERIFICATION

If you receive a response to your dispute that says the listing is verified and stays "as reported," you have the right to request the bureau's method of verification. Call the bureau and record the conversation. It's faster, cheaper, and more efficient than writing. And the conversation might lead to additional actionable violations of law. "Actionable" is legalese meaning you can sue. If you feel uncomfortable on the phone, write, and ask how they verified the information you disputed.

When I speak with the CRAs, I'm always particularly interested in the answer to the question, "How did you verify my dispute?"

When you're disputing public records, the CRA representative will always try to get rid of you by either referring you to the Recorder's Office or the court. If they didn't delete the public record you disputed, if you call instead of re-disputing with another letter, your conversation with the

CRA representative should go something like this. (Record the conversation.)

You say:

"How was my dispute verified?"

They will say either:

"Through the court" or "Recorder's Office."

You say:

"I'm not asking where I am asking how. Did someone physically go to the courthouse or was it done electronically with an email?"

They will say:

"It was verified by a third-party vendor."

Your follow up question is:

"How did the third-party vendor verify it? Did the third party physically visit the court, did they speak to someone or did they do it electronically?"

They will say:

"Electronically."

Then you ask:

"Did they send an email to the court? Is that how they verified the information?"

They will say either:

"The vendor verified it electronically."
OR
"They used PACER."

As I outlined previously, PACER is stale information. It isn't adequate to use PACER to meet the legal requirements for verifying the information you've disputed.

With non-public records, like a credit card, mortgage, auto loans, repossessions, or foreclosure, your conversation will go something like this:

You say:

"How was my dispute verified?"

They will say:

"Through e-Oscar."

You say:

"What's e-Oscar?"

They will say:

"e-Oscar is an electronic online solution for processing automated credit disputes."

You say:

"Did you get a copy of my signed contract or copies of my personal checks for payment?"

"How was it verified?"

"Did they simply compare my name and social to a name and social they have on their files and since they compared they said it's mine? Isn't that what fraud is, someone using your name and social to get credit?"

They will say:

"Are you saying the account is fraudulent?"

"Did you fill out a police report indicating fraud?"

You say:

"No, it's not my job to file a police report. According to the Fair Credit Reporting Act, it's your job and the information furnisher's job to make sure what's reported is accurate and in fact mine!"

Once you have this recorded either of these conversations, terminate the call and have a consumers' rights attorney listen to these recordings to see if there is a violation of the Fair Credit Reporting Act.

Ask the following ONLY if you sent documentation with your dispute: "Was all the documentation and the reasons for my dispute forwarded to the information furnisher?"

In most cases, they will say "No" and possibly tell you it was turned into a numeric code, but will indicate that your specific dispute wording and documents were not sent.

Terminate the call and get the recording to a consumer's rights attorney.

TO RECAP

If what you disputed was a matter of public record, if it isn't removed, they will say that it was verified by a third party. The third party is usually a company called LexisNexis. All LexisNexis does is view an online service called PACER, an acronym for "Public Access to Court Electronic Records." In the case of records like judgments and tax liens, these records, specifically, the balances, are never updated. Because interest is accruing or because payments you made are not included, the information regarding the balance is incorrect a month after the date it is reported.

If the disputed item was something other than a public record, they will indicate it was verified by e-Oscar. All e-Oscar is, is an email.

The representative at the credit bureau, who may be in India, the Philippines, or South America and whose first language isn't English, assigns a code and emails the information furnisher that code. Except in the case where you are disputing medical debt and sometimes not even then, the information furnisher rarely sees your dispute letter or the documentation it took you days, weeks, or even months to compile.

According to the Fair Credit Reporting Act, the methods CRAs use to "verify" the accuracy of a disputed account are insufficient for the CRAs to use and then claim the disputed item has been verified.

The third-party vendor looked up old, maybe years old, information on the internet that has never been updated and repeated the ancient information PACER reports. Once you have this conversation recorded, along with the letter they sent you saying, "We verified the accuracy as reported, the item will remain" or similar wording, you now have a situation where you should contact a consumers' rights attorney.

You probably have an actionable violation of the FCRA, a lawsuit worth $1,000, possibly more. (Just in case you're unfamiliar with the word "actionable," it's legalese, meaning you have the basis for a lawsuit.) The CRAs do not follow the law with their verification methodology. What I just described is exactly my basis for three suits that I won, one each against Equifax, Experian, and TransUnion.

This is an excerpt from the law they violated:

> §611. Procedure in case of disputed accuracy { 15USC § 1681i}
>
> (5) Treatment of Inaccurate or Unverifiable Information
>
> (A) In general, if after any reinvestigation . . . of any information disputed by a consumer, an item of information is found to be inaccurate or incomplete OR CANNOT BE VERIFIED, the consumer reporting agency shall
>
> (i) promptly delete that item of information from the file of the consumer . . .

The procedure they admit they use doesn't legally verify anything.

Chapter 5
INCREASE YOUR CREDIT SCORE

Pay On Time

Contrary to what every so-called credit expert will tell you, your credit score will not be affected by missing one payment. A single past due payment will never show up on any credit report. The trigger point is thirty days past due, and that happens when you're two payments past due.

The primary factor in all scoring systems is paying on time. This is how it works for reporting purposes:

> 1–29 days overdue (1 payment)—Nothing is reported
>
> 30–59 days overdue (2 payments)—Reported as 30 days past due
>
> 60–89 days overdue (3 payments)—Reported as 60 days past due
>
> 90–119 days overdue (4 payments)—Reported as 90 days past due

If you have internet access, set up anything that can be paid online so you can pay it online. It's faster, more reliable, and unlike regular mail, it's free. That way you have a dated email receipt for your payments. If you use snail mail, without paying for a return receipt, you don't have any dated proof of when the creditor received your payment. Unscrupulous lenders have been known to hold payments so they can hit you with a late charge. Providian settled a class action lawsuit for $105 million, in part because they were allegedly holding payments past the due date to assess late fees.

The suit states in "although Providian's promotional materials advertised credit repair through the use of a Providian credit card, the lawsuit contended that Providian's payment-processing procedures led to the improper assessment of late fees that instead of helping, damaged customers' credit."

The best way to make sure that you're never late is to set up automated payments. Make sure the money for the payment is in the account so the lender can electronically make a timely withdrawal.

Never Go Over Your Credit Line

Almost equally important as paying on time is how much of your lines of credit you carry over from month to month. In credit scoring, this is commonly called usage or utilization. So-called credit experts vary in their opinion as to what percentage of a credit line usage will adversely affect your credit score. They seem to recommend figures between 10 percent and 30 percent. All they are doing is giving opinions. Being the inquisitive type, and not wanting to give inaccurate info, I tested the theory. I didn't just want to say, "Trust me, this is the way it works." I did the research. Carrying any balance will negatively affect your credit. I went ahead and used 10 percent, then 28 percent, 50 percent, and 90 percent of my limits; nothing else changed. So, the only thing that could have had a negative impact on my report was the credit usage. Here's a breakdown of what happened.

Ten percent usage dropped my score seventeen points. Then I specifically used 28 percent to keep my usage under the often stated, "It's OK to use up to 30 percent of your credit limits" advice. My FICO score dropped from 765 to 701. It is NOT OK to use up to 30 percent of your outstanding credit limits! That sixty-four-point drop would cost me tens of thousands of dollars on a mortgage and thousands on the average auto loan. Using 50 percent dropped it 119 points. Using 90 percent dropped it 181 points.

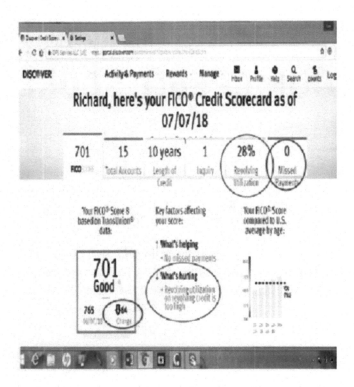

As you can see, the credit score decreases are significant. Keep in mind that your credit report and mine have other variables, so your score won't drop exactly like mine did. I gave you these figures as an example of how usage affects scores. For credit scoring purposes it's as significant as paying on time.

Any drop in your credit score can be significant. There are specific trigger points that lenders use to determine rates, especially mortgage companies and auto loan lenders. The difference between a 699 score and a 700 can be substantial. If you are financially able, pay off or pay down as much debt as possible before applying for additional credit. If you can, do it at least a month, and don't cheat, I mean an entire thirty days, prior to a major financing request like a mortgage or auto loan.

Ideally, you will never carry any balances from month to month. I know that's sometimes hard to do, but as far as your credit score is concerned, that's the ideal. Even if you never go past due, carrying balances has a negative impact on your score.

Have Your Credit Limits Raised Before You Need It

Regardless of what other credit "experts" think, it's best not to carry any balances if possible. Not even a 10 percent usage. Your circumstances may force you to, but it will substantially affect your score. The "experts" giving out the advice, that it's OK to carry 10 percent, are doing it based on theory, not fact. Remember, anything I tell you to do or to avoid doing, I did! Credit scoring systems all regard carrying any balance, from one month to the next, as a negative.

There are two "usage" calculations: usage based on an individual card and overall usage. They can both be damaging. Overall usage is calculated based on the total available as a percentage of your total usage. For example, if you have five cards with total limits adding up to $5,000 and you're using one card, in the amount of $500, or five for $100 each, the total "usage" calculation is the same. You're using $500 of the total available of $5,000 or 10 percent of the total possible. To decrease the amount in use, always accept credit limit increases if offered. If they aren't offered or automatically given, request increases every twelve months or as needed. It always seems easier to get a limit raised when you don't need it then when you do. An increase request may result in a hard inquiry. Hard inquiries usually result in a score drop of two or three points. If two to three points is important, ask your lender if they perform a hard inquiry for line increases.

Did you ever wonder why your credit utilization isn't zero when you pay the balances due on your credit cards every month? It's because your due date and "report date" are not necessarily the same. Call your credit card company and ask what day of the month they report to the credit bureaus. Adjust when you pay that bill accordingly.

APPLYING FOR CREDIT LIMIT INCREASES

Don't go crazy with the amount of any requested increase. Don't ask for an additional $3,000 on an existing $1,000 line. If you ask for an addition to your credit limit, the lenders will evaluate:

- Your payment record with them
- How long you've had the card
- The usage of that card
- If they perform a hard pull of your credit report and/or score, they'll consider other credit line amounts, overall payment history, and ultimately your credit score.

You should wait twelve months between requests for an increase in your lines of credit. If that's too soon for your lender, they'll usually let you know. Some lenders may offer you a lower amount than requested.

If possible, when applying for a credit limit increase try not to have a balance near or at your credit limit, and make sure you have been making more than minimum payments for the prior six months. Again, these are ideal times to apply for increases. Sometimes you need the increase when it wasn't anticipated. Go ahead and apply if you need the increase. The worst that can happen is they turn down the request. If you handle your credit cards properly, a lender may raise your limit without you applying.

Mix It Up!

All credit scoring systems are heavily weighted toward calculating higher scores for people who have a mixture of borrowings: for instance, credit cards, auto loans, and a mortgage—not just a mortgage or just a credit card. If all that you have ever done in the credit world is use a credit card, your FICO and VantageScores will rise more slowly than if you had a variety of borrowings.

This is not to say that strictly having credit cards won't work: It will. It'll just take longer to maximize your scores. Lenders and credit scoring analytics like to see that you have handled a range of different types of loans in a satisfactory manner.

Chapter 6
REMOVING NEGATIVE INFORMATION: DISPUTES WILL REPAIR YOUR CREDIT REPORT

The following is from the Fair Credit Reporting Act (FCRA): 15USC § 1681i(a) Reinvestigation of Disputed Information.

I'll condense the relevant part of the lengthy FCRA. Although I'm NOT an attorney, I personally sued and settled enough cases to understand and translate the legalese. "If after any reinvestigation . . . any information disputed by a consumer is found to be inaccurate, incomplete or cannot be verified, the consumer reporting agency shall delete or modify as appropriate." In plain English, they have to prove it or remove it.

When a consumer disputes the completeness or accuracy of any information contained on their credit report, the credit reporting agency (CRA) must conduct what's legally termed a reinvestigation. I found the term reinvestigation odd, but I did get clarification from all three bureaus. They indicated that even your first dispute is called a reinvestigation. Personally, I would have termed the review of the first dispute an investigation and all subsequent reviews reinvestigations, but I guess that's just me.

Per, 15USC § 1681i(a), if the reinvestigation reveals that the information is inaccurate or can't be verified, the CRA must promptly delete or update the information, and notify you of the results of your dispute. In the case of *Cushman v. TransUnion*, the courts ruled that a failure to conduct a reasonable reinvestigation violates the Fair Credit Reporting Act (FCRA). They also ruled that the burden to conduct the reinvestigation is exclusively on the credit reporting agency. It can't be shifted back to the consumer.

What that means is that no one should be asking you for documentation to prove your disputes. You aren't required to do their job. They're required do a reasonable reinvestigation based on the information you provided, if any, and to prove it or remove it. In the case where you're saying that it isn't your account, there's nothing you can provide to prove it's not your account. Tell them to prove it or remove it. My letters, formatted in the appendix, include a demand to remove unverifiable items.

Cushman v. TransUnion (caselaw.findlaw.com/us-3rd-circuit/1434033.html) outlines the credit bureaus' and creditors' procedural responsibility for verification during a dispute. In another lawsuit, *Hinkle v. Midland Credit Management, Inc.*, the court said, during a dispute and subsequent reinvestigation with the original creditor, collector, or a credit bureau, that the original creditor or collector must be able to provide "account-level documentation." That means an original contract or similar proof, not just a printout of the payments that were made. Keep in mind that when you apply for credit online there is no signed contract. The lender or collector even if they sue you is not required to supply a signed contract. There is a legal doctrine called an account stated. It basically says if you made a payment on an account, you have admitted the account is yours. There's a detailed explanation of an account stated in chapter 20. Two things to be said here. The court said similar proof. They didn't say the credit bureau had to provide documents. The bureaus never have documents. The bureaus are simply repositories for information reported to them by banks, credit card issuers, collection agencies, and in the case of services like Experian Boost you're self-reporting. When you file a dispute with a credit bureau, they're required to contact the information furnisher. They must tell the information furnisher what you're disputing and relay the documentation you included if any. The bureaus rely on the information furnisher to have documentation that confirms what they are reporting is correct. If you are going to demand documents, they must be requested from the information furnisher/creditor after, and I repeat, after your dispute is processed by the credit bureau. If you go directly to the creditor before disputing an item with the credit bureau, you lose your right to sue.

My first dispute letter always states, "Not my account." Any credit bureau you send that letter to may ask if you are claiming fraud. When I receive that as a response, I immediately call the bureau. I tell them, "I'm not claiming anything. What I'm saying is this isn't my account. You can define what that means any way you want." They probably will tell you to file a police report. There is no legal requirement for you to do so. The FCRA says it's their job to prove that what you're disputing is correct. It's not your job to prove it isn't.

The courts have repeatedly ruled that the "grave responsibility" imposed by § 1681i(a) of the Fair Credit Reporting Act must consist of something more than merely repeating, or as the court terms it, "parroting," information received from other sources. A "reinvestigation" that merely shifts the burden back to the consumer cannot fulfill the obligations required by the FCRA. In plain English, that means, when there is a dispute, the information furnishers are the ones obligated to prove you owe the money and it is not your job to prove you don't.

I disputed a past due utility bill that appeared on my Experian credit report from APS, Arizona Public Service. In response, Experian sent me a letter indicating APS verified the account was mine and it would remain on my report.

I called APS to ask how they identified me as the consumer of their services. As it turned out, they didn't; there was no way they could have. The account had been opened with a phone call. The utility never saw ID and never had anyone sign a contract. Someone had used my Social Security number and made payments in cash. Because of the cash payments, they didn't even have a paper trail. They had nothing that indicated that I was the user of their services. Yet, the utility company said they

"thought" it was me and repeatedly insisted I file a police report. I repeatedly insisted that the Fair Credit Reporting Act doesn't require me to file a report and I wouldn't file one.

I sued and we went to arbitration. The case was settled before going to trial for an amount I am legally prohibited from disclosing. The delinquency they claimed was mine was removed from my credit report.

There are two things my conversation and subsequent arbitration with APS proved. It proved beyond a shadow of a doubt that creditors will try to bully you into thinking you must have a police report. You do not need a police report! It's easier, a slam-dunk, if you have a police report, but you don't necessarily need one. Second, creditors are clueless about what the FCRA obligates them to do to prove a debt is yours. It definitely isn't the rep saying, "We think it's yours." The Fair Credit Reporting Act does not say that you need a police report to dispute a debt. Creditors try to create the illusion that it's up to you to prove you don't owe the money. That's not your job. Again, and this is important, it's not your job to prove you don't owe the money. It's their job to prove that you do.

It's important to note that before I spoke to the original creditor, the utility company, I disputed the debt with Experian first. It's a sequence that legally must be followed to preserve your right to sue: Dispute the listing with at least one of the bureaus first. If the outcome of the dispute doesn't resolve the problem in your favor, then ask for an investigation by the original creditor.

During my phone call with APS, their entire basis for concluding I was the person who owed them the money was that they matched my name and Social Security number on a credit report to the name and Social Security number they received during a call from someone claiming to be me. Based on that alone, they concluded it must be my account. To which my response is "No kidding my Social Security number matches. That's what fraud is. Somebody using my name and Social Security number to obtain credit. How about a copy of an application with my signature?"

Filling out a police report could have easily remedied the problem, but that wasn't my goal. My goal in addition to getting my credit report corrected was to prove that even though they make it sound like filing a police report is mandatory, it isn't.

In *Hinkle v. Midland Credit Management, Inc.* the court said the collector must provide "account-level documentation." This means an original contract or similar documentation that would hold up in court when presented to a jury. It means they can't just send you a printout, or a computer-generated accounting of a payment history and or a current balance statement and claim that's sufficient to prove that it's your account. It isn't proof of anything. At best it proves someone made payments. At worst, it's simply a piece of paper with words and numbers, proving someone has typing skills and access to blank paper. It is not proof you owe money. It's not proof that the debt is yours.

As part of any reinvestigation, a CRA must provide the information furnisher with notification of exactly what the consumer is disputing. The CRA must also note on your credit report that the account is disputed.

You can dispute without documentation. I never include docs. And there are reasons I don't ever supply documents. First, in most cases, I don't have any. Second, if you claim the account doesn't belong to you, the date of last payment is wrong, the opening date is wrong, there is no such thing as a document that proves any of those types of claims. Third, the only time I did have proof was on my state tax lien. I wanted to get what I knew would be a fraudulent reply of "Verified" and then sue. When I received that "Verified will remain as reported" letter as I knew I would, I sued and won. You can see the suits against Experian and Equifax listed as #1 and #2 respectively on PACER in Figure 1.

Here is the state tax lien story. It shows a blatant disregard of the law by the credit bureaus.

I knew my state tax lien was paid. I disputed the balance with all three bureaus. I received letters from all three stating the balance was correct and would remain as reported. Since the state doesn't send paid in full letters, I immediately went to the Arizona State Department of Revenue. They said it was paid in full. I knew I still owed four cents. Apparently, they don't consider four cents a balance. I offered the four cents; they didn't take it, suggesting instead that I could wait about three hours to see an agent who would give me a paid letter. There was no way I was going to wait for three hours, so I left without it.

I immediately sent second dispute letters to Equifax, Experian, and TransUnion. I disputed my state tax lien again, telling them my balance was incorrect as reported. Had I waited three hours for that paid letter, I could have sent documentation along with the disputes and the bureaus would have updated my report as paid. But I wanted to prove they can't verify public records, in this case, a state tax lien, so I sent the disputes without any documentation.

As a response to my dispute, I received letters from Equifax and Experian saying, "Verified, will remain as reported." Experian even went so far as to say they would NEVER investigate the dispute (see Figure 12). The second paragraph says, "Unless you send us relevant information to support your claim we will not investigate this information again." Knowing it was paid, I knew they couldn't have possibly performed a reasonable investigation. Equifax and Experian had violated the FCRA by not following the legally mandated dispute investigation procedure. I had proven my point; bureaus can't and don't verify public information. I sued and won.

TransUnion didn't even reply. Another violation, so I sued them too. Had I sent the documentation proving my claim, they would have removed the lien information, but I couldn't have sued. I settled both the Equifax and Experian suits for a total of over $11,000 and TransUnion for more than $3,000. Figure 13 shows the cover sheet for the lawsuit.

The Fair Debt Collection Practices Act and Fair Credit Reporting Act delineate violations for collectors and credit reporting agencies under federal law. In addition some states have their own version of the FDCPA and FCRA, including California, Massachusetts, Florida, and Texas. Under federal law, violations of the FDCPA are capped at $1,000 and you can only sue collection agencies. State consumer protection laws are usually much more generous allowing suits for up $10,000 and may allow you to sue the original creditor.

Prepared for: **RICHARD J MANSFIELD**
Date: **July 29, 2013**
Report number: **1294-5252-41**

information to determine the accuracy and completeness of any disputed item by contacting the source of the disputed information and informing them of all relevant information regarding the consumer's dispute. If the issue is not resolved, then the consumer credit reporting company must offer to include a consumer statement on the personal credit report. The Consumer Financial Protection Bureau (the government agency charged with enforcement of the FCRA) does not require that the consumer credit reporting company obtain documentation such as the actual signed sales slips, signature cards, contracts, etc.; nor does it require that consumer credit reporting companies act as mediators or negotiators in account disputes.

Unless you send us relevant information to support your claim, we will not investigate this information again and you will not receive this notice again regarding this particular dispute.

MARICOPA COUNTY RECORDER

Sincerely,

Experian
NCAC
P.O. Box 2002
Allen TX 75013

FIGURE 12

You can sue under both federal and state FDCPAs for the identical violation. When you win, you can get paid under both laws!

Clearly what the bureaus had done was outsource their responsibility to verify my lien to a third party. And they do it every time to everyone. The third party simply looked at an online source called PACER (Public Access to Court Electronic Records) and decided the tax lien was owed and still had a $7,000+ balance. The bad news for them is PACER balances are so rarely updated, to the point where it's valid to say they're never updated.

This is especially important when disputing any public information such as tax liens, bankruptcies, and judgments. I've never seen public record balances updated. Third-party vendors, hired by the CRAs, simply repeat information from online sites such as PACER. Based on the court's ruling in *Cushman v. TransUnion*, this is legally insufficient and is the basis to have all public records removed from your credit reports.

This is how I removed two tax liens, a bankruptcy, and judgments from my credit reports.

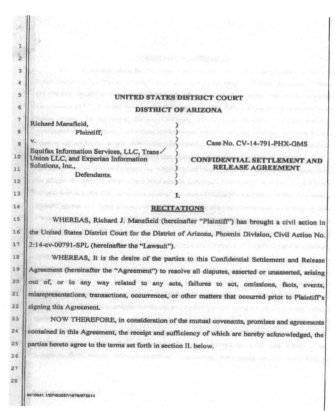

FIGURE 13

And I will say this again: You can get a bankruptcy removed from your credit report, but don't! Much too much effort and not enough reward. I removed my bankruptcy simply to prove it could be done for this book. I explained why you should NOT remove it and how to reestablish credit, after a bankruptcy in chapter 4. If you didn't read it and you want to know why you shouldn't remove a bankruptcy, go back and read it now.

Never File a Dispute Online

Anyone who disputes online is giving up their right to sue. Once you've waived that right, you've lost your leverage and the bureaus don't have any motivation to resolve disputes in your favor. All credit bureaus have very wordy disclaimers that you automatically agree to because you used the online dispute process. For example, Equifax has a disclaimer that's 1,323 words of unintelligible babble that says you have no right to sue them or be part of a class action lawsuit. It's buried in Section 35, of a document totaling eleven thousand words, that most attorneys would struggle to understand. You would be agreeing to mandatory binding arbitration, meaning you forfeit your right to sue. Don't ever dispute online.

Make sure to mail every dispute letter certified. Request a return receipt. The day that the letter is received starts the clock ticking for the thirty days the bureaus have to respond. If your disputing with a collection agency, they do NOT have to respond. A collection agency has two options once they receive a dispute letter. They can choose to respond, or stop all collection activity. Collection activity includes mails, emails, texts, phone calls, suing you, and credit reporting.

If they don't respond then pull a credit report thirty days after they signed for your letter. Make sure they haven't continued to report.

The following is the minimum information required to process a dispute:

- The full name of the creditor, collection agency, public record, or other information furnisher that you're disputing.

- The number of the account in question as shown on the credit report.

- A description of what you're disputing and why.

- Proper identification is required. A government issued picture ID, and a Social Security card are the norm. If either of these are unavailable, call the bureau in question and ask what they accept.

They are not required to investigate your dispute unless it includes all the above. Don't worry about giving them your Social Security card. Your Social Security number is already part of the file they have on you. They ask for it as part of the process to validate that you are who you say you are.

The following is directly from the Fair Credit Reporting Act. The section I italicized clearly states that disputes must come from the consumer. I never send a dispute letter for a client. I make calls to collection agencies and credit bureaus on a client's behalf and compose letters for clients to mail. My coaching complies with the requirements of the FCRA! This is one of the many reasons why my process works and companies like Lexington Law who mail disputes for consumers often don't accomplish anything. Bureaus can ignore disputes sent out by anyone other than the consumer themselves!

> § 611. Procedure in case of disputed accuracy [15USC § 1681i]
>
> (a) Reinvestigations of disputed information.
>
> (1) Reinvestigation required.
>
> (A) In general. If the completeness or accuracy of any item of information contained in a consumer's file at a consumer reporting agency is *disputed by the consumer and the consumer notifies the agency directly of such dispute*, the agency shall reinvestigate free of charge and record the current status of the disputed information, or delete the item from the file in accordance with paragraph (5), *before the end of the 30-day period beginning on the date on which the agency receives the notice of the dispute from the consumer.*

If you have proof backing up your dispute and all you are looking to do is get your credit report corrected, send the proof. But remember, proof is not required. It's not your job to assist them in doing their job. The burden to conduct the reinvestigation is on the credit reporting agency and the information furnisher. It cannot be shifted back to you.

Keep a diary exclusively to document all your efforts. Mail everything certified with a return receipt requested. The date they sign the receipt is the date that starts the clock ticking for their response. Keep a copy of every letter you send and the original of every letter you receive.

There is proof for everything I say that I did, copies of checks for suit settlements, letters from the credit bureaus and collection agencies, here in the book, and you can scroll through my Twitter account (@DebtAssassin15).

In the appendix there are examples of letters you can use for general and specific disputes. Use the letters as a guide to say what you want to say to get what you want accomplished. It's recommended that you don't copy the letters word for word. The bureaus don't want any dispute letters sent to look like form letters. They want the disputes to come directly from you. They are legally allowed to refuse to investigate or reinvestigate disputes they think are credit repair company generated or not written by the consumer.

Since you control when the letters are sent and how fast you follow up on the replies, your credit improves much more quickly than using a traditional credit repair company. Traditional credit repair organizations have no incentive to do anything quickly. They make money by charging monthly. They drag their feet to increase their revenue.

Keep Track of All Your Communications

All communication means phone calls, letters, smoke signals, or carrier pigeons: ALL COMMUNICATION. Record every conversation. Send all mail certified. If you file a lawsuit, and in the rare event it goes in front of a judge, you need documentation. The legal system works based on proof. Make sure you have written documents and recordings. It's better to have them and not need them than need them and not have them.

Keep a diary. The diary should include the dates and results of all your recorded phone calls with collectors and credit bureaus, both incoming and outgoing. Have a file for all the letters you send and receive. Your diary should include follow-up dates and a short description of what you spoke about.

Before you call a collector or credit bureau, make a list of questions you want to ask. In chapter 2, I listed a few general questions you might want to ask a collector. Be creative and feel free to add your own. The more they talk, the more likely they are to screw up.

Keep a written record of where you kept your recordings so that you can locate a specific conversation, without having to listen to every recording to find the one you want.

Keep your postal receipts as evidence of your mailings. Keep the signed, dated receipts (green cards) to document the start of the thirty-day clock ticking that requires the recipient to answer.

Collectors must have "account-level documentation," meaning a copy or original signed contract or something similar. If the original transaction was completed over the internet, signed contracts don't exist. Lenders rely on the legal concept of an "account stated." An accounted stated is based on the fact that a consumer received a bill and made payments without disputing the debt. When you made payments, you acknowledged the debt as yours. (A detailed explanation of the account stated is in chapter 20.) But they can't simply produce a computer-generated printout. If they rely on the account stated doctrine, they must produce evidence of a canceled check or some form of an electronic funds transfer payment from you, not a money order or a Western Union money transfer that could have come from anyone.

Documentation for everything you do is very important. Ninety-nine percent of these consumer suits are resolved by mediation, or a settlement prior to mediation or a trial. In that extremely rare instance that a case goes in front of a judge and jury, the side with the most documentation usually wins.

If you get a reply to your dispute that says they "verified" the disputed item, there are two ways to go. You can call the credit bureau. That entire scenario, what you should ask, is spelled out in detail toward the end of chapter 4. If you feel comfortable you can veer off the script provided to accomplish your particular goals. Or send another letter disputing something else. For instance, if you said in your first dispute letter "not my account," send another one saying the balance is wrong. If they say they verified the balance, send another letter saying the high credit is wrong, or the date of last payment is incorrect. Don't give up, keep disputing. Sometimes this turns into a marathon and the person with the most stamina wins!

Eventually:

- They will acknowledge your dispute is valid
- Be unable to verify correct information with the information furnisher
- Fail to answer your dispute.

All these scenarios result in the item being removed. If they fail to answer within the thirty days mandated by the FCRA or don't answer at all, you can sue, make up to a thousand dollars, and get the item removed.

Make sure you use a different reason on each dispute, or they can disregard the dispute as "frivolous." Disputes can legally be regarded as "frivolous" if you use the same reason twice, for the same account, with the same bureau. If they deem the dispute frivolous, they aren't required to do a reinvestigation unless you send additional proof not included in your previous dispute. If they refuse to reinvestigate, they must notify you of that fact and the reasoning behind it.

Anything an Information Furnisher (Creditor) Lists You Can Dispute

Here are some of the common negative reported items you'll want to challenge:

- Foreclosure
- Repossessions (voluntary repossessions are also negatives)
- Legally settled for less than the full balance
- Accounts that are or were late (thirty/sixty/ninety/etc. days)
- Accounts reported by a collection agency
- Judgments
- Tax liens (federal and state)
- Student loans
- Medical bills
- Any account in collections.

The status is what you dispute. This is how you can dispute every negative item that shows up, not just the ones listed above. You can say:

- Not my account
- I didn't pay late that month
- Wrong terms
- Wrong balance
- Wrong balance history
- Wrong payment amount
- Wrong account number
- Wrong date of last payment
- Wrong opening date
- Wrong original creditor
- Wrong credit limit
- I was only an authorized user and therefore not financially responsible.

The negative items reported by the original creditor (OC) are the most difficult to remove, but not impossible: They screw up too. Dispute those just like you would any other account. But keep in mind, you must dispute anything that's reported by the OC with the credit bureau first before you dispute it directly with the original creditor.

Don't forget that if the original creditor or a collection agency has NOT notified you that they are going to or have reported negative information, they are in violation of the Fair and Accurate Credit Transaction Act, aka FACTA. It's important to note that they are only required to notify you the first time they report a delinquency, not every time. Here's an explanation of the FACTA's Notice of Negative Information requirement.

Notice of Negative Information

A provision of the FACTA regulations is the notice of negative information provision, covered in section 623(A) (7) of the act.

FACTA (the Fair and Accurate Credit Transactions Act) requires creditors to give you a "warning" notice, before reporting your account as being past due. The notice might alert you to the fact that:

- A payment you thought was made was never received
- Someone opened an account in your name or
- You simply didn't make a payment.

A Notice of Negative Information isn't necessarily a separate mailing. They only need to notify you one time. It's usually included with your first monthly billing. As noted by the Federal Trade Commission at https://www.ftc.gov/tips-advice/business-center/guidance/how-comply-privacy-consumer-financial-information-rule-gramm#whois (see under the "Are you a financial institution?" heading), collection agencies and student loan servicers are among the groups that must send the notice.

All financial institutions that extend credit and report to a credit bureau are required to send the notice before they report, or no later than thirty days after the negative information is furnished to a credit bureau. Negative information includes late payments, missed payments, partial payments, over your credit limit, or any type of default or deficiency on an account.

They're not required to give the notice every time they report a negative; it's a one-time notice. You are only entitled to the notice the first time they report. A financial institution can continue to report negative information, without additional notice. Even if you bring the account up to date and then fall behind again, they aren't required to give another notice. If you have multiple accounts with the same institution, they are required to give a separate alert on each account.

One of the reasons behind the law is to give a heads up to people that there may have been fraud.

Unfortunately, you can't sue if you never received the notice of negative reporting. But you can file a complaint with the FTC or CFPB.

Write the creditor or collection agency. Tell them their failure to give notice that they were going to report negative information is a violation of the Fair and Accurate Credit Transactions Act (FACTA). Inform them of your intent to file a complaint with the FTC and/or the CFPB. Sometimes the notification of your intention is enough to get a negative item deleted. Keep in mind that the "Notice of Negative Information" doesn't usually come in a separate mailing or even on a separate piece of paper. It's usually buried somewhere in a billing statement or something else the average consumer would normally ignore.

Date of First Delinquency

On your credit report this is noted a few ways depending on which report you're looking at. It may be noted as "DoFD" or "first date past due," or "past due as of," or they may indicate something like "this item will remain on your report until" and insert a date.

This is a very important date. This is the date that starts the seven-year time frame a negative is legally allowed to remain on your credit report. This is how that date is calculated.

The calculation for DoFD for installment loans or lines of credit is slightly different. Installment loans are ones you have a fixed monthly payment for a specific number of months. For instance personal, auto loans, and mortgages. The financial world refers to these as closed-end loans. The first time you are past due, and you never make-up that past due payment is the date that starts the clock ticking. As an illustration, if you're a full or even a partial payment past due in March of 2016 and never bring the account current, by making up that missed payment, March of 2016 is the date of first delinquency. The bad news is, if that past due March payment continues to be past due during the scheduled life of the loan and you never pay the account current, by for instance making two payments in a given month, they will hit you with a late charge every month. The good news is, they can't report your account as delinquent solely based on late charges or a single past due payment. Even if after you missed that March payment, you made every other payment on time, if you never made up that payment, meaning your account was always past due for that one March payment, that's the date that started the clock . . . tick, tock, tick, tock!

The date of first delinquency is calculated differently on revolving credit, credit cards, and lines of credit, all known as open-end credit You know, the ones where monthly balances and payment amounts can vary. On revolving credit, let's say you miss the March payment; the April bill will show you owe $75. That total due may include $25 for March, the payment you missed, and $30 for April, the current month, and a $20 late charge. They usually won't break it down that way. It will just show a total amount due. If you pay $74 and not $75 you're still past due. If you never bring the account current by paying the total amount requested or more, the start date for your date of your first delinquency is March. If at any time you pay the total amount requested you have brought the account current. The whole process would restart for calculating your date of first delinquency if you went past due again.

There are negative financial items that can be reported longer than seven years from the date of first delinquency:

- Judgments—Seven years from the date they're paid.

- Discharged Chapter 7 bankruptcies—ten years (discharged means you went bankrupt)

- Tax Liens—Seven years from the date they're paid or immediately on the "Automatic Release Date." The release date is the date indicated on the lien recording.

Dismissed or withdrawn Chapter 7s and Chapter 13 bankruptcies are seven years from the date they were filed.

Keep in mind for all bankruptcies, the clock starts ticking as soon as the application to go bankrupt is filed with the court, not on the date of discharge, dismissal, or withdrawal.

Don't confuse how long a negative item can remain on your credit report with the statute of limitations (SOL). They're two separate issues. The statute of limitations varies from state to state and varies based on the type of debt.

The statute of limitations only governs the amount of time they can collect an account by suing you. Keep in mind, they can still sue, but you can go to court and point out to the judge that the account is beyond the statute. It's called an affirmative defense, and the judge should throw out the case. Do not expect the judge to look at dates to determine the legitimacy of the suit. You must show up and present your case or you will lose.

The statement I just made about the possibility of being sued beyond the SOL is true as of the writing of this book in October 2021. That having been said, Congress and local and state governments are all talking about legislation that would prohibit initiating lawsuits on out of statute debt. Filing suits on expired SOL debt is sleazy and deceptive; some collection agencies love to do it!

In the appendix, I include letters that I used. You may not find a letter that says everything, word for word, for your situation. Remember, the bureaus are legally allowed to refuse to investigate or reinvestigate disputes they think are computer or credit repair company generated. So change the language in the letters to make it personal but use them as a guide to express what you want to be done. Just make sure, that if I refer to a legal document, for example when I say, "Legally it is known as 15USC §1681i" or "§611 (5)(a)" or reference case law like "In *Hinkle v. Midland Credit Management, Inc.*," include those terms or phrases word for word. It lets them know that you know what you're talking about.

Read your letters before mailing them. Don't just copy and paste them. If you do, you may not be successful in getting your goals accomplished. The letters in this book are sample letters and are meant to give you guidance with cited case law references. Don't worry about writing a perfect letter. They will get the gist when you include cited legal references.

The bureaus get thousands of dispute letters every day, and that volume works in your favor. They are unable to investigate each one as specifically required by law.

Disputing Negative Items, Including the (OC) Original Creditor

The original creditor (OC) is the institution who made the loan. Although we don't view doctors or hospitals as having extended credit, under the Fair Credit Reporting Act, for the purpose of credit reporting, the government says medical providers are original creditors too. In the case of a student loan, the government may guarantee the loan, but the institution that dispersed the money is the OC.

The original creditor may attempt to collect past due balances on their own. If they do, they cannot use a name other than their own. If they did, it would be considered deceptive, as it may imply that a third-party collector is collecting the debt.

The OC may hire a debt collector or sell the account to a debt buyer. A debt collector is anyone other than the OC reporting and/or trying to collect a debt. Collection agencies are third parties who have been contracted specifically to collect your account or someone who has purchased your delinquent debt. You can send a dispute directly to any collector or credit bureau, but you can only dispute an account with the OC after you have disputed it with at least one of the bureaus that lists it.

Here is the procedure to use when disputing an account with the original creditor.

First, dispute the listing with any credit bureau that has the derogatory item listed. Use certified mail with a return receipt requested, never online. You lose important rights, like your right to sue, by disputing a debt online.

Wait for the results of the credit bureau's investigation.

If the listing is deleted or modified to your satisfaction, you're done. If not, you have options:

Continue disputing using a different reason for the dispute. You can dispute anything that they report. There is a list of ten possible dispute reasons later in this chapter and in chapter 2, or you can use a reason of your own. Again, anything they report you can say is wrong.

After you file a dispute with a credit reporting agency, if your dispute isn't resolved in your favor, call the origin creditor. During the call, ask the OC what specific proof they provided to the credit bureau. If they don't have proof of the negative information, demand that they remove the disputed item.

If they have proof of the specific item you disputed, go back and dispute something else with the credit bureau.

If at any time, the credit bureau says that the results of the investigation show the negative information is accurate, but your call to the OC shows they don't have documentation, then you have the grounds for a lawsuit against the OC and/or credit bureau for an FCRA violation. At that point contact a consumers' rights attorney in your state.

There's a specific sequence that must be followed when disputing accounts. By law, disputes with third parties, for instance, collections agencies, are handled differently than the procedure you must follow when disputing with the original creditor (OC). If you decide you are going to dispute an item furnished by the original creditor, you must dispute that item with the credit reporting agency before contacting the original creditor. If you dispute anything on your credit report with the OC, before you dispute it with the credit bureau, you lose your ability to sue. If your dispute is with anyone other than the original creditor, you can deal with them directly or the bureau, in either order.

If the original creditor is no longer the owner of the account, they will either show up on your credit report as a zero balance or not at all. When the account has been sold, the debt purchaser will, in most cases, send the account to a collection agency. The collection agency, not the debt buyer, will usually appear on your credit report with the current balance due.

If you duplicate the reason for a dispute, with anyone, the credit bureau, collection agency, or original creditor, they can simply disregard it as "frivolous." If they deem the dispute frivolous, they aren't required to look into the dispute unless you send additional proof not included in a previous dispute. Within five days of receiving your dispute, if they view it as frivolous, they're required to send you regular mail or an email advising you they view the dispute as frivolous.

That doesn't mean you can't use the same reason with each separate information furnisher. You could tell every one of your creditors that the date of last payment is wrong, or the account numbers are wrong, or the account they're reporting isn't yours. What it does mean is that you can't use the same reason for the dispute, for the same account, with the same information furnisher twice, unless you include additional documentation or information not in the original dispute.

You don't need to prove your claim. It's their obligation to investigate or reinvestigate and verify that what they report is accurate. It's not your job to do their job. If you have documents, go ahead, and send copies; make sure to keep the originals.

Don't Let Them Bully You: You Don't Need a Police Report

I had a ten-minute conversation with APS, Arizona Public Service, a supplier of electricity for parts of the state. They attempted to shift the burden of proof onto me, to prove an account wasn't mine. They kept telling me to file a police report. I kept telling them, I am not required by law to file a report. Ultimately they refused to remove the negative listing from my credit report without a police report. I refused to file the report, but what I did file was a lawsuit and they settled it! The negative item was removed from my credit report and I got some cash.

Here's a photocopy of the court document from Public Access Court Electronic Records (PACER). It shows the suit I filed regarding the previously mentioned conversation with Arizona Public Service (APS). I sued APS for not taking the negative off my credit report when they couldn't prove it was mine. In the following document the notice of settlement is indicated next to the numbers 43, 44, and 45.

All because I knew my rights, sent a letter, and recorded my conversations. Collection agencies, creditors, and credit bureaus try to bully people that don't know their rights!

You Don't Need Proof to File a Dispute

It's never your responsibility to provide proof of anything in a dispute. It's the bureau's job to prove that what they report is accurate. If you claim an item on your report isn't your account, the bureaus and collection agencies will try to make it seem like you're required to file a police report. They will repeatedly ask if you are claiming fraud. I tell them I'm not claiming anything. I am stating this isn't my account. No matter how many times they ask and how they try to reword the question, my answer always is, "You word it any way that makes you feel comfortable. All I am saying is, this isn't my account."

If fraud did happen, and you feel like going through the effort of taking five or six hours out of your life, then file a police report. On the other hand, don't let them bluff you. It's their job to prove that it's your account and reported correctly, not your job to prove it isn't.

You'll get one of two letters in response to any dispute letter. The letter will say, "Our investigation of the dispute you submitted is now complete. The results are listed below." The result will either be "Verified" or "Deleted." Deleted will mean it's gone, and you've accomplished your goal.

The letter that says "Verified" tells you that nothing has changed on your credit report. If you get the verified letter, that says the item isn't being deleted; then write a follow-up letter with a different dispute reason. Or call the bureau. Record the conversation. Ask them what documentation the creditor provided as verification that your dispute had no basis. Then send another letter, disputing something else, for instance, date of last payment, the balance, or the total amount of the debt. Or call the OC and ask that they send you the documentation they relied on, to assure the credit bureau that your dispute was baseless.

Just talking to the bureaus can lead to unexpected riches. I've won lawsuits based on the follow-up calls themselves. I've made calls to ask how they validated the debt I disputed, and in that conversation a new FCRA violation occurred that had nothing to do with the reason I was calling.

The follow-up call, to a "Verified" letter, is to question the bureau's method of verification. In other words, what documentation did the creditor/collector have that disproves your dispute? As always record the call. If you decide to call, your conversation regarding a public record item should go something similar to the first dialogue, noted here as Conversation 1, and every other call will be close to the one noted as Conversation 2. They're similar, yet slightly different.

Conversation 1

You say:

"How was my dispute verified?"

They will say either:

"Through the Court" or "Through the County Recorder's office," or something similar.

You say:

"I'm not asking who, I am asking how. Was it done electronically with an email or did someone physically go to the (Court or County Recorder's office etc.)?"

They will say:

"It was verified by a third-party vendor."

My follow-up questions are:

"What did the third party do to verify that the information as reported was correct?"

"Did the third party talk to (Court or County Recorder's office etc.)? Did they speak to someone?" or "Did they do it electronically?"

CRA rep's reply will be:

"Yes, the vendor verified it electronically."

Electronically means the third party went on the internet, to a website called PACER (Public Access to Electronic Court Records). PACER is never updated and insufficient to meet the legal requirement of a "reasonable reinvestigation" required under the FCRA. At this point terminate the call and contact a consumers' right attorney. Ask the attorney to review the recorded conversation.

Conversation 2

After being connected to a bureau representative and they identify you . . .

You'll say:

"How was my dispute verified?"

They will say either:

"Through the collection agency."

or

"Through the creditor" or something similar.

You say:

"I'm not asking who verified it, I am asking how. Was it done electronically with an email or did someone call and speak with a representative?"

They will say:

"It was done electronically."

(If you included documents, you ask):

"Did you send them all my proof?"

They'll say:

"No."

(If you didn't include documents, don't say the above just continue with the conversation below.)

You say:

"Did you send them a copy of my dispute letter?"

They will say:

"No."

You say:

"What did they send you proving this is my account? Did they send you a signed contract? Did they verify my signature? Did they provide an original application? How did they verify it was me?"

They will say:

"No. they didn't send us any documentation, they notified us saying they verified it as your account."

At this point terminate the call and contact the information furnisher who's reporting your disputed item. When you speak to them, tell them you disputed what they're reporting to the credit bureau. Ask what documentation they have that your disputed information is correct. If they ask you if you are saying this is fraud, tell them, you are not commenting on the account until they provide documentation. RECORD the conversation!

Here's why you are questioning both the bureau and the creditor. You're getting the bureau to admit that they used e-Oscar to send and receive an answer to your dispute. If they accepted the information furnisher's validation electronically, it's a violation of *Cushman v. TransUnion*. Secondly, you question the creditor / information provider, to determine if they have "account-level documentation." If they don't and reported any negative item on your credit report, they are in violation of *Hinkle v. Midland Credit Management, Inc.*

In an actual conversation with Equifax, an agent told me they had someone physically go to the Maricopa County Recorder's Office. They never do. I called the Recorder's Office, and they said there is no contact between their office and the credit bureaus. Here I am, calling to find out information on an unrelated matter, and while we were speaking, the representative violates the FCRA by erroneously telling me that they physically went to the Recorder's Office. I sued and won again!

I understand some people don't want to make phone calls, or get an attorney involved, or personally handle a lawsuit. If you're simply looking to clear up your credit and you received a letter saying they reinvestigated your dispute and the negative item will remain as reported, write another letter using a different reason for your next dispute. But I urge you, if your rights have been violated, contact a consumers' rights attorney. They won't bite and won't charge you anything to review or handle your case. Attorneys want to hear from potential clients.

Here's the list again showing some reasons you can use for disputing the status of an account. The status that the information furnisher reports is what you dispute.

Not my account

I didn't pay late that month

Wrong balance

Wrong payment amount

Wrong account number

Wrong date of last payment

Wrong opening date

Wrong original creditor

Wrong credit limit

I was an authorized user; this should not appear on my report

For example, the first time you challenge a listing, you might say the account is "not mine." The second letter could say "never late." The third dispute might be "wrong balance," the fourth "wrong credit limit"—you get the idea.

If you hit on the right dispute, the listing will get completely removed from your report. If you don't, you'll need to change the reason for every subsequent reinvestigation. If you don't change the reason for the dispute, they can consider it frivolous. If they deem the dispute frivolous, they aren't required to do a reinvestigation unless you send additional proof or information not included in a prior dispute.

On the following pages are copies of just two of the many deletion letters that I've received. They're the ones that say they investigated your dispute and they deleted the derogatory item. If the removed item ever gets re-reported, the credit bureau is required by law to send you another letter, telling you it will reappear and the reason why. If they don't send that letter, and they re-report the deleted information, you can sue. I never had anything re-reported. Collection agencies and debt purchasers rarely re-report. For them, it's a numbers game. There are too many fish in the sea to worry about your one account. Collectors dial three hundred to five hundred accounts a day (it's automated dialing). They probably get to talk to ten debtors and hope to make payment arrangements with two or three.

The first letter (Figure 14) is from TransUnion removing two disputed accounts; the second letter (Figure 15) is from Equifax, advising me the disputed judgment was removed. The Equifax letter notes that they deleted the disputed information toward the middle of the letter. It says, "THE RESULTS OF OUR REINVESTIGATION IS AS FOLLOWS." The exact wording is, "We have reviewed the judgment information. Case or ID# - CC2008105167RC. The Results are: The Item has been DELETED from your credit file."

The results of our investigation of your dispute consists of two sections: 1) the Investigation Results Summary which appears below, and 2) the attached view of how the disputed item(s) that remain on your credit report now appear(s). If an item you disputed is not listed, it means that the item was not appearing in your credit report or it already reflected the requested status at the time of our investigation. Items deleted from your credit report will not appear in the attached credit report detail and if no credit report detail is attached following the Investigation Results summary, you may view a free full copy of your credit report by visiting www.transunion.com/fullreport.

The following key provides you a more complete description of our investigation results of the items you disputed:

DELETED: The disputed item was removed from your credit report.

DISPUTE NOT SPECIFIC; VERIFIED AND UPDATED: The item was verified as belonging to you and other account information has changed or the item was updated to reflect recent activity.

DISPUTED INFORMATION UPDATED: A change was made to the item based on your dispute.

DISPUTED INFORMATION UPDATED AND OTHER INFORMATION UPDATED: A change was made to the item based on your dispute and other information unrelated to your dispute has changed.

INFORMATION DELETED: The item was removed from your credit report.

INFORMATION UPDATED: A change was made to the item.

NO UPDATE NECESSARY: The disputed information already reflects the requested status.

REINSERTED: This previously deleted item has now been verified; therefore, it has been reinserted into your credit report.

VERIFIED AS ACCURATE: The disputed information was verified as accurate and no change was made to the item.

VERIFIED AS ACCURATE AND UPDATED: The disputed information was verified as accurate; however, other information has changed and/or the item was updated to reflect recent activity.

Investigation Results Summary

ITEM	DESCRIPTION	RESULTS
CREDIT ONE BANK PO BOX 98872 LAS VEGAS, NV 89193-8872 (877) 825-3242	# 444796218079****	DELETED
SYNCB/WAL-MART PO BOX 965024 ORLANDO, FL 32896-5024 (877) 294-7880	# 603220140377****	DELETED

FIGURE 14

As indicated in the Equifax letter, it was a judgment. Judgments are a matter of public record. As I said before, they have no way of verifying a current balance on any public record. Balances on tax liens, bankruptcies, judgments, etc. are never updated. Credit bureaus must prove that what's being reported is reported correctly.

Make Sure You Follow Up Any Letter That Doesn't Delete Your Disputed Item

By law, your dispute must be answered within thirty days. The following is the exact wording of the Fair Credit Reporting Act.

§ 611. Procedure in case of disputed accuracy 15USC § 1681i]

Reinvestigations of Disputed Information

Reinvestigation Required

In general-

Subject to subsection (f), if the completeness or accuracy of any item of information

---

EQUIFAX

CREDIT FILE : February 19, 2014
Confirmation # 4043041376

Dear Richard J Mansfield:

Below are the results of your reinvestigation request and, as applicable, any revisions to your credit file. If you have additional questions regarding the reinvestigated items, please contact the source of that information directly. You may also contact Equifax regarding the specific information contained within this letter or report within the next 60 days by visiting us at www.investigate.equifax.com or by calling a Customer Representative at (888) 425-7961 from 9:00am to 5:00pm Monday-Friday in your time zone.

For an added convenience, use one of the below options to start an investigation or check the status of your dispute.

Please note, when you provide documents, including a letter, to Equifax as part of your dispute, the documents may be submitted to one or more companies whose information are the subject of your dispute.

Visit us at www.equifax.com/CreditReportAssistance or Call us at 866-349-5186.

Thank you for giving Equifax the opportunity to serve you.

The Results Of Our Reinvestigation

Public Record Information (This section includes public record items obtained from local, state and federal courts.)

>>> **We have reviewed the judgement information. Case or ID # - CC2008105167RC The results are:** This item has been deleted from the credit file. If you have additional questions about this item please contact: *South Mesa Gilbert Justice, 1837 S Mesa Dr, Mesa AZ 85210-6219*

Notice to Consumers

You may request a description of the procedure used to determine the accuracy and completeness of the information, including the business name and address of the furnisher of information contacted, and if reasonably available the telephone number.

If the reinvestigation does not resolve your dispute, you have the right to add a statement to your credit file disputing the accuracy or completeness of the information; the statement should be brief and may be limited to not more than one hundred words (two hundred words for Maine residents) explaining the nature of your dispute.

If the reinvestigation results in the deletion of disputed information, or you submit a statement in accordance with the preceding paragraph, you have the right to request that we send your revised credit file to any company specifically designated by you that received your credit report in the past six months (twelve months for California, Colorado, Maryland, New Jersey and New York residents) for any purpose or in the past two years for employment purposes.

(Continued On Next Page)   Page 1 of 2   4043041376ICR-001592558- 5392 - 6820 - AS

005392

001592558-5392
Richard J Mansfield
PO Box 40652
Mesa, AZ 85274-0652

P. O. Box 105518
Atlanta, GA 30348

FIGURE 15

contained in a consumer's file at a consumer reporting agency is disputed by the consumer and the consumer notifies the agency directly, or indirectly through a reseller, of such dispute, the agency shall, free of charge, conduct a reasonable reinvestigation to determine whether the disputed information is inaccurate and record the current status of the disputed information, or delete the item from the file in accordance with paragraph (5), before the end of the 30-day period beginning on the date on which the agency receives the notice of the dispute from the consumer or reseller.

The reason to mail your disputes certified mail, return receipt requested, is the day they sign for your mailing starts the thirty-day clock ticking. If you don't get a response by day thirty, you can call a consumers' rights attorney on day thirty-one, but in most cases, allowing for regular mail, they'll probably want to wait until day forty or so to start your lawsuit.

Keep in mind, a reputable attorney, in any consumers' rights case, including but not limited to FCRA, FDCPA, and Telephone Consumer Protection Act (TCPA) cases, will not ask you for money. When you win, the attorney's costs, fee, and any monetary award or settlement for you will all come from the defendant. Consumer affairs attorneys only take cases they are sure they'll win. But even if they lost, in these types of cases you aren't responsible for any outlay of cash, win or lose.

A credit bureau response to your dispute will read "deleted," "verified, the item is correct and will remain as reported," or similar wording It will also indicate that "you may request a description of how the investigation was conducted along with the name, address and telephone number, if any, of the source of the information."

All three bureaus will use different wording to express the same idea. Regardless of the wording, if you receive a letter that indicates the disputed item is going to stay on your credit report, what you do next will separate you from the average consumer. After an unsuccessful dispute letter, the uninformed may think it's the end of the road and give up. After an unsuccessful first letter, don't give up. That's what they count on. Mail another dispute using a different reason. Don't be one of those people that gives up. Persistence is often the key. The credit bureaus rely on consumers not knowing what to

do, getting frustrated, and accepting a negative outcome. You are now one of the few that know what to do. Do it!

If the bureau doesn't resolve your dispute, call the information furnisher and record the conversation. Tell the furnisher you filed a dispute with the credit bureau and the bureau informed you that they (the information furnisher) verified what you disputed was correct. If your dispute said not my account, ask them what documentation they have proving this is your debt. If they claim to have proof, tell them you want to see it. If you disputed anything else, ask them what proof they have for verifying that and ask to see proof. Demand documentation.

If you said this wasn't your debt, they'll ask if you're claiming fraud. Tell them you're not claiming anything; you are asking for documentation of what they're reporting. If your dispute said that this wasn't your account, they will likely tell you to file a police report. Tell them the Fair Credit Reporting Act doesn't require you to file a police report but, as outlined in *Hinkle vs. Midland Credit Management, Inc.*, it does require the information furnisher have documentation to support what they report. If they refuse to produce proof, contact a consumers' rights attorney. Tell the attorney that the information furnisher is unable or unwilling to provide documentation and is in violation of the FCRA as outlined in *Hinkle v. Midland Credit Management, Inc.*

If the creditor/collection agency agrees to remove the disputed item, tell them you want an email or snail mail indicating it has been removed. If they do not agree to remove the negative listing, tell them you will file suit: Let them respond to that comment. If the response isn't what you want to hear, just say "OK then I am filing a lawsuit"; verify their name and title again. Ask for the phone number and address of their legal department and terminate the call. Then, contact a consumers' rights attorney in your area, or refer to the section in this book that walks you through filing a lawsuit on your own.

What Is e-Oscar?

When you're absolutely sure mistakes are being reported, e-Oscar may be the reason your credit dispute was verified as accurate. Credit reporting agencies created e-Oscar as an automated shortcut for communicating with creditors regarding disputes. Congress doesn't like shortcuts; they like accuracy.

Instead of the bureaus calling the creditor to review your dispute, the credit bureaus handle the dispute process using e-Oscar (Electronic-Online Solution for Complete and Accurate Reporting). It's a glorified email system that sums up your entire dispute in a two- or three-digit code. Disputes are outsourced to places like India, Guatemala, or the Philippines, places where English isn't even their first language.

The e-Oscar system is utilized when consumers send in disputes with or without supporting documents. So that detailed dispute you sent the bureau, that took you months to compile, is reduced to a numeric code, a code assigned by a representative who looked at your letter and documents for 240 seconds. That's right, a person whose first language isn't even English takes approximately four minutes to read your entire letter and *"carefully"* examine all the documents you submitted. Once this *"thorough, meticulous"* 240-second *"scrutiny"* of your dispute and documentation is completed, the rep who doesn't speak English as a first language assigns the dispute a numeric code. Wow! Maybe it's just me, but somehow that doesn't sound extremely efficient. I'm sure that's not what Congress had in mind when they included the words "reasonable investigation" in the Fair Credit Reporting Act. This is an absolute failure on their part to perform a reasonable reinvestigation.

As part of the settlement of a suit brought by the New York State Attorney General, the three major credit bureaus agreed to have medical disputes examined by a trained document review specialist. They will then forward medical disputes to the information furnisher. Whether the CRAs follow through on that commitment is another matter entirely. Judging from the bureaus' past track record, I have my doubts. Only time will tell. I'm sure there will be hundreds of suits filed when the bureaus don't comply with the agreement. AND. . . this only covers medical disputes. If the bureaus follow through on the agreement, it still means their dispute resolution methods, for everything other than medical records, are still inadequate.

People are unaware of their consumer protection rights. The few that do know their rights are at a loss as to what to do when they're violated. Leonard Bennett, an attorney specializing in credit reporting litigation said, "I see hundreds of consumers with similar problems each year."

Consumers will dispute a negative credit item, then receive a letter saying that the debt will remain on their credit report and believe there's nothing they can do. A National Consumer Law Center (NCLC) report discusses how some creditors and information providers avoid their federally mandated responsibility to investigate. The investigations these companies perform consists primarily of ensuring "data conformity" between the data maintained by the credit bureaus and the information furnisher's records. In plain English, all they do is compare the bureau's info with the information furnisher's data, to make sure they substantially match up. They are, in many cases, verifying errors on your credit report against the same errors the information furnisher has on record and saying they have confirmed it's your account. Once again, I'm sure that's not what Congress had in mind, when in the Fair Credit Reporting Act, they included the phrase "reasonable investigation."

Credit bureaus are simply "parroting" the information furnisher's data. The credit bureaus have zero incentive to perform proper investigations. Creditors are the bureaus' primary paying customers, not consumers. Disputes are costly and simply a pain in the butt for the bureaus. They lower their costs by outsourcing the dispute process. According to a bureau insider, one of the bureaus pays a third party in the Philippines fifty-seven cents per dispute. Each dispute is broken down into a numeric code and supporting docs are rarely, except in the case of some medical disputes, sent to the information furnisher.

The bureaus and information furnisher compare data. If the information is close, the CRA will consider it "valid" and verify the debt as being yours and it will remain as reported. Even Social Security numbers and dates of birth don't need to be identical. Social Security numbers can be off by as many as four digits and the month, day, or year can be incorrect for your date of birth.

Addresses don't need to match at all. If a credit reporting agency is notified of a totally different address, from for instance, a credit card application, they will simply update their files with that address. Valid or not, it will suddenly become the current address on your credit file.

If three portions of the items that are listed as a "match," then your debt has just been verified. That's all the CRAs do. They match possibly fraudulent information to possibly bad or stolen information and conclude that it's you.

There's good news about how new information gets "updated" and input on your credit report.

If you happen to be trying to hide from a creditor or let's say the repo man, you can apply for credit, using a totally erroneous address on a credit application. Magically that becomes the new address on your credit report. That's where anyone pulling a credit report to locate your address, for example, the repo guy, will be looking for you. Now I'm not suggesting that you do that, but I also can't tell you what not to do.

Check Your State Laws

States usually have separate but similar laws to the federal FDCPA that govern debt collectors. For instance, California has the Rosenthal Act and Texas has the Finance Code. Collection agencies are governed by both federal and state laws. Whichever one is more beneficial to consumers is the one they're required to abide by. The state law that applies is the state you live in at the time a violation takes place.

Many consumers never use their state laws or state's attorney general (AG) to settle issues. It's a valuable resource to settle issues with debt collectors. It forces debt collectors to respond to the attorney general. The AG will always let you know the outcome of the response they receive. Collection agencies (CAs) never ignore inquiries from an attorney general. The other thing about complaints to the AG's office is that if the collection agency can't give the AG's office a satisfactory response, the collection agency will usually close your account.

Dealing with Credit Bureaus

When disputing items with the bureaus, the FCRA requires them to do an actual investigation to confirm the accuracy of what they're reporting. They rarely do, even when consumers send supporting documents along with their disputes.

The credit bureaus simply send a three-digit code to the furnisher of information and the furnisher of information verifies the code. No real investigation is done. This is not a reinvestigation and violates the Fair Credit Reporting Act. Credit bureaus can be sued if a reasonable investigation hasn't been conducted and they continue to report inaccurate information. Remember e-Oscar is legally not true validation. Also, keep in mind, when it comes to public records like judgments, tax liens, bankruptcy, etc., they don't even attempt to contact the courts

or recorder, where all public records are kept. They use a third-party vendor, who looks at outdated information on the internet called PACER and claim that's validation. Per the FCRA that's not validation.

I recorded a phone call to TransUnion. The representative told me they use a third party, who actually visits the courthouse, to confirm that the reported public record information is correct. Of course, that never happens. I sued for the misrepresentation of the verification process and won.

How and When Can You Dispute Directly with the Original Creditor/Information Furnishers?

The information furnisher is not always the original creditor (OC). In fact, if you are severely past due, for instance, more than six payments, the information furnisher is rarely the OC. The OC is the institution that gave you the loan. Anyone other than that is not the original creditor.

Under Section 623 of the FRCA, you can dispute directly with the furnisher of information. Disputing directly with the furnisher of information puts the responsibility of investigating disputes directly with the company that placed the negative mark on your credit. This makes them accountable for reporting erroneous or inaccurate information to the credit bureaus.

An information provider, in the case of derogatory items, is usually a collection agency, law firm, court, or the IRS and/or state in the case of tax liens. If the information provider is the OC, keep in mind that to preserve your right to sue, you are legally obligated to dispute the listing with the credit reporting agency first.

The information furnisher has thirty days to respond to the dispute or remove the disputed item. If they don't respond or remove within that time frame, you can sue.

If they do verify the information as accurate, call them and ask them to provide you with the documentation that was used to verify the disputed information as being accurate. Ask them for a detailed accounting of how they arrived at the amount they claim you owe. They can't simply supply a bill. If you ask for it, they must account for how the balance was calculated, including ongoing balances, payments made, interest accrued, and late charges assessed. If you ask for it, they must be able to show the contractual authority that allows them to add any of the charges that they have. In *Hinkle v. Midland Credit Management, Inc.*, the courts said, during a dispute and subsequent reinvestigation, with the original creditor, collector, or a credit bureau, that the original creditor or collector must be able to provide "account-level documentation." That means an original contract or similar proof, not just a printout of the payments that were made.

Dispute e-Oscar

When a consumer disputes an item on their credit report, the credit bureaus legally must conduct a "reasonable" investigation. Reasonable includes contacting whoever supplied the information, for example, a credit card company, collection agency, or mortgage company. It doesn't happen. The credit bureaus submit the dispute through e-Oscar. In most cases, there isn't any contact with the information furnisher, other than a questionable e-Oscar email with a numeric code.

The courts have said that this method of investigation doesn't comply with the law. In *Cushman v. TransUnion*, *Stevenson v. TRW* (Experian), and *Richardson v. Fleet, Equifax, et al.*, the courts ruled that the CRA couldn't merely "parrot" information from the creditors and collection agencies. They must conduct an independent reasonable investigation to ensure the validity of the debt in question. e-Oscar is not regarded by the courts as a reasonable investigation.

WHAT'S ON A CREDIT BUREAU VERIFICATION FORM?
On the left side of the form, Equifax fills in the information they have on file. The checkboxes, on the right, are there for the information furnishers. The credit bureau and information furnishers may be comparing erroneous or even fraudulent information and saying it matches, and since it matches it must be you! All they do is review their records to see if the info matches what they have on file. If it DOESN'T match, they fill in what their computers have on the right side and then check the box.

If the information is even close, the CRA will consider it a match and verify the debt. Social security numbers and dates of birth don't need to be exact. Addresses don't need to match at all. The bureaus will simply update their files with the address the information furnisher provides (collection agency or creditor). If they provide a different address, the new address (valid or not) will magically become the current address on your credit file. If three pieces of information on the above form are listed as a match, your debt has just been verified. It's scary how this works. And remember if your Social Security number or date of birth is off by two or three digits, they assume it's a typo and consider that a match! That's why you will sometimes have to threaten to sue or go ahead and sue. See chapter 19 on "How to Start a Lawsuit."

Identity Theft: An Instructive Example

Consider this identity theft situation. An Arizona resident sees tradelines on their credit report from a boutique in New York. This is a line of credit that can only be used in that specific store. The consumer receives copies of the charges. She sees there are charges for fifty-four days that she can prove she was at work in Arizona. She gets a notarized statement from her employer that verifies she was at work on those days. The consumer also sends copies of Arizona utility bills, Arizona driver's license, and a property tax bill to prove residency. The consumer points out that charges were incurred in New York on the same day as legitimate charges were incurred in Arizona. The CRA simply reduces the consumer complaint to a "not mine" code and asks the creditor to verify.

In the above scenario, the bureau didn't forward the consumer's documents or the specific details of the dispute to the creditor/information furnisher. It's impossible for them to have a legitimate claim that they performed the "reasonable" reinvestigation that Congress intended when they passed the Fair Credit Reporting Act. Assigning the dispute a three-digit code that reduced the complaint to "not mine" absolutely isn't reasonable. Information furnishers may try to defend themselves by saying they didn't get sufficient info from the bureau. If that's true, they should ask the bureau for all the documents they received from the consumer. If this happens to you, there is a solution. Call the information furnisher. Ask them what documentation they have that proves what they're reporting is accurate. If they claim to have documentation, tell them you want copies. If they don't have documentation or refuse to supply you with them, sue. I had a similar scenario with APS: sued and settled.

Another client wrote about their experience with an electronic dispute method saying: "I recently had my credit bank some inaccurate info. To prove they sent it to the CRAs, they sent me copies of a 'Universal Data Form' (UDF) which is apparently a standard form that the information furnishers use to send in data. Oddly enough, there is a box that starts with the question 'If the change makes the trade current [in credit bureau language "trade" means account] is previous delinquent history to be deleted? check off YES or NO.'"

Obviously, the information furnisher in many cases controls how your account shows up on your credit report. In many cases, they will try to tell you they can't change the status: Obviously, they can.

Chapter 7

WHAT'S A CREDIT SCORE AND HOW DOES IT DIFFER FROM A CREDIT REPORT?

Your credit score is a numeric grade based on your credit report. A credit report breaks down how you've paid on specific extensions of credit: the good, the bad, and the ugly. Your credit score gives the lender one specific numeric grade by analyzing all your credit report information. FICO 8, the most widely used score, ranges from 300 to 850.

Ideally, obtain a credit report and score four months prior to any major purchase like a home or a car, or at a minimum twice a year. This will give you sufficient time to correct errors or remove negatives from your report using the advice here. Prior to the pandemic you could only obtain a free credit report from each of the three major bureaus once every 365 days, by going to www.annual creditreport.com. All three bureaus changed the frequency you could get free reports to weekly during the height of COVID-19. The last I looked it was still weekly. Check www.annualcreditreport.com to see what the rules are now. There are exceptions to the once-a-year rule: for instance you were looking for a job, turned down for credit based on a credit report, or a victim of ID theft. This site is just for free credit reports.

You can get free reports AND scores without a credit card or any gimmicks at: www.CreditKarma.com. Reports and scores are based on Equifax and TransUnion credit reports.

These scores are not the ones any lender will see, but they give you an approximation of where you are score-wise.

You can get a more accurate assessment of your scores by going directly to www.myFico.com. A word of caution. You'll have to pay for your scores and scores can change daily. Plus, there are a number of industry-specific scores. There are different FICO scores that may be accessed by mortgage lenders, auto lenders, credit cards, etc. FICO will give you an option to see all the industry-specific scores.

The scores may be different from each site. There are so many different scores that the scores you get for free are as good an indication of where you stand financially as the scores you'd pay for. The reality is, any credit scores you see will never be the one the lenders see, even if you pay for it. Don't be alarmed and don't get hung up on the specific number; just use them as an approximation of where you stand with potential lenders.

Most of us already know whether our credit is good, bad, or somewhere in between without getting a score. Knowing your score is a starting point that allows you to measure your progress later. When you compare scores always compare apples to apples. Never compare a score from a free score site to a score directly from FICO; compare FICO to FICO or the specific free site you used to that specific free site again.

The number is important to lenders. They will ultimately use it to evaluate the risk of making you a loan. The lower the score the higher the risk. The higher the risk, the higher the interest rate. If the risk is too high, they won't extend you credit at all.

In the past, everyone used the FICO scoring systems, but that's changing. VantageScore is edging its way in, but FICO is still the gold standard and dominates the market. FICO, as of October 2021, has forty-nine industry-specific scoring systems. What is the same for every score is that the higher the score, the better off you are.

Most lenders will look at the score and not pay much attention to what makes it up. One of the few times that what composes the score makes a difference is when you're applying for a mortgage. Mortgage lenders look at everything. Keep in mind that even though it's the score that's important, the only way you can change the score is to change the credit report components used to calculate the score. As negative items are corrected or deleted from your report, your score will increase. It's up to you to correct reported errors. Using the credit rehabilitation tools, techniques, and knowledge outlined here, you can legally remove negative information.

Because of a quirk in the law, you'll be able to get rid of negatives that really are yours. That's what I set out to prove, and it absolutely works. Derogatory remarks on credit reports don't magically disappear by themselves. There is that seven-year limitation that most negative items can legally appear, but sometimes that doesn't even get them removed. It takes knowledge of how the system works and hands-on involvement on your part to make sure you optimize your ability to get approved for any loan you need and at the best rates possible.

Anybody can tell you how to remove the items that are incorrect. The difference between our program and everyone else is that ours allows you to get rid of some, if not all, of the negatives that appear on your credit report. Clearing up everything is what separates us from the other guys. I show you what I did to get rid of the negatives that were mine but that were reported incorrectly or were unverifiable by the credit bureau. It's all legal. The FDCPA and FCRA were instituted to protect consumers.

Most people are aware that their credit score affects whether or not they qualify for loans or credit cards, interest rates, and the size of their credit lines. But there are some less obvious consequences of poor credit: higher car insurance rates, higher down payment requirements, more stringent leasing requirements for housing rentals, and in some states not getting a specific job or promoted in a job you already have. I know that may sound crazy, but read the following 2008 story from the *LA Times*:

LOS ANGELES - Mark Manzo never thought he'd struggle to provide for his two daughters. "We weren't rich, but we were comfortable," he tells CBS News correspondent Ben Tracy. "We had a house. We paid all our bills on time. I had excellent credit."

He and his wife Kristin were making $96,000 a year. But last year the stalled economy forced Manzo to shut down his car rental business near Los Angeles. Without a paycheck, he couldn't pay the bills. The bank foreclosed on the family's condominium. Their credit was wrecked.

"As a man, I feel bad, honestly," Manzo said. "I feel like I can't provide for my kids. I can't find a job."

Manzo says his damaged credit is why he's been rejected eight times for recent jobs. "They sent me a letter stating that because of information on my credit report, I was not being considered for a position."

He said his heart sank. "I just thought, what am I going to do, what else can I do?"

Sixty percent of employers say they now run credit checks on some or all of their job candidates. It's legal as long as the job candidates agree to it, and employers tell them their credit is the reason they're not being hired.

Business owners often say credit histories indicate someone's reliability and integrity. They say bad credit can be a sign of someone prone to things like corruption and bribery.

"If you're stocking shelves, if you're cleaning rooms, if you're a cook—any of those positions—you do not need a credit check," said California state assemblyman Tony Mendoza. Mendoza wrote a California law, which takes effect in January, banning the use of credit checks in hiring. The ban will not apply to jobs in law enforcement or management, or jobs involving large amounts of cash.

"I don't think that a person's credit score or a person's history is indicative of a person's trustworthiness or their work ethic," Mendoza said.

California joined five other states—Maryland, Hawaii, Illinois, Oregon, and Washington—in prohibiting the use of credit information by employers by enacting new legislation placing restrictions on so-called credit checks by employers that use the credit report or credit history of job applicants or employees for employment decisions.

Manzo stopped opening bills he can't pay. "I can't give up," he said. "I have two little kids. That's not an option for me, I have to keep going."

Without a job, Manzo said he could be facing bankruptcy. So, he tried a new strategy. In his last interview, he brought up the credit problem and explained it. It worked, and he got a job.

As of October 2021, New York City, Washington, DC, Philadelphia, Pennsylvania, and the following states don't allow credit reports or scores to be used for employment purposes: California, Colorado, Connecticut, Delaware, Hawaii, Illinois, Maryland, Nevada, Oregon, Vermont, and Washington. There may be exceptions when they're allowed in each city or state. The laws in this area are constantly changing. If this is something that affects you, Google, "Exemptions to state laws on employer use of credit reports."

Chapter 8

HOW LONG DOES BAD CREDIT STAY ON YOUR RECORD? JUDGMENTS, BANKRUPTCY, DELINQUENCIES, AND MORE

Contrary to what every other so-called credit expert will tell you, missing one payment does not affect your credit report. The trigger point is missing that second payment and becoming two payments overdue. Any type of an account that requires monthly payments and is two payments past due will show up on your credit report as thirty days past due. It doesn't matter what two months you miss; it could be January and October. It's the bureaus' way of saying you're two payments past due. There's a detailed explanation of how past dues are reported in chapter 5. Certain types of bills, for instance medical bills, utility bills, cellphones, and gym memberships, don't report monthly transactions. They normally won't show up until they're sent to a collection agency. Paying non-reported items on time won't establish credit, but if they're sent to a collection agency they will have a negative effect.

I've never seen a bad item linger for more than seven years, although legally, seven years and six months (not seven years as we are led to believe) is the length of time a credit report can show an accurate negative mark. The clock starts ticking from the date you were first delinquent and never paid the account up to date, not from the date it's reported, charged off, sold, or resold. There is no way the date of first delinquency that starts that seven-year reporting limit can be restarted.

But...

There are some exceptions to the that seven-year reporting limit and the way the seven years is calculated.

- Chapter 13 bankruptcy—Ten years from the initial filing, NOT the date of discharge or dismissal.

- Judgments—Seven years from the date it was filed even if they're paid/satisfied.

- State and federal tax liens—Seven years from the date they're paid.

If you have an IRS tax lien, they instituted a program called Fresh Start. If you paid your lien in full or have an ongoing agreement to pay and are up to date with that arrangement, you can probably get the lien removed by getting a "Lien Withdrawal" letter from the IRS. Send the Lien Withdrawal letter to the bureaus that have the lien listed.

What Are the Reporting Time Limits for Charge-Offs?

Just like most other delinquencies, there is a seven-year reporting window. The seven years starts when you first became past due on the account and never paid it up to date. It doesn't restart for any reason. The charge-off date doesn't affect the starting date and neither does the account being sold. Once that original past due date is established, it's that date forever.

The reporting start date for the seven-year time frame needs some explanation. You have a loan that has a fixed monthly payment. In January of 2015, you missed a payment. You made payments after that, on the due date every month for a year but never caught up that past due payment. You were always one payment behind. Now it's January of 2016 and you stop paying completely. The account is charged off by the lender in May of 2016 and is immediately reported to the credit bureaus. The seven-year clock started ticking not on the date of the charge-off and not on the date of the last payment, but the first time you became delinquent and never paid your account current: January of 2015.

Keep in mind that the previous scenario is for a fixed payment loan, like auto, mortgage, and personal loans. If you are paying on a variable monthly basis, for instance, a credit card or some form of line of credit, the monthly bill you will get will be for your past due amount plus the minimum due for the current month. In those cases, if you make the minimum payment requested, you are bringing the account current. But the same rules apply. If your monthly credit card bill asks for a minimum payment of $50, and you send $49 and never pay at least the minimum amount requested, the first time you didn't pay the minimum is your start date. If you make up the missed payment or payments, bringing the account current, the seven-year clock restarts on the date you miss another payment and don't make up that payment.

Bankruptcy

If you filed for bankruptcy, the information can be reported on your credit history for the following time limits: ten years on a discharged Chapter 7 and seven years for a Chapter 13 or a dismissed or withdrawn Chapter 7. Be aware that your bankruptcy does not have to be affirmed/finalized to be reported. Even if the bankruptcy is denied or you withdraw the bankruptcy petition, the bankruptcy filing itself remains as a negative on your credit report. The fact that you considered going bankrupt makes potential future lenders wonder if you will go bankrupt after they make you a new loan. I outlined an in-depth explanation regarding credit reporting and bankruptcy in chapter 4. If the subject is important to you and you didn't read it, go back and read it.

Tax Liens

Due to a lawsuit I am proud to say I was a part of, many tax liens have been removed from consumers' credit reports. As I've preached for years, because of redacted Social Security numbers, most are unable to be attributed to an individual consumer. Those that still remain on your credit report can be removed. I address how to remove those in chapter 5. Tax liens can remain on your credit report for seven years from the date you pay off the lien. I removed two tax liens and sued Experian and Equifax. They sent me a "will remain as listed" letter claiming they verified the debt when I had paid documents in my possession. I settled the suits for more than $8,000. Tax liens and most public records like judgments can be deleted (see the appendix for the appropriate letter).

Government Guaranteed Student Loan Default

Default, deferment, forbearance, forgiveness, rehabilitation, consolidation, income-driven repayment, and yes, now even bankruptcy . . . I'm not sure anyone, especially the loan servicers, know where to start or satisfactorily explain what's going on with student loans. What I do know is how to remove them from a credit report before they are due to come off, and how to wipe them out in the entirety without paying them.

If you default on a government guaranteed student loan, the loan will appear on your report for seven years from the original date of delinquency. The original delinquency date is the date the first payment was missed that led to a claim being filed with the government.

However, even if a student loan no longer shows up on your credit report, the government might still come after you. I've been very successful in coaching clients through getting student loans removed from their credit reports and wiping out the debt entirely. Student loans, guaranteed by the government, have no statute of limitations. Private student loans do, and that clock is governed by state law. If you are trying to determine if a statute of limitation has run, you must know when the clock starts ticking. For most student loans, it would fall under a "breach of contract." The limitation period starts running when you first defaulted on the terms of the contract. For student loans, if you never made a payment, the default date would be when you were scheduled to start paying. If you started paying, the default date starts when you stopped.

Judgments

Judgments can appear on your credit history for seven years or for the period specified for your state in the statute of limitations for judgment "enforcement," whichever is longer. The good news is that they are easily removed from your credit report. The bad news is removing judgments from your credit report doesn't mean judgment creditors can't still legally pursue you for payment. That's a different scenario. The time frame that a creditor can legally collect money based on a judgment, legally termed enforcing the judgment, is different from state to state. Here's the best explanation of how and when judgments can be enforced.

The statute of limitations on judgment "enforcement" is different from the statute of limitations, which limits the time you can be sued. Enforcement comes into play when they already have sued you, won and obtained a judgment. Some states allow judgments to be renewed one or more times. Renewal will substantially extend the enforceability of a judgment. If the judgment creditor is on top of the renewals, this can result in a permanent legal obligation until it's paid. In simple terms, you can get a judgment removed from your credit report but still need to be aware that they may be able to legally still come after you for payment . . . if they renew the judgment.

You may have an idea about what your credit report contains, but you'd be surprised to find that there may be errors on your report. Errors are easily corrected. The hard part is getting rid of stuff that's legitimate and truly does belong there. Getting those legally removed without paying them off, that's the genius of this system. That's the difference between the credit restoration tools described here and everyone else. You should order copies of all three of your credit histories from the major reporting bureaus: Equifax, Experian, and TransUnion. Prior to the pandemic, everyone had the right to receive one free copy of each from www.annualcreditreport.com. As of October 2021, you can get them weekly.

You can also get a free report for up to sixty days after you have been denied credit, denied a job, or even if you are approved for financing and didn't get the best terms available because of a credit report. You should always ask the lender or broker if you are getting the best terms available and if not, why not. The denial letter, from any creditor that turned you down, or didn't give you the best rate available because of a credit report, will tell you how to get a free credit report.

Chapter 9
OBTAINING REPORTS AND SCORES

Credit reports and credit scores can cost money. If you're ordering them frequently, throughout the credit restoration process, you can easily spend a couple hundred dollars. It's a good thing there are places that you can get your credit reports and scores free. Here are a few.

www.annualcreditreport.com

A free credit report, no credit score. No credit card required. No gimmicks. Free weekly as of April 2020 and until they stop!

You can get all three major credit reports, all three at once or spacing them out if that suits you better. You are allowed by law to get a free report from each agency once a year, and they do calculate it at exactly 365 days between reports.

Other sites like FreeCreditScore.com try to rope you into pay services for things like credit scores, credit monitoring, and alerts. If you want those, go ahead and pay. If you want a free credit report without an attempt to sell other services, go to annualcreditreport.com or one of the sites below.

FICO scores

This is current as of October 2021 (these deals seem to change by the minute). Google "Free FICO score." If you get the score for free, there are usually strings attached, but you can untie the strings. The last time I pulled a free FICO, it was through FreeScore360. As soon as I received my scores, I immediately called and canceled the service. This way I wasn't charged for an ongoing product I didn't want. If you don't cancel the service, your debit/credit card will be charged an ongoing monthly fee.

Keep in mind that FICO has forty-nine different scores. Each one is specifically tailored to a specific industry: for instance mortgages, auto loans or leases, and credit cards. The FICO you see is never the one the lender will see. It will simply give you an approximation of the one any individual lender will view.

www.CreditKarma.com

Your free report and score is based on Equifax and TransUnion credit reports.

The law says that under specific circumstances you are allowed free credit reports directly from the credit bureaus. Here are a few of the more common reasons:

You Are Entitled to a Free Credit Report If Based on Your Report . . .

- You were turned down for credit
- Didn't get the best deal possible on a credit application (higher interest rate, lower credit line, larger down payment, etc.)
- They increased your insurance premium
- You didn't get a job
- You didn't get a promotion
- You were denied housing or required to leave a larger deposit than normal.

You must ask for the report within sixty days of receiving a notice of negative action. The company that took adverse action will send you a letter of denial or a notice that you didn't get the best terms possible. That letter should give you the name, address, and phone number of the credit reporting agency they used to make their decision and a notice that you are entitled to a free report from the bureau they used.

You're also entitled to one free report a year, if you're unemployed and plan to look for a job within sixty days, or you're on welfare, or if your report is inaccurate because of fraud or identity theft.

The Inside Scoop on Credit Scores

FICO isn't the only number in town. The score that counts is the one the lender uses. There are numerous "scores" in use. The major player, FICO, allows lenders to individualize the type of score they request. Different lenders key in on various aspects of your credit history, to produce different scores. In addition, each of the credit bureaus—Experian, Equifax, and TransUnion—have their own exclusive scoring model. In addition to each bureau having a proprietary score, they joined together to design VantageScore. This was done a few years ago to compete with FICO. It all boils down to FICO being far and away the most used while everyone else is fighting for a small piece of the pie.

FICO scores range from 300 to 850. You'll need about 760 or better for the best mortgage rates, but a score of 720 should be sufficient to get you a good deal on an auto loan. FICO is still the industry leader, but a small percentage of lenders now use VantageScore. The older VantageScore model ranged from 501 to 990 and had corresponding letter grades from A to F. The new VantageScore 3.0 has come in line with FICO with scores now also ranging from 300 to 850. If you're denied a loan or given less than the best rate, a lender must tell you the score they used, along with the corresponding score range and factors that adversely affected your score. They will not tell you specifically which accounts had the negative impact. What they will say is something generic like "late payments or judgments" and leave it up to you to figure out how to remedy the situation.

Your Fiscal Health Is a Very Close Second in Importance to Your Physical Health

You can monitor your credit by requesting a copy of your credit report from any of the numerous free report sites such as Credit Karma, Discover, or Capital One. Discover does it for everyone, not just their cardholders.

Honestly, it's a waste of money to pay for any score, even FICO. The scores you see, from any scoring model, are never the ones that the lender will see. It's usually close, but keep in mind the lender pulls a score specifically designed for its own industry.

Scores can change daily, for better or worse. As an example, most mortgage bankers get commission based on the loans they get approved. If your credit score is borderline, they'll pull a score for ten consecutive days or more, hoping to get a score that can get you approved.

You should track your scores. If you're seriously in the market for a loan, not just curious, go to www.myFICO.com. If you just want a general idea you can use any one of the free sites available.

When you are tracking your score fluctuations as you try to repair your credit, make sure you are comparing the same scoring models to each other. For instance, don't compare FICO to VantageScore. Always compare apples to apples.

Every scoring algorithm usesthe same factors from the information in your credit file to calculate your score, payment history, credit usage, the length of your credit history, credit mix, and inquiries. Credit scoring systems view late payments and heavy usage of your credit lines as the biggest no-nos. FICO considers your payment history as 35 percent of your score and usage as thirty percent.

Your score is an indication as to whether they can be confident about getting paid on time or paid at all. Try to keep your credit-utilization ratio low. Be aware of the amount of debt you owe, as a percentage of the amount of available credit you have. If you are living at the top of your credit lines, that's a major red flag for lenders. It indicates to potential lenders you may be having financial problems.

Be aware that any credit line usage, carried over to the next billing cycle, will be detrimental to your score; even a single point decrease in a score can affect loan rates. There are trigger points for lenders that alter loan rates. The difference between 719 and 720 can cost you thousands.

A history of paying your bills on time is critical. Having a variety of loans, for example, a revolving line of credit such as a credit card, a car payment, and a mortgage, will boost your score. Lenders like to see a mix.

The information in your credit files is continually changing; consequently so do your scores. If you're going to apply for a loan, check your reports for mistakes and removable negative items that could impact your score. Pay down balances as much as possible. Dispute every negative notation.

Why Should You Get Your Credit Report?

Your credit report contains all the information that determines whether you have a good or bad credit score, which, in turn, determines the risk a lender perceives in lending you money. When you receive each report, go over every single line of information and check it for accuracy. Any incorrect information should be disputed with each bureau on which it appears. When I say all information, that's exactly what I mean. The slightest error can negatively affect your score. I'm not just talking about the obviously harmful notations like the number of days past due or an account being handled by a collection agency. You also want to correct the misreported things like opening date, credit line, maximum credit in use, and even the type of account.

Never dispute anything with the online or printed forms provided by the credit bureaus. Buried in a lengthy document, provided by all three of the major bureaus, is wording that says by using their online service, you waive your right to sue. If you dispute online and they violate the Fair Credit Reporting Act (FCRA), failing to make changes as required by law, you have waived your right to sue. Once you've waived your right to take them to court, you've lost the most important credit restoration tool you have! Use the letters in the appendix as a guide for writing your own. Send all disputes by certified mail, return receipt requested. The date they sign for your mail is the date that starts the thirty-day clock ticking for their reply. (The return receipt is the green card from the post office.)

You always want a paper trail, or recording, as proof of what you did. If you speak with someone, always record the conversation. Keep a diary noting the date, what the conversation was about, and exactly where the recording of that conversation is stored. If you don't have documentation and you need to sue, the court will view it as if it never happened.

The bureaus are required to investigate all reported inaccuracies, and if the creditor does not respond within thirty days, the information must be dropped from your report.

Unfortunately, credit reports aren't the easiest documents to understand. When you're checking your credit report for the first time, you may be confused by the layout and the information that's being reported. Chapter 10 will give you information about reading a credit report.

Take your time. They have a guide on the report that explains everything. It may be confusing at first. I'm sure they make it intentionally confusing to discourage us. After a while, you'll get the hang of it. Persistence is the key to success. Don't give up. They rely on people not knowing their rights, getting frustrated, and giving up. Don't be one of those easily discouraged people. Don't let them win!

Chapter 10

UNDERSTANDING YOUR CREDIT REPORT

You're preparing to clean up your credit or simply want to increase your credit score, and you're looking at your report. But, if you are like most people, you have a hard time understanding what the heck your credit report says, let alone interpreting all the information it contains. They give you a guide as to what each notation means, but it's all still a jumble. The three major bureaus vary slightly, but they all contain basically the same categories of information. I can imagine the average consumer struggling to understand what the heck they're talking about. That having been said, here are the basic categories of information found in your credit report and a basic guide on how to interpret what they mean.

Identifying Information

They all have your name, address, Social Security number, and date of birth. If you're married or divorced, you could have a few versions of your name. This section will also show any nicknames, misspellings, typos, and abbreviations of your name that might be out there. Your past and present addresses and phone numbers will be included as well. These factors are not used in credit scoring. Updates to this information come from the information you supplied to lenders on applications, even if the loan request was denied. Information may also come from collection agencies, people with similar names, or even someone fraudulently applying for credit in your name. There's a human component to all data. Humans make mistakes. Misspellings, wrong middle initials, wrong Social Security numbers, wrong dates of birth, and locations where you have never lived may appear.

YOU NEVER KNOW WHO MAY BE LOOKING FOR YOU
Collectors, repossessors, and even bounty hunters will use credit reports to locate you. Some people put down an incorrect address on a credit application in an attempt to avoid a summons or to send the repo guy or process server to the wrong address. That new address will show up as a current address on the consumer's credit report. But the smart ones will go back to previous addresses too. So, if you want to send them to the wrong address, you can, but you've probably only bought yourself some time.

Summary Sections

Summaries vary by credit report, but typically they will give a listing of the negative information on your report. It will include the number of negative accounts you have and the total amount past due. The summary section may also provide information about your total credit age and the total amount of your debt balances. Credit age is one of those factors that may need an explanation. In its simplest form it's the average age of all your accounts.

The largest section of your credit report details all your accounts individually. For each credit card, loan, collection account, etc., the same basic information is reported:

Information Furnishers / Lenders / Creditors Supply

Information in these sections may include:

- Status of the account, for example, are you current or past due
- Date the account was opened

- Last time the account was updated

- Type of account, for example, installment, revolving, collection

- Monthly payment

- Type of account responsibility, for instance joint, individual, or authorized user

- Credit limit or original loan amount

- High balance (this is the highest balance ever charged on the account or original amount of the loan)

- Current balance

- Date of the last payment

- Date of first delinquency

- Account history for the past seven years

- Your personal statement on your account, if any.

Keep in mind as you read the following that your credit report is your financial payment history. Your credit score is a numeric calculation obtained by evaluating what's on your credit report. In many cases, the lender only looks at the score and doesn't care what went into arriving at the score. In some cases, for instance a mortgage or auto loan, the lender will look more deeply into what's on the report itself along with the score.

ACCOUNTS ON YOUR CREDIT REPORT MAY HAVE NOTATIONS SUCH AS:

- Disputed by the consumer—This is meaningless to your score but could be a negative to a lender if there's more than one. Numerous disputes will be a problem if you apply for a mortgage. The mortgage lenders will go over your credit report line-by-line. They will question all the disputes that are unresolved. Every dispute should be removed or noted as "resolved" or similar wording prior to applying for a mortgage. It can be accomplished by calling or writing the bureaus. If you haven't done this prior to applying for a mortgage, most mortgage brokers will do it for you or walk you through the process.

- Closed by creditor—The effect on your credit score is slightly negative. If the creditor closed the account, that usually indicates there was a problem or you weren't using the card.

- Closed by consumer—The effect on your score is neutral unless there is a balance past due, then this notation becomes a scoring negative.

- Legally settled for less than full balance—The effect on credit score is slightly negative but better than an unpaid collection account.

- Account(s) being paid through a consumer counseling service—The effect on your credit score is neutral but may be considered a negative by a lender looking at your credit report, not just the score. It's a red flag that you were unable to handle your finances. A counseling service may be paying partial payments for you, and the partial payment scenario would be negative because this probably would result in your account being past due.

In the section showing the negative items, the accounts will be listed showing when a late payment occurred and how late it is/was, thirty/sixty/ninety days and so on. Usually, the credit reports will have a "Payment History Legend" that will explain all the possible notations that a creditor will use, and they will often be color-coded: green for good, yellow for bad, red for very bad, and black for no data. The "ND" or no data notation usually indicates that the lender didn't report that month because you didn't have a balance. Even though the credit gurus will tell you to "be careful, never miss a payment, it will affect your credit report," missing a single payment doesn't affect your credit and here's why.

You will never see an account listed less than thirty days past due. Thirty days past due is two payments. If you are late for a single payment, you are from one to possibly twenty-nine days past due. The triggering mechanism for all lenders is missing that second payment. That's when your account gets reported as thirty days past due. For credit reporting purposes, you can miss making a single payment, on time, forever, and it won't ever affect your credit report.

If an account is placed with or sold to a collection agency, the address, name, and phone number of the agency will be listed. Collection agencies that are simply collecting for the original creditor usually won't report. If you call the original creditor, regarding an account that has been placed with an agency, they usually won't discuss the account. They will usually advise you to contact the collection agency. If your account was sold to a collection agency, it will almost always appear with all the contact information for the agency; contact them directly if needed. If an account has been sold, the original creditor will always refer you to the debt purchaser and will never discuss payments.

The institution that reports the negative on the report is the only one that can remove it. A collection agency cannot remove the lenders' negative notations and the lender cannot remove a collection agency notation. The company reporting the data is referred to as the "Information Furnisher."

TRADELINES

These are all your loans, including mortgages, credit cards, student loans, and auto loans. Lenders report separately on each account that you have with them. They report the type of account, the date you opened the account, your credit limit, the highest balance you have ever had, the current account balance, and your payment history. Most but not every lender sends your data to every credit bureau.

SECURED BY REAL ESTATE

There are three basic types of account classifications for borrowings: Mortgages, Revolving Credit, and Installment Loans. Some of these will overlap into two categories. These include first mortgages, second mortgages, home equity loans (noted on your credit report as HELOC / Home Equity Line of Credit), and any other loans you may have secured by real estate.

REVOLVING ACCOUNTS

Revolving accounts are credit cards and lines of credit. Payments and balances vary from month to month. If there is any balance on the account, they require a minimum payment every month. This includes most credit cards. Your credit report will show your monthly payment, total amount due, and current balances that will vary based on the monthly activity. These are often referred to as open-ended lines of credit. These include credit cards, Home Equity Lines of Credit (HELOCs), and unsecured lines of credit accessed by simply writing a check.

A common mistake people make on open-ended credit is thinking they've pre-paid months in advance. For example, they have a minimum payment of $25 and pay $50 and assume they paid the following month's payment. You cannot prepay monthly payments on any revolving form of credit like a credit card or line of credit. It's recommended to pay more than the monthly minimum, but it won't take care of the following month's mandatory minimum. You are required to make at least the minimum payment every month that you have a balance.

INSTALLMENT LOANS

Installment loans, also referred to as closed end loans, include mortgages, personal loans, and car loans. These loans have the same payment due each month. As timely payments are made the loan balance declines. The loan terms, payment amount, due date, interest rate, and length of the loan are spelled out in the loan contract. These usually can be paid in advance. For instance, if you are current and due for your May payment of $100 and you pay $200, you've paid May and June.

Always ask the lender or read your contract to make sure you can pre-pay payments or pay the balance in full without penalty. Mistakes can be very costly and severely damage your credit. It's one thing for your credit to be damaged because of your inability to pay, it's another thing totally if your credit is damaged simply because you didn't understand the contract. If you are in doubt, call and ask the lender for clarification before you do anything you're uncertain about.

People will often misunderstand promotional credit purchases. Be careful. When those ads say, "Interest-free for 12 months," it doesn't mean you can go twelve months without paying. You have to make timely monthly payments. Interest is accruing all the time the loan has a balance. The interest is waived when you make the final payment, assuming ALL monthly installments were made on time. If you miss one payment, by one day, they'll add all the interest that's being accumulated. You have to make at least the minimum payments due, on time, for it to be interest-free. At the end, if you did everything the contract called for, they'll waive the interest. When you are approved for this type of loan, ask how it works.

CREDIT INQUIRIES

Inquiries will show up as either hard or soft.

Hard inquiries are when you apply for a loan and you authorize the lender to request a copy of your credit report. The inquiries section contains a list of lenders who accessed your credit report within the last two years. Typically, you will see a list of voluntary or hard inquiries, generated by your requests for credit, followed by a list of involuntary or soft inquiries.

Soft inquiries are a result of creditors running your report, prior to sending you pre-qualified offers for credit. Employers, insurance companies, and owners of rental apartments will do soft inquiries. In the soft inquiry section, it will also show people that are trying to locate you, for instance, a collection agency, repossessor, process server, even a bounty hunter. Soft inquiries never affect your credit score; hard inquiries always do.

Lenders are leery of multiple "hard" inquiries over a short period of time. It often leads to being turned down for credit. The exceptions to this rule are car loans and mortgages. Lenders are aware that multiple recent inquiries will exist, for mortgages and cars, where people shop for rates. Lenders realize that most people aren't buying four cars or three houses at once. Every credit scoring algorithm treats multiple car and mortgage inquiries, within fifteen to thirty days, as a single inquiry.

PUBLIC RECORDS AND COLLECTION ACCOUNTS
Credit reporting agencies report public record information obtained from federal, state, or county courts, or county recorders. This information is compiled by a third party such as www.LexisNexis .com. Public record information includes bankruptcies, foreclosures, liens, and judgments. These are the negative notations that people usually think will be the most difficult to erase. If you know your rights, they can easily be removed. I deleted three judgments and a bankruptcy along with state and IRS tax liens. I recommend NOT removing a discharged bankruptcy. I did it just to prove I could for research on this book.

If you're one of those people who skim through books like this and didn't read the section on bankruptcy, you can go back to chapter 4. I explain why you shouldn't remove a discharged BK.

SATISFACTORY ACCOUNTS VERSUS NEGATIVE ITEMS
All three of the major credit reporting agencies—TransUnion, Equifax, and Experian—will usually segregate positive accounts from the negative ones. The report usually gives a "Credit Summary" which provides a rundown of all your open accounts, as well as some useful summary statistics, such as total debt by account type, debt to credit ratio by account type, and length of credit history.

Never follow the guidelines that any of the bureaus give you for disputing "inaccuracies." Never dispute online. Always dispute through the mail, certified, return receipt requested. You should always have a paper trail as proof of anything you do. If you dispute online, there's a waiver you agree to, in small print of course, that says you are waiving your right to sue. Once you've given up that right, you've lost your leverage to get them to do anything.

WHAT DOES CHARGED OFF MEAN?
Charge-offs usually occur when an account is five to seven payments past due. The credit report may note it as C/O or 120, 150, or 180 days. It depends on the lender and state or federal law as to how long a lender will carry an account before they're required to charge it off. A charge-off allows the bank to write off the debt as a loss and take the associated tax deduction. Sooner or later, most financial institutions will sell charged-off loans. A charge-off doesn't mean you no longer owe the money; it usually just means you owe it to someone else.

If sold, the original creditor should show up on your credit report as a zero balance and a debt buyer, usually, a collection agency, will now show up with the balance you owe. Don't be alarmed if they both show up. Even though they may both appear on your report, only the one with the balance affects your score. If they both appear, and both have a balance, write a letter to the bureau, telling them to remove the balance for the original creditor. You can't owe them both.

WHAT IS PLACED FOR COLLECTIONS?
This indicates that your account is now being serviced by a collection agency. The account may be pre–charge-off, or already charged off and/or sold.

CLOSED BY CREDIT GRANTOR
The credit card company shut down your ability to access any more of your credit line. This sometimes happens if you are defaulting on other cards or more often you are past due on payments directly to them. It will also happen if you don't use a card for an extended period. To guard against cards being closed for a lack of use, put cards that you don't regularly use in a rotation so you use them at least twice a year.

CLOSED BY BORROWER
The borrower closed the account. It may or may not have a balance. Never close accounts, unless there is a yearly fee and you don't want to or are financially unable to pay the fee. Even if you aren't using it, having the available line of credit will always help

your credit usage ratio. Closing a past due account never helps your credit score. If you are closing it because there is an authorized user that you no longer want to have access to your credit, call the lender: They'll remove that party and send you a new credit card.

ACCOUNT BALANCE

This is the amount owed on the debt.

HIGH BALANCE

This is the most you ever owed on the debt. It could be more than your credit line due to interest or late charges or the financial institution allowing you to exceed your line of credit.

DATE OF LAST ACTIVITY

This will be specified on the report as "last updated" or "last activity." It's the last date any account activity occurred. Typically, it's the last time you made a payment or a charge.

DATE OF FIRST DELINQUENCY (DOFD)

This is the most important date on your report. The DoFD is the date you became delinquent and never made up the payment. After you miss a payment and never become current, the reporting clock starts ticking for how long this negative item can be reported. If you pay the account current and miss another payment that you never make up, the clock restarts, and that date becomes the new DoFD.

The reporting start date for the seven-year time frame needs some explanation. You have a loan that has a fixed monthly payment. January of 2015 you missed a payment. You made payments after that, on the due date every month for a year but never caught up the past due payment. You were always one payment behind. In January of 2016, you stop paying completely. The account is charged off by the lender in May of 2016 and is then reported to the credit bureaus. The seven-year clock started ticking not the date of the charge-off, not the date of the last payment, but the first time you became delinquent and never paid your account current: January of 2015.

Keep in mind the previous scenario is for a fixed payment loan, like auto or personal loans. If you are paying on a credit card or some form of a line of credit, the monthly bill you'll receive will be for any past due amount and the minimum due for the current month. If you make the minimum payment requested, you're bringing the account current. But the same rules apply. If your monthly credit card bill asks for a minimum payment of $50, and you send $49 but never pay at least the minimum amount requested, the first time you didn't pay the minimum and continued never paying the minimum, that's your start date or "Date of First Delinquency."

Chapter 11
COMMON QUESTIONS CONCERNING CREDIT REPORTS

How Often Should You Check Your Credit Report?

As a rule of thumb, you should check your credit report at least twice a year. If you are planning any major purchase, for instance, a house or car, it's a good idea to check your credit report as early as you can anticipate that major purchase. This way you don't have any surprises during the loan process, and plenty of time to correct errors. Using the credit restoration tools outlined here, not only can you correct errors, but you can legally remove correctly reported, but unverifiable, negative items.

Why Are My Scores Different on Different Credit Reports?

If you compare your credit reports side-by-side, you may notice they're not always identical. It's because not all businesses report to all the bureaus. Different bureaus will often generate different credit scores.

What Affects My Credit Score?

Your credit report is a detailed record of your borrowings, including your payment history, credit limits, highest balance ever used, the average age of all your accounts, and assorted public information. Your credit score is a numeric representation of your credit history. Lenders may have a specific report as their primary source. As an example, Chase may use Equifax, Wells Fargo, Experian, and GM TransUnion. Mortgage lenders always pull all three reports and the affiliated scores. If a lender views multiple scores, they usually throw out the high and the low scores and rely on the middle score.

Will My Spouse's Credit Affect My Credit Score?

Your credit report will contain only your credit, even in a community property state. It does include joint accounts, authorized user, and the ones you've co-signed.

I'm an Authorized User. Am I Responsible for Paying the Debt?

The fact that you are an "authorized user" (AU) does not make you financially responsible for payment. If you co-sign, that's totally different. As co-signer, you are equally as responsible as the primary signer.

Can They Force Me to Pay If I'm Only the Co-signer?

If you are a co-signer, you are the strength of the loan. The lender would not have extended the credit without your OK (signature). By co-signing you are stating that if the primary borrower defaults you will be responsible for paying the loan. A collection agency or other creditor will pursue all signers on any debt. A co-signer is guaranteeing the loan. It will affect your credit score.

What Hurts Your Credit Score?

DELINQUENT ACCOUNTS
Delinquencies and public records (bankruptcy, judgments, and tax liens) adversely affect your score. If you're one payment past due, it will not show up on your credit report. The trigger point, for a past due payment to be reported, is thirty days. When you are one to twenty-nine days past due, you're still below the two payments past due trigger point. When you become thirty days past due, two

payments, the delinquency is reported. Your payment history and public records are 35 percent of your credit score.

Any unpaid bill can become a credit problem, even if it's not from what we would consider a traditional lender like a credit card, mortgage, or loan. Many businesses send even the smallest debts to a collection agency. Once the collector receives the debt, they, not the original creditor, can report the delinquency and it may adversely affect your credit score. A parking ticket, cellphone bill, gym membership, or even a fine for an overdue library book may end up on your credit report. For credit scoring purposes, the amount may be insignificant. The severity of the effect of the negative notation isn't based on the amount in question; it's the age of the delinquency—thirty, sixty, ninety days past due, or other notation like collection account or charge-off.

USING TOO MUCH OF YOUR AVAILABLE CREDIT

The second-most important part of a credit score is your credit card balances. The closer your credit card balances are to your credit limit, the worse it is for your credit score. Most experts recommend using no more than 30 percent of your available credit line to improve or maintain your credit score. I found that to be totally untrue. Even using 5 percent had an adverse effect on my credit score. Again, everything I tell you about, I've done. I'm not just some "credit expert" telling you about a theory. I put my money where my mouth is!

CLOSED ACCOUNTS WITH BALANCES

It's common for people to close their credit cards because they don't want the temptation the card presents or because they're upset with the credit card company. Closing the card doesn't hurt the credit card company but may hurt your credit score. Once your credit card is closed, your credit limit is reported as $0. If your credit card has a balance, it looks like you're maxed-out, when all you've really done is close the account. Conversely, if it's open with a zero balance in use, it helps your "credit utilization" ratio and has a positive effect on your score. Of course, if you aren't using the card and there's a yearly fee, that may be a financial consideration. But closing a credit card never helps your credit score.

TOO MANY "HARD" INQUIRIES WILL HURT YOUR CREDIT

Hard inquiries are ones where you applied for credit. Inquiries count for approximately 10 percent of your credit score. Your score takes a hit whenever you apply for several credit cards or loans in a short period of time. Even though hard inquiries can remain for two years, the effects lessen dramatically after about six months. Auto loans and mortgages are treated differently than other inquiries. Credit score algorithms take into consideration, in those two instances, that people shop for rates, and multiple inquiries commonly show up. The rule of thumb is, for credit scoring purposes, multiple auto or mortgage inquiries that show up within a fifteen- to thirty-day period count as one inquiry.

Keep in mind, there is a difference between soft inquiries and hard inquiries. A soft inquiry is one appearing from someone who has the legal right to access your info, like a collection agency, employer, or insurance company, but you have not applied for credit. Often credit card companies will "pull" thousands of reports for people meeting specific credit criteria, so they can solicit them to apply for their card. These are referred to as pre-screened solicitations and are soft inquiries. Hard inquiries are only the ones where you have applied for credit. Soft inquiries don't affect your score; hard ones do.

NEWLY OPENED CREDIT CARDS OR LOANS

Approximately 15 percent of your credit score is based on the age of your file. This means the amount of time since you opened your first account and the average age of all your accounts. Opening a new account lowers the average age of your accounts. Opening a new account will have a short-term, minor negative effect on your scores. This is another consideration when closing out an unwanted or unused credit card. How will it affect the "age" of your credit file?

TAX LIENS

Partially because of a lawsuit I participated in, and the subsequent settlement, many tax liens and judgments have been removed from thousands of credit reports. If you are one of the unlucky ones, where they still appear, liens will remain on your credit report for seven years from the date you pay off the debt. I used the credit rehab and restoration tools outlined here to remove four tax liens from my credit report years prior to the date they were due to come off. If you have lien problems. review chapters 4 and 5.

JUDGMENTS

These will show up at your County Court or at the County Recorder's Office. A judgment can be reported on your credit report for seven years from its origination date or for the period specified in the statute of limitations for your state, whichever is longer. I removed three judgments. See the appendix for judgment removal letters.

GOVERNMENT GUARANTEED LOAN DEFAULT

In most cases, the government doesn't make loans. They guarantee loans made by approved lenders. What that means is for a student loan, SBA, or FHA loan, if you default, the government pays the lender and the government takes ownership of the debt. The government will attempt to collect the debt directly or indirectly through a collection agency. Collection efforts may include calls, letters, garnishment of wages, attaching bank accounts and tax returns, along with placing liens on current and future property. Garnisheeing your wages means they take a percentage of your income every time you get paid. Attaching a bank account, keeps you from accessing any funds from the account if and until you reach an agreement with the collector. If you own property, the lien must be paid on sale of the property. If you try to purchase property, for instance a home, the lender may require the lien to be paid as a condition for obtaining a mortgage.

The good news is, you can dispute these just like any other negative item on a credit report, and they are just as likely to mishandle the response to a dispute as a bank, collection agency, or credit card company. Negative student loan items can be removed, but they will still be able to pursue you for the debt.

Now I guess your question is, "What good is removing it if they're still going to come after me anyway?" The answer is that having a clean credit report allows you to do a number of things that will help you pay that loan off and help you with your financial life in general.

Chapter 12
CONSUMER PROTECTION LAWS

The Fair Credit Reporting Act (FCRA)

The FCRA outlines what can and can't appear on your credit report. The FCRA says that inaccurate, incomplete, unverifiable, or outdated information can't be listed on your credit report. You have the right to dispute credit reporting errors either with the credit bureau, or the company that lists the information on your report.

The Fair and Accurate Credit Transactions Act (FACTA)

FACTA was a 2003 amendment to the FCRA. It entitles you to annual credit reports through the federally mandated website www.annualcreditreport.com. It also added a few requirements to the FCRA that relate to credit fraud. Most notably, it required notification that a creditor is reporting the first-time delinquency to a credit bureau. This requirement is known as the Notice of Negative Information and is described in detail in chapter 6. FACTA also established your right to dispute negative credit bureau entries directly with the original creditor.

FACTA requires all credit reporting agencies to block any information in a consumer's file that the consumer identifies as being a result of identity theft. The CRA must block the information within four days of receiving a copy of an identity theft police report. Included with the police report a consumer should include a statement indicating the specific fraudulent information, and a statement that the information is not a result of a transaction they initiated.

The Fair Debt Collection Practices Act (FDCPA)

The FDCPA restricts what debt collectors can and can't do. And there's a long list of things they can't do. For example, they can't call you before 8:00 a.m. or after 9:00 p.m., your time. They can't call if you've already told them it's an inconvenient time or place. They can't call you at work if you've told them your employer doesn't approve of calls at work, or even if another employee, like the switchboard operator said you "can't get personal calls at work." There are also specific requirements as to what they must and what they can't say when leaving messages. For example, they can't say, "This is Joe. I have an important message. Please call me." That message is worth $1,000 in your pocket!

In the appendix there's a Cheat Sheet for Common FDCPA Violations. Have a consumers' rights attorney review all recorded calls, left messages, emails, texts, and letters . . . any communication or attempt at contacting you by a collector.

The Telephone Consumer Protection Practices Act (TCPA)

The TCPA was created to enable consumers to restrict calls to landlines, cellphones, and fax machines. Collectors don't have a right to call your cell if they haven't been given permission by you. Don't get overly excited. They may have permission to call. If you filled out an application that gave the original creditor the OK, that right is passed on when a collector is employed by the original creditor or they purchase the account. But here's the thing: If you get calls from a collector for someone other than you, a wrong number, where the previous owner of your cell number did give permission, but you didn't . . . you can sue. Contact a consumers' rights attorney. Let them listen to the recording if you have one or tell them about the call and see if you have a case. I got a check for $500 when a collector called me looking for someone else.

The Fair Credit Billing Act (FCBA)

The FCBA was created to help consumers correct billing errors from credit card companies. Billing errors include unauthorized charges, unposted payments, and charges for merchandise that wasn't received at all or wasn't as promised. You have sixty days from the date of the billing error to make a dispute directly to the credit card company. The credit card company must investigate the dispute. In the meantime, you don't have to pay for the disputed charges, and you can't receive any penalty when you don't pay while a dispute is in process. If you owe money for legitimate charges, it must be paid even while the dispute is ongoing.

Without these five consumer protection laws, the only thing that would repair credit would be the passage of time. We wouldn't have a shot at repairing our own reports. The critical aspect of these laws is they give us a "private right of action," which means that we, as individuals, can sue to recover money when these laws are violated. Many other laws don't allow an individual to sue. Numerous laws reserve the right to litigate for government agencies, like the attorney general, the Federal Trade Commission, or the Consumer Financial Protection Bureau. I've used consumer protection laws to win or settle over $127,000 in lawsuits and cleaned up my credit at the same time.

I've used consumers' rights attorneys and sued on my own. Consumers' rights attorneys don't charge you anything. They don't take cases unless they're sure they'll win. When they do win, the entity you sued pays the legal costs. You'll get a check minus court costs and fees.

Occasionally, an attorney won't take your case because there's not enough money in it for them. Don't let that discourage you. You can sue on your own as I did. The Small Claims Court procedure is outlined in chapter 19.

These are a few of the laws that can make you money while clearing up your credit report. In the appendix, I included a list of the most common violations that will make you some cash.

IS MY SETTLEMENT TAXABLE INCOME? AND WHEN NOT TO PAY

When you settle an account for less than the full balance, if you "save" $600 or more, the collection agency or original lender may send you a 1099C.

It may be a consideration for income tax purposes. You might want to settle it for more than agreed so that you only "save" $599 and avoid the tax problem that may occur if you save $600. Let's say you owe $1,000. They offer to settle it for $400. Don't take that settlement. Pay them $401, so that you only saved $599 and won't get a 1099C.

Another way around having an earned income tax liability on settled debt is the Tax Code Section 108, the Continued Insolvency Exclusion.

Here's how that works. Add up the value of all your assets on the day before you intend to settle your debt. Then add up all your obligations, including your mortgage, car loans, credit card debt, student loans . . . balances on anything you owe on that day. Include the full amount of the debt being settled, not the settlement amount, as something you owe. If your debts exceed your assets, you meet the Continued Insolvency Exclusion. If your debts exceed your assets, all or part of the 1099C income IS NOT taxable. There's a form to fill out (Form 982) for the exclusion. Don't take my word for it: Ask your accountant or tax advisor, or you can look it up by Googling 1099C Continued Insolvency Exclusion or going to https://www.irs.gov/publications/p4681/.

Another tidbit so-called credit experts never mention is, by paying, even a single penny, you may be restarting or extending the statute of limitations (SOL). If the statute had expired, and you pay anything or even acknowledge the debt, the SOL may be back in play; they may again be legally allowed to sue you. Making a payment, of any amount, and in some states even acknowledging a debt, may restart or extend the clock for the statute.

Arrangements made with a collection agency, under the stress of a collection call, often can't be kept. You have great intentions. You made an agreement to pay, then something comes up making it impossible to keep the arrangement. All you've accomplished is an extension of the SOL, If you intend to pay an account to a collection agency, wait until you have money to discuss paying a settlement or the balance in full.

Once your account is placed with a collection agency, since making any payment restarts the statute, there is seldom an advantage to making any payment. The fact that you are making payments may not even be reflected on your credit report. When an account is settled, or paid in full, that gets reported. It's reported as "Legally paid for less than full balance" or "Paid in full." I have never seen payments reported by a collection agency.

Remember there is a difference between the time a delinquency can be reported on your credit report, usually seven years, and the SOL which varies from state to state and dictates the time frame within which creditors can win a suit: two totally different situations, different countdown clocks for their expiration dates, and a very important distinction.

Chapter 13

MEDICAL BILLS—WHAT YOU KNOW AND WHEN YOU KNOW IT MAKES ALL THE DIFFERENCE

When possible, just like you do before work is done on your car or a home repair, get an estimate in writing for any interaction with a doctor or hospital. Ask the question, "How much of this bill will I be responsible for and how much will my insurance cover?"

When possible get answers and documentation prior to anything that involves a hospital stay or outpatient procedure. Of course, if you're in the ER and possibly losing a limb, you probably don't care about the answer to those questions. But when you get that bill for $50,000 and you were told that you'd only be responsible for a $100 copay, it may be too late. When that person in the billing office says, "No one from this office would have ever told you that" or "Oh, Marty Smith, the person who assured you that was your copay, is no longer employed here," won't it be nice to have some documentation? If you don't have proof, you may be out of luck. Anything you can get documentation for, do it. As always, it's better to have it and not need it, then to need it and not have it.

Medical bills, both hospital and doctor bills, will go to a collection agency more quickly than any other bill. It's a matter of staffing. Most doctors and hospitals don't have an internal collection staff. What they do have is a billing department. Billing departments send bills and letters or in some cases possibly make a call or two. If they don't get a satisfactory response or payment arrangement, the account will be sent to a collection agency. The good news is, as of 2014, a medical-related bill can't be reported to a credit bureau until it's 180 days overdue. The bad news is that medical bills will go to collection agencies as soon as they're thirty days past due. Lenders like banks and credit card companies will often wait 180 days or more before a collection agency gets involved, but lending institutions normally report delinquencies as soon as thirty days past due.

If the hospital or doctor's billing department is calling, they are considered the original creditor (OC) and are not governed by the FDCPA but are terrified by the Health Insurance Portability and Accountability Act (HIPAA).

When your bill is placed with a collection agency, how does a collector avoid violating HIPAA when reporting the bill to a credit bureau? When asking for payment, how can a collector verify the accuracy of your bill as required under the FDCPA without violating your HIPAA privacy rights? It's tricky for them.

Medical bills are mostly unintelligible and riddled with errors. HIPAA violation penalties are extreme and designed to be punitive. Violations carry fines of up to $250,000 and ten years in jail. Make the doctor, hospital, or collector prove you owe the bill. Ask for written, itemized proof that you owe it. For instance, if you were in the hospital, ask for proof that they used thirty syringes or fifteen thermometers. You get the idea: Challenge every item on the bill. Tell them you want a detailed billing and dispute everything. Be creative.

Here's the story and documentation for how I handled my medical bills. I sent a dispute letter to Experian, the one from this book's appendix, indicating that the item reported wasn't my account. In return I received a letter from Experian saying the account was deleted. It had been removed from my credit report because the information furnisher didn't respond to Experian, yet I was still getting calls. So I sent another certified letter return receipt requested, this time directly to the collection agency. I waited the mandatory thirty days, still no reply from the agency. Once the collector received the letter within the thirty-day validation window, all collection activity should have ceased. Yet, the collection calls continued in violation of the FDCPA.

Here is that very effective sample letter. I used it four times to get medical items removed from my credit reports and the bills themselves wiped out. All four times I sent it to the collection agency. They didn't respond at all and continued collection calls, a violation of the FDCPA.

Date: September 30, 2013

Creditor: Collection Service Bur
Balance: $1,010.00
Account: Ending in 85067

Sir/Madam,

The above captioned medical bill, listed on my Experian credit report, is not mine. Simply verifying that someone used my name, Social Security number and/or address is insufficient to confirm that I am the person in question and owe this debt.

The court has ruled in *Hinkle v. Midland Credit Management, Inc.*, that during a dispute and subsequent investigation with the original creditor, collector or a credit bureau, that the original creditor or collector, must provide "account-level documentation" that would hold up when presented to a jury. That means an original contract or similar proof. To this end, I am demanding an itemized bill to include but not limited to:

The diagnosis and procedure performed that I am being billed for
Dates of said procedure(s)
Cost of any medication you may have provided
Cost of any medical devices you may have provided
Office visits
Consultation
Hospital visits
Miscellany

As I am not the person who owes this bill. I am aware that providing the information requested may lead to third-party disclosure; a HIPAA violation. That's your problem, not mine. Do not tell me I am required to fill out a police report since the Fair Credit Reporting Act nor the Fair Collection Practices Act require a consumer to do so.

In addition, a provision of the FACTA regulations is the Notice of Negative Information provision, covered in section 623(A)(7).

I have never received notification that this had been or was going to be listed with a credit reporting agency. FACTA (Fair and Accurate Credit Transactions Act) requires creditors, including doctors and hospitals, to give the consumer a "warning" notice, so the matter can be addressed before a negative item such as this is reported in error.

I also am requesting a copy of your in-house procedures that enable you to avoid the problems that lead to the improper identification of consumers and the subsequent misreporting to the credit bureaus.

In lieu of supplying the information I'm demanding, you can simply stop all collection activity, including but not limited to removing this item from all the credit bureaus to which it has been reported. If this is not done within 30 days of the receipt of this letter, I will proceed to exercise all my legal rights, including litigation, to protect my good name.

I look forward to your immediate cooperation.
(Your name printed)
(Signature)
(Social Security Number)
For Identification purposes, I am enclosing copies of:
1-My Social Security Card
2-My Driver's License (or other government issued picture ID)

I sent this letter to the collector, Collection Service Bureau. They removed their negative item from my credit report based on the letter, but in violation of the Fair Debt Collections Practices Act (FDCPA), they continued to call. I sued and settled for $1,001.

The following documents are:

- The check I received for the settlement (Figure 16)

- Collection Service Bur (Bureau) on my credit report (Figure 17)

- The letter from Experian deleting Collection Service Bur from my credit report (Figure 18)

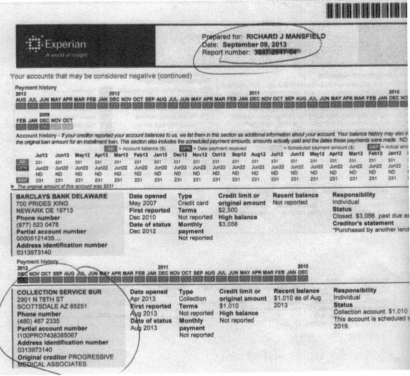

FIGURE 16

FIGURE 17

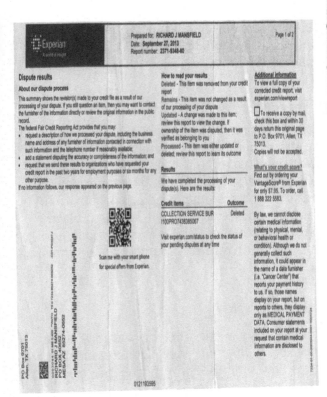

FIGURE 18

I sent the same letter to another collector, the Bureau of Medical Economics, with the exact same results. They removed the account from my credit report, the debt was wiped out, and I settled that suit for $800.

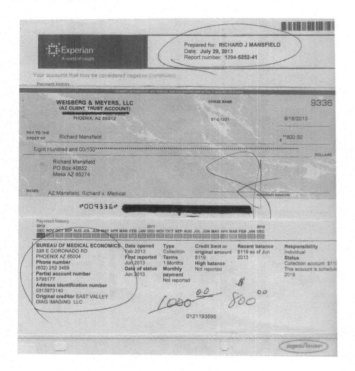

Medical bills are a major reason for many bankruptcies. There are numerous options and resources available to get help with hospital bills. Some of the following suggestions will work even if a hospital bill is already in collection.

Requirements for Hospitals

The Patient Protection and Affordable Care Act (PPACA) added a new section known as 501(r) to the tax code. 501(r) imposes four additional requirements on not-for-profit hospitals that want to qualify for tax exemption under the tax code. Approximately three out of five hospitals are considered nonprofits. There are new criteria that must be met for hospitals to qualify as exempt.

Hospitals must make reasonable efforts to determine whether an individual is eligible for assistance, under the hospital's financial assistance policy, before engaging in extraordinary collection actions against the individual and refrain from certain extraordinary collection tactics. They must establish written financial assistance and emergency medical care policies and limit amounts charged for

emergency or other medically necessary care to individuals eligible for assistance under the hospital's financial assistance policy.

Not-for-profit hospitals are required to have their policies in writing and available to the public. When you are compiling your dispute information, ask the hospital for copies of their billing procedures and dispute resolution policies. The more paperwork you create, the less they'll want to deal with you, the better your outcome will be.

Hospitals have at least one financial assistance expert on staff. Go to the financial aid office as soon as you are able, immediately upon discharge if possible. Tell them you will have a problem paying the bill, and ask if there is help. If they offer you a payment plan, other than wiping out the bill, don't agree to anything immediately. Tell them you want something in writing. Take it home and carefully read it all. Never agree to their first repayment plan. You can usually get a better one. Their first offer is rarely their best offer. If you accept a plan and keep the arrangement, the hospital will leave you alone. The financial aid office can also offer help with insurance. They can, for example, often set you up with a county or state insurance plan that you've never even heard of.

The financial aid office is also the gatekeeper for charity applications. If a charity application gets approved, then a portion of your bills, maybe even all the bills, will wind up paid or forgiven. Sometimes bills that have already been sent to collections can be taken care of too.

Victims of Crimes Debt Relief

Record all conversations when possible.

These programs are only available for the victims; they don't cover the criminals. Again, the hospital's financial aid office will have information on getting in touch with the local Victims of Crime Programs office. Even if your bill has been placed with a debt collector, sometimes it's not too late to get help—ask. There are time limitations for filing. Be proactive!

Workers' Compensation

If your injury was work related, you may have a workers' compensation case. Understand that these cases take time. Keep your case information number handy at all times.

Document everything. Record every conversation when possible. Many workers' compensation cases are sent to collections before being resolved. Make sure you notify any collector that the delinquency is a result of a comp case and make sure you dispute the billing immediately.

Notify the collection agency in writing, certified mail with a return receipt. Ask your compensation caseworker or attorney for specifics on how to proceed so that this doesn't affect your credit.

Laws have been enacted that prevent medical providers from reporting delinquent billings to a credit bureau for a minimum of 180 days. It can be extended indefinitely if there is an insurance or workers' comp case, pending, but it's up to the consumer to notify and document the situation for the creditor.

Auto Accidents

In most states, since multiple insurance companies and/or individuals are often involved, there's a specific order of liability when it comes to auto accidents. In numerous states, most of "Who has to pay what" depends on the circumstances of the accident. Get every shred of documentation to the appropriate party at the hospital or collection agency, so they can get paid and leave you alone.

It's not unusual for insurance companies to deny your initial claim. If they deny coverage and you don't follow up, it's money they don't have to lay out. Often, an initial turndown of coverage has a very simple solution. A very common problem is a coordination of benefits (COB), when two or more insurance companies are working together to pay claims for the same person. Often a fax or email outlining your situation solves the problem.

Sometimes the reason you're in collection is as simple as a wrong Social Security number, the wrong form submitted by the hospital, or an encoding problem. Never accept the initial rejection by your insurance company. Contact someone at the insurance company and argue your case. If possible, speak directly with someone who has the authority to make the decision. As a last resort, ask the person you're speaking with for the address of the state insurance board: They hate that question. Sometimes just the inference that you are filing a complaint is enough to get the problem resolved. If not, then go ahead and file a complaint. Record all calls.. Your state insurance board will love to hear the conversation.

When you successfully treat a major medical problem, it often leads to major medical bills. Medical bills are the most common reason for bankruptcies. Knowing that doesn't make the process any more pleasant or less damaging to your credit. This may seem obvious, but people become so frustrated and stressed over the enormity of medical bills that they throw in the towel and decide bankruptcy is the answer. Going bankrupt should be the last resort. Having information before incurring any medical bill is half the battle. If you have the time to do it, look into all bill-paying help options before arranging for treatment. Often, time is not a luxury that's available. If that's the case, get treated, get well, and handle the bills as best you can. Life is more important than a credit score. Being alive is a necessary component to fixing your credit. If your account does wind up in collections, demand a copy of the bill and dispute everything—item by item—down to you only used one Band-Aid and they charged you for two.

Seriously, just to get rid of the headache you're creating for them, and to avoid potential HIPAA violations, they may drastically reduce the bill or drop it altogether. I got rid of two ER billings that way. I also sued the collection agency for FCRA and FDCPA violations and pocketed $1,800. The medical bills were zeroed out and removed from my credit reports.

More Hospital Inside Info

As stated above, hospitals must wait for a minimum of 180 days before they report delinquencies to a credit bureau.

In addition, regulations passed in 2015 limit Extraordinary Collection Actions (ECAs) by hospitals. The regulations define ECAs to include the prohibition of reporting individuals to credit bureaus, filing liens, foreclosure, attachments, garnishments, and selling the debt. The regulations created exceptions. For instance, a hospital can attach the proceeds of a judgment from personal injury cases. Hospitals are required to recall the debt if the debtor is found eligible for financial assistance. If the debtor is found to be eligible for financial assistance, the debt must be reduced or eliminated to reflect the financial assistance, and any negative reported to a credit bureau must be erased.

A hospital cannot deny medically necessary emergency care because of a failure to pay for previously provided care. They also can't require payment before providing medically necessary emergency care because of an unpaid bill. A hospital may still require the payment of copays or other payments in advance of providing non-emergency care, as long as those are required from all patients, not just ones with unpaid bills. If you're not experiencing an emergency, and you don't have medical insurance or the ability to pay, the hospital emergency room may not be legally required to treat you. Again, they can refuse treatment in a non-emergency situation. I've never seen it done but they can.

If you decide to do battle with a hospital, tell them you want copies of every billing and collection procedure policy, along with their policy for people who are uninsured and unable to pay. The more paperwork you create, the more likely they are to lower or drop the bill entirely just to get rid of you.

You may not be aware, but there are generally at least two hospital billing standards, one for patients who pay out of pocket and those with insurance. And contrary to what you might think, they charge patients who are paying on their own more than the insured. If you are physically able, when you are leaving the hospital, go to the billing office and ask which rate is lower and insist you be billed at the lower rate. Record the conversation if you are able, or at least take notes and get what you can in writing. Always get the name and title of the person you're speaking with. If you can't do this yourself, get someone to go in your place and give them written, notarized authority to act on your behalf.

Financial Aid Patients (FAP) are those individuals who are eligible for emergency care at little or no charge. In the case where you may be FAP-eligible but haven't applied for assistance, the hospital can charge you the amount generally billed (AGB), provided the hospital is complying with all the requirements regarding the notification of individuals about the possibility that they may be FAP-eligible. If an individual is later found to be FAP-eligible, the hospital must correct the amount charged and reverse any extraordinary collection actions previously initiated.

What actions are considered "extraordinary collection actions" and the "reasonable efforts" a hospital facility must make to determine FAP-eligibility before engaging in such actions?

The sections of the proposed regulations generating the most interest are those related to debt collection. Under the current IRS regulations, non-profit hospitals are required to make a "reasonable effort" to determine if a patient qualifies for financial assistance. The proposed regulations define what "reasonable" means. A hospital must provide any patient who might qualify for charity care with a 120-day "notification period" that commences with the first bill during which the hospital must communicate its financial assistance policy. This must be followed with another 120-day "application period" during which the patient is allowed to submit a financial assistance application. Only after these two periods have expired can a hospital engage in "extraordinary collection actions."

Under the proposed refinement of the regulations, reporting a patient's delinquent debt to a credit bureau would now be considered an "extraordinary collection action," as it currently is in some states.

In addition, the new regulations would also include a prohibition of selling a patient's debt to a third party as an extraordinary collection action. While a not-for-profit hospital can contract with a third party to collect a debt, the proposed regulations forbid it from selling that debt until it has definitively determined, beyond a reasonable doubt, that the debtor does not qualify for financial assistance.

The list of extraordinary collection actions also includes, but is not limited to:

- Placing a lien on an individual's property
- Foreclosing on an individual's real property
- Attaching or seizing an individual's bank account or any other personal property
- Commencing a civil action against an individual
- Garnishing an individual's wages
- Causing an individual to be subject to a writ of attachment.

In most cases the hospital must wait 240 days after the patient is provided with the first post-discharge billing statement before it can engage in "extraordinary collection actions."

Chapter 14

BUREAUS THAT TRACK PRESCRIPTION DRUGS, EMPLOYMENT HISTORY, INSURANCE CLAIMS, GAMBLING HABITS, AND MORE

When Should You Order a Specialty Report?

Directions on to how to go about obtaining these "specialty bureau" reports are in the appendix. There's a description of the various bureaus and what they track.

The info there is current, as of 2021. Since bureaus seem to try to be moving targets, they seem to change their mailing addresses quite often. Before mailing anything, you might want to call and verify the address or Google the name of the agency to make sure the information is still valid.

SPECIALTY BUREAUS TRACK

- Banking Transactions—overdrawn checking accounts, bounced checks, or bank fraud
- Apartment rentals and eviction history
- Auto and homeowner's insurance claims
- Payday loans
- Utilities payments and disconnects
- Employment history
- Pharmacy records
- Gambling transactions at casinos (extensions of credit through the casino, NOT what you gamble on or how much you bet—although, internally, the casinos keep those records)

Occasionally, you may want to review the information that's on a specialty consumer report. You might find inaccuracies that could result in the loss of financial benefits, employment opportunities, or even indicate fraud. Ordering all those reports is time-consuming. Even though most are free, there's no need to spend the time and expense of the ink and postage to get every report available.

Choose the reports you want based on your potential need. Here's my input on when you may want to order a specific specialty report:

If you are shopping for insurance, get a copy of your CLUE or A-Plus claims report. If you ever filed a claim, it's a good idea to review one or both the reports. Make sure the reports have the accurate information.

If you've ever had a problem cashing a check or opening a bank account, you may want to order your check writing history from a company like ChexSystems. If you are in good standing, they won't have anything. Only negative check transactions appear and usually only for five years.

If you are applying for a job or your current employer wants your permission to run a background check, find out the name of the screening company they use. Ask another employee who might know or post the question on one or more social media sites. Somebody knows the answer. Or if you feel comfortable asking your employer—ask. Contact the company that will supply the report and get a copy. It's not uncommon for those reports to have outdated and incorrect information. Information that's on your credit report will often be repeated, in its entirety or in part, on specialty reports.

If you're going to rent an apartment or house, go to social media and ask if anyone knows the screening company the landlord uses or ask the landlord.

Tell them you know the screening companies aren't perfect and you want to make sure the report is current and accurate.

ARE YOU APPLYING FOR PRIVATE HEALTH INSURANCE?
Get a copy of your MIB report from the Medical Information Bureau. If your report contains erroneous information, you will want to make sure it is corrected before you apply for any form of private health insurance.

APPLYING FOR A NEW JOB?
You might want to see your Employment Data Report from the Work Number. If you have ever worked for a company that uses them, they'll have data about you. Additionally, you may want to review a report from LexisNexis known as a "Full File Disclosure" file. You'll never know what erroneous and possibly negative info is on any report until you see it. It's better to be proactive so you can be aware of questions that may come up. You never want to be blindsided. Better to have it and not need it.

For a good overall data checkup, you should order your LexisNexis Full File Disclosure along with a Lexis-Nexis Accurint Person Report. Go to all of the following and decide what you want to pull.

https://personalreports.lexisnexis.com/fact_act_claims_bundle/landing.jsp

www.lexisnexis.com/privacy/for-consumers/request-personal-information.aspx

www.lexisnexis.com/privacy/for-consumer/CD307_Accurint_Person_Report_Info_Form.pdf

You are entitled to a FREE one of each report, once a year. They will compute the year as 365 days since the last request.

Chapter 15
AUTHORIZED USER

Becoming an Authorized User Is a Great Tool

If you're working on restoring your credit, being an authorized user (AU) on a credit card is a great option. Here are the pros and cons.

Being an AU on a credit card is an excellent way to give your credit a major boost. When you are added as an AU, the credit reporting agencies will add the entire tradeline for the card you're added onto. This includes the payment history, usage, opening date for the card, and credit limit. It's very important that you realize that all the years of history for that card automatically counts as yours.

But be careful. Your credit can also be negatively affected if the primary account holder doesn't make on-time payments or uses too much of their credit line.

When you are considering becoming an AU, here's what you need to know.

Being an authorized user means you can use someone else's credit card as if it were your own. To make you an authorized user, the primary account holder simply adds your name to the credit card by calling the card company or online.

As an authorized user, you are NOT legally responsible to pay the credit card. Payment is still the primary account holder's responsibility. The primary account holder's actions will impact your credit score for better or for worse. If the primary account holder has a history of on-time payments, it will have a positive impact on your credit. If the account's credit utilization rate is low, it will be good for your credit too.

The cardholder's overall utilization has nothing to do with yours. The primary cardholder's payment history on their other credit obligations is also meaningless to your score.

The only thing you will have in common is the history of that AU card. Your credit reports and scores are separate. If the primary account holder

becomes delinquent on the card, your credit will take a hit. Late payments of thirty days or more will hurt your credit score. The same goes for high credit utilization on the account.

Make sure you select someone you can trust and who practices great credit habits, a person who pays bills on time and keeps their credit usage/utilization low. In the financial world you'll see utilization and usage used interchangeably. You can determine your usage by dividing how much credit card debt you carry from month to month by the total amount of available credit you have.

If the primary cardholder goes off the deep end, becomes delinquent, or overuses the card, your credit score will take a hit. If that happens you can have yourself removed as an AU. There's a letter in the appendix for that purpose.

Mortgage lenders often advise people that to qualify for better interest rates they need to lower their usage. Lowering usage requires paying off or paying down debt. It may be very expensive. As an alternative to paying down your debt you can become an AU. I provide this service for my clients.

Collection Efforts and the Authorized User

If a creditor or collector tells you that you are required to pay a past due credit card, but you think that you're only an "Authorized User," what do you do?

First, make sure that's all you are. Review your credit report. There are numerous places to get free reports. The best is www.AnnualCreditReport.com. There you can get all three reports directly from the bureaus themselves. When you look at the report, it will describe your responsibility on the account in question as one of the following:

- Individual—meaning you are solely responsible for payments.

- Joint Accountholder or Co-signer—meaning you and someone else are equally responsible for payments

- Authorized User—meaning you are NOT responsible for payments ever, even if the individual who is the primary cardholder doesn't pay or dies!

If you're positive or have confirmed your status as an authorized user, you have two options. First, call the collection agency; record the call, tell them you're only an authorized user and not responsible for any payments. If the account is being reported by them as delinquent, tell them that you want it removed and terminate the call. If they acknowledged that you're only an AU, that should end the drama. No more calls, letters, and removal from your credit report.

Do not tell them not to call. After advising them of your AU status, and recording the call, I'd love for them to call and ask for money. If I received another past due notice or collection call, it's game on; I'm suing! If, after notifying anyone, original creditor, or collector, that you are merely an authorized user and they insist on money, contact an attorney immediately. They're in violation of the FDCPA and possibly the FCRA.

The other alternative is to notify the bureaus that list the account as delinquent. Tell them you're an authorized user and have them remove the item. If they refuse, sue them too.

There are always two ways to approach the removal of any collection account. Mine is to simultaneously clean up my credit report and make money. If all you are looking to do is improve your credit score, then by all means, go ahead and do it. If that's the case, in this specific instance, call the collector or credit bureau, tell them you're simply the AU. Follow it up with a certified letter and be done with it. If the past due account is on your credit

report, just dispute it, indicating you are simply the AU and demand that the CRA remove it.

I never write or tell a collector to stop calling. Heck, you don't have to answer the phone. The messages they leave can often result in violations of the FDCPA resulting in debt removal and cash! The so-called credit experts who tell people to "Have the collector stop calling" or to send a cease and desist letter clearly don't understand how the game is played. In every case, when I'm dealing with a collector or credit bureau, I'm not just looking to get my credit straightened out, I'm looking to pocket some cash. I've settled suits for $127,000 doing this and raised my score from 461 to 742, and it's still going up!

It's not brain surgery or rocket science. It's a matter of knowing your rights and knowing what to do when your rights are violated. Don't be intimidated by collectors or credit bureaus.

I am going to repeat this, so there's no confusion, I never send letters to advise anyone that they are breaking a consumer protection law. I call and record conversations. You can tell them to stop calling or not; it depends on what your ultimate goals are. If they do call, after you've recorded the fact that you told them you're only the authorized user, I'd sue. It would be considered an actionable violation under the FDCPA. If you speak with an attorney, regarding a lawsuit, they'll use the word "actionable." It simply means you have a case.

Again, it's up to you. If you want to sue, Google, "consumers' rights attorney" or go to www.lawyers .com/consumer-law/find-law-firms-by-location/. Find an attorney in your area, call them, and get the recordings to them immediately. If you have a case, you'll usually wind up with a check for up to $1,000 with zero out-of-pocket expenses.

If any consumers' rights attorney asks you to pay any money up front, call a different attorney. Reputable consumers' rights lawyers don't ask you for money.

Chapter 16
THE HOA NIGHTMARE

I'm going to address the Arizona situation because that's the place I have a home with a homeowners' association (HOA). Each state has slightly different laws specific to that state. Many Arizona homeowners are surprised to discover that Arizona does allow an HOA to foreclose on a lien against a homeowner . . . sometimes. This is not true in every state and wasn't always the case in Arizona. Lawmakers amended the Arizona Revised Statutes. To avoid losing your home to your homeowners' association, you should understand your rights. HOA laws are tricky and subject to change, so contact an attorney if you have an HOA-related problem.

Fortunately, Arizona law does not allow a homeowners' association to foreclose against a homeowner for unpaid fines.

If a homeowner in Arizona fails to pay assessments, and if the assessments remain unpaid for one year or the unpaid amount exceeds $1,200, the HOA will have an automatic lien, meaning they can file the lien without taking you to court and it can be foreclosed on.

Fines, as opposed to assessments, are the penalties that HOAs charge for violations of the homeowners' association's covenants, conditions, and restrictions (CC&Rs) or other governing documents. Common fines stem from a failure to maintain landscaping, running a business from your home, changing the oil in your car on your driveway, or possibly painting your rocks pink! Unpaid fines do not result in an automatic lien and require that the HOA sue the homeowner to obtain a judgment. Only after they have this judgment can they file a lien against your property. Even after obtaining a judgment and recording the lien, however, the HOA cannot seek to foreclose on the home for unpaid fines.

Even though a homeowners' association has a right to foreclose for assessments, it often doesn't make sense for the HOA to do so. HOA liens in seventeen states are what's known as "Super Liens." These are complex and vary state by state. In this instance, the word super means superior. As hard as this may be to believe, in states that have super liens they are required to be paid before any other lien including your mortgage.

In Arizona, they take priority over every lien except the first mortgage.

HOA lien and foreclosure proceedings are very complicated. In Arizona, if there isn't sufficient equity to pay off the mortgage and satisfy the HOA lien, foreclosure may not be in their best interest. Homeowners must understand that failing to pay assessments could result in the loss of their home.

The HOA may still pursue foreclosure even when it's not financially to their benefit. If they do try to foreclose and there is NO equity, definitely contact an attorney. An attorney may be able to fight the foreclosure on the basis of it being discriminatory, selective prosecution, and/or punitive—especially if the HOA does not normally foreclose in a situation where there is no equity. Now I know you are probably saying, "If I could afford an attorney, I could probably pay my HOA assessments and fees." I don't know your situation. It's your decision.

In many cases, there are allowable defenses, but they must be presented to a judge before an adverse decision rendered by a court. A judge needs to see both sides of any case. If they only get one side, they make their decision based on the side that presents itself. You always want your side to be heard.

Chapter 17
THE STUDENT LOAN HORROR STORY

Congress, under both Trump and Biden, appear to be trying to work out programs to help student loan borrowers. It's reached the point where the massive amounts of student loan debt aren't only negatively affecting the individual borrowers, but it affects the national economy. President Trump talked about proposing a bill that would limit the payback period for federally insured student loans. For undergrads, the remaining debt would be forgiven after fifteen years. President Biden has talked about wiping-out student loan debts in their entirety. For people who can't wait for Congress to act, you can at least get student loans off your credit report.

Anything, including student loans, that shows up on your credit report can be disputed and removed using the credit restoration tools outlined here. I've coached clients through not only having student loans removed from their credit reports but the loans eliminated too. If you want to contact me, my contact information is at the beginning of the book.

Some Consequences of a Student Loan Default

The consequences of a default can be severe:

- The entire unpaid balance of your loan and any interest is immediately due and payable.

- You lose eligibility for deferment, forbearance, and repayment plans.

- You lose eligibility for additional federal student aid.

- Your account could be assigned to a collection agency.

- The loan will be reported as delinquent to credit bureaus, damaging your credit rating. This may affect your ability to buy a car, house, or to even get a credit card or a job.

- Your federal and state taxes may be withheld through a tax offset. This means that the IRS can take your federal and state tax refund to collect defaulted student loan debt.

- Your student loan debt could increase because of the late fees, additional interest, court costs, collection fees, attorney's fees, and any other costs associated with the collection process.

- Your employer may be required to withhold money from your pay and send the money to the government. This process is called wage garnishment.

- The lender or debt purchaser can take legal action against you, and you may not be able to purchase or sell assets such as real estate.

- Federal employees face the possibility of having 15 percent of their disposable pay offset by their employer toward repayment of their loan through Federal Salary Offset.

If the student loans can be wiped out by bankruptcy, lenders will more carefully examine loan applications. More diligent oversight is needed because many students use student loan proceeds for a variety of things totally unrelated to education.

If a student loan can be refinanced into some sort of personal loan, paying off the student loan, that subsequent loan, no longer guaranteed by the government, can usually be wiped out in a bankruptcy.

Generally, your payment amount under an income-driven repayment arrangement is a percentage of after-expenses, discretionary income. The percentage differs depending on the plan and when you took out your student loans. If you have a large family and a low income, you may not have to pay anything.

The "Pay as You Earn" program allows eligible student-loan borrowers to cap monthly payments to 10 percent of their discretionary income, and have their loans forgiven after twenty years. An earlier version of the program capped payments at 15 percent and offered forgiveness after twenty-five years.

The Pay as You Earn program also offers loan forgiveness after ten years to those involved in public service who have made all their payments on time.

The Department of Education developed a tool allowing borrowers to have their tax data transmitted directly from the Internal Revenue Service into their Income-Based Repayment application.

You can dispute student loans just like any other loan. Remember to always dispute with the CRA first. Student loans just like any other derogatory listing only stay on your credit report for seven years from the date you first went delinquent and never made up that payment. Keep in mind having it off your credit report will help your credit score but, even if it's gone from your credit report, they can still come after you.

Chapter 18

NOW YOU CAN'T SAY, "IF I ONLY KNEW."

Notice of Negative Information

A provision of the FACTA regulations is the notice of negative information provision, covered in section 623(A)(7).

FACTA (Fair and Accurate Credit Transactions Act) now requires creditors to give you a "warning" notice. The notice might alert you that a payment you thought was made was never received or that someone opened an account in your name, or you flat out just didn't make a payment. You may have to look closely to even see the notice. It is not necessarily a separate notice. Lenders sometimes will include it with other mailings they send.

This started in December 2004. All financial institutions that extend credit began being required to send you a notice before or no later than thirty days after the negative information is furnished to a credit bureau. Negative information includes late payments, partial payments, over your credit limit, or any type of default on the account.

If they send this notice, make the payment and or dispute it immediately. The only time you will get this notice is the first time you were ever past due on the account.

They are not required to give this notice EVERY TIME they report a negative. It's a one-time notice. You are only entitled to the notice the FIRST time they report. They can notify you before or within thirty days after the first late payment is reported. The financial institution can continue to report negative information about the same account without another notice. The good news is that collection agencies are required to send this notice, but they never do. This would be a great angle to use to get rid of the collector and the negative on your credit report. The bad news is that there is no right to individual action under this section of the law. That means you can't sue. Only a government agency like the FTC, CFPB, state, or federal attorneys general can! Your only recourse for not receiving this notice would be to file a complaint with one or more of the entities that can sue.

Date of First Delinquency

This is a very important date. This date starts the seven-year time frame that a negative is legally allowed to be reported. The date of first delinquency is the date you first became past due and never caught up to date. If you are past due and then pay the account up to date, the clock for the date of first delinquency restarts if you ever became past due again and never bring the account up to date. There is a detailed explanation of the Date of First Delinquency at the end of chapter 10. If you're interested and didn't read it, you can go there and take a look.

DO NOT confuse how long a negative item can remain on your credit report with the statute of limitations (SOL). They are two separate issues. The SOL varies from state to state and varies based on the type of debt: credit card, verbal, contractual, etc. The SOL only governs the amount of time that they can collect an account by suing you. Keep in mind they can still sue you, but you can go to court and point out to the judge that the account is beyond the SOL. It's called an affirmative defense and the judge should dismiss the case. You must show up if you get a summons or you lose. Put the name of the state you're in now and Google it along with statute of limitations on debt. That will give you a breakdown of how long a creditor can win a lawsuit for various types of debts.

Can a Creditor Take Money from My Bank Accounts?

There are situations when a creditor can take money from your bank account. In most cases it requires that the creditor obtained a judgment or a court order, but there are exceptions.

If you have a past due loan with your bank, the bank may take money from any account you have with them, to make payment on any loans you have with that bank. This is called the "right of offset."

The IRS and judgment creditors will never let you know beforehand that they're attaching your bank account. You'll simply get a notice from the bank that your account is "frozen." Normally the financial institution will give you an opportunity to call the creditor to pay whatever you owe and release the rest of your money.

The IRS and all government guaranteed loans including student loans and mortgages, plus alimony and child support, can attach Social Security dollars. If you get a direct deposit from Social Security, most private creditors can't touch the equivalent of the sum of two benefit deposits. Anything more than that can be taken by a judgment creditor. Don't commingle money in bank accounts. If you do, it will be up to you to prove which money is Social Security–related and which isn't. The money that isn't is fair game for judgment creditors.

Can a Collector Charge Me for Making a Payment Over the Phone?

The Fair Debt Collection Practices Act (FDCPA) regulates debt collectors. The pertinent part of the FDCPA is section 1692(f)(1), which prohibits debt collectors from collecting, "any amount, including any interest, fee, charge, or expense incidental to the principal obligation unless such amount is expressly authorized by the agreement creating the debt or permitted by law." Many courts interpret this section as prohibiting debt collectors from passing transaction fees along to consumers, including credit and debit card payments, checks over the phone, and wires, yet there are some courts that say it's OK.

There are more than ten states that passed laws that specifically prohibit debt collectors from passing on transaction fees to consumers. They can't tack on a transaction fee for a credit or debit card or a check given over the phone. This fee is especially questionable when they tell you "The only way we accept payments is debit, credit, check over the phone."

If this has happened or happens to you in the future, call a consumers' rights attorney and tell them about it. See if you have a case. I sued based on the collector telling me it was the "only" way I could pay, and they would charge me a fee for a check over the phone and gave me the deadline to pay . . . "right now." I won $1,000 and had the account removed from my credit report. You can see the email in question that was the basis for my lawsuit and the check I received as part of the settlement in Figure 19 and Figure 20.

Alpha Recovery Corp.
5660 Greenwood Plaza Blvd, Suite 101
Greenwood Village, CO 80111
Toll Free 877-359-8714

12/31/2012

393013
Richard J Mansfield
PO BOX 40652,
MESA, AZ 852740652

RE:	Creditor:	JEFFERSON CAPITAL SYSTEMS, LLC.
	Acct Number:	393013
	Original Creditor:	JUNIPER MASTERCARD
	Original Creditor Account No.:	5140218028115879
	Current Balance Claimed Due:	$3,056.07

Dear Richard Mansfield,

Our client, JEFFERSON CAPITAL SYSTEMS, LLC., has authorized this office to offer you an opportunity to pay less than the amount due to satisfy your delinquent account. This settlement, as offered shall be in the total amount of $1,410.00.

This settlement offer will expire unless we receive your payment of $1,410.00 due in our office on or before 12/31/2012. In the event that you are unable to make the settlement payment within the time frame indicated, call our office prior to the deadline date. It may be possible to extend the deadline under certain circumstances. If you fail to comply with the above terms this office will, without further notice, declare the entire balance due immediately and proceed accordingly. Upon clearance of funds, this account will be considered satisfied.

If you have any questions relative to the above referenced settlement, please do not hesitate to contact our office toll free at 877-359-8714, Monday through Friday 8:00am-5:00pm Mountain time. Please refer to the account number indicated above.

Alpha Recovery Corp.

This is an attempt to collect a debt. Any information obtained will be used for that purpose.

This is a communication from a debt collector.

**A $9.95 convenience fee will be charged on all credit/debit cards and ACH transactions except in CO, CT, ID, MA, MN, WA, or WI.

FIGURE 19

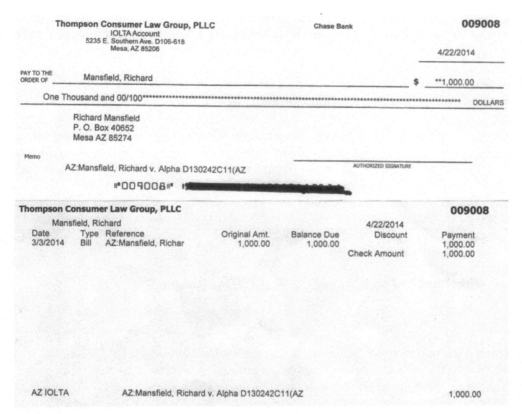

Thompson Consumer Law Group, PLLC
IOLTA Account
5235 E. Southern Ave. D106-618
Mesa, AZ 85206

Chase Bank

009008

4/22/2014

PAY TO THE
ORDER OF   Mansfield, Richard

$ **1,000.00

One Thousand and 00/100**   DOLLARS

Richard Mansfield
P. O. Box 40652
Mesa AZ 85274

Memo

AZ:Mansfield, Richard v. Alpha D130242C11(AZ   AUTHORIZED SIGNATURE

⑈009008⑈

Thompson Consumer Law Group, PLLC   009008

Mansfield, Richard   4/22/2014

Date	Type	Reference	Original Amt.	Balance Due	Discount	Payment
3/3/2014	Bill	AZ:Mansfield, Richar	1,000.00	1,000.00		1,000.00
					Check Amount	1,000.00

AZ IOLTA   AZ:Mansfield, Richard v. Alpha D130242C11(AZ   1,000.00

FIGURE 20

Know your rights. It could be $1,000 in your pocket, for every violation. A consumers' rights attorney will never charge you to ask if your case is an "actionable" violation. Actionable is legalese for "You can sue." Any reputable attorney that regularly handles these types of lawsuits won't charge you for pursuing a company that's violating the FDCPA, FACTA, FCRA, or TCPA. If they tell you they are going to charge you anything, call another lawyer.

Keep Records of EVERYTHING!

If you don't have documentation, the courts will view it like it didn't happen.

Keep track of everything that happens. Keep a diary of all contacts. Keep dates of all correspondence, dates and times of calls, the collection agency name, the name of who you spoke with, what was said, and possible violations. Keep a record of the dates you should follow up, and the results of everything you do. Record every conversation. Keep every letter they send you. No matter how insignificant it seems, keep everything and record everything. Better to have it and not need it than need it and not have it!

Writing a letter is the first step in ensuring your rights are preserved under most consumer protection laws. Make sure you send all letters, certified mail with a return receipt requested (green card) so that you have dated proof of your mailing and the receipt. There are several reasons that you may want to send a letter. You may want to advise a collection agency, the original creditor, or a credit bureau of a dispute, or their violation and/or your intent to sue. Personally, I rarely advise them of my intent to sue; I just sue. But, if your sole goal is to clean up your credit report, and not to file suit, then you may want to advise the collectors, creditors, or credit bureaus of their liability and the potential that you will, "See them in court," if necessary.

You have rights that are outlined in a few different laws. The most commonly violated laws are included in the FDCPA (Fair Debt Collection Practices Act), the FCRA (Fair Credit Reporting Act), FACTA (Fair and Accurate Credit Transactions Act), and TCPA (Telephone Consumer Protection Act). If you are curious about any of these individual laws, you can Google them and read the entire text for each one. If you don't feel like doing that, there are specific sections of each law that are commonly violated. I listed them in the appendix.

You can win $500 for every single TCPA violation and $1,000 from violators of the FDCPA and FCRA/FACTA. GLBA and the CARD Act violations aren't "actionable" by individuals. They can be used as leverage to get negative items removed from your credit report but only governmental agencies, like the FTC, CFPB, and state attorneys general can take legal action. There's no money to be made, but they're useful.

If the violations appear to be widespread, in other words, they are not just doing this to you, but a lot of other people too, these amounts may increase substantially in a class action lawsuit. Your attorney can advise you about the difference between an individual suit by you and a class action.

Figure 21 is the letter I sent to Midland Credit Management. See Figure 22 for the letter they sent back, removing the account. They were reporting to TransUnion, Equifax, and Experian. If a creditor removes an item from one report, they must remove it from each CRA to which it had been reported.

June 26, 2011

Midland Credit Mgmt. Inc. #853730**** Original Creditor: HSBC Bank Nevada NA

To Whom It May Concern:

This letter is sent regarding a TransUnion credit report. I am requesting that you provide validation of this debt per FDCPA § 1692 g(B) Collector must cease collection efforts until the debt is validated (Credit Reporting is an attempt to collect a debt). True validation should not be simply verifying the original creditor, my name, and Social Security number. Validation must have the requisites to enable it to be recognized and enforced by law. To this end, I am asking for a copy of the original contract you alleged that I signed, the related payment history to include an accounting of all charges added to the original balance and the contractual authority referenced that allows these added charges.

Validation must also include copies of all payments made and an accounting of how these payments were applied to include but not limited to how much went to the principal, late charges or other fees. If you cannot provide the requested validation, I demand that ALL credit bureau notations regarding this account be removed. This would include but not be limited to Experian, Equifax, and TransUnion.

If you do not comply with this request by July 26, 2011, I will immediately file a complaint with the Federal Trade Commission, the appropriate State Attorneys General offices and civil claims will be pursued for monetary compensation.

Sincerely,

R J Mansfield
PO Box 40652
Mesa, AZ 85274
SSN 116-xxx-xxx

FIGURE 21

07-20-2011

Contact Information: Tel (800) 825-8131

Hours of Operation: M-Th 6am - 7pm;
Fri-Sat 6am - 5pm PST
Current Owner: Midland Funding LLC
Original Creditor: HSBC BANK NEVADA. N.A.
Original Account No.: 5155970043207873

MCM Account No.: 8537300723

*BWNHLTH
#0000 08   00 7237#
RICHARD J   SFIELD
PO BOX 40
MESA, AZ   -0652

2044-352

Dear RICHARD J MAN   D,

Based on the information   ded to us, we have instructed the three major credit reporting agencies to delete the above referenced MCM account   our credit file. Please be advised, our credit reporting does not affect any credit reporting of this account by the origina   tor.

If you have any questions r   g your credit report being updated, you may contact the credit reporting agencies in writing or by calling:

Equifax/CBI
PO Box 740241
Atlanta, GA 30374-0241
(800)685-1111
www.equifax.com

Experian
PO Box 2002
Allen, TX 75013
(888)397-3742
www.experian.com/reportaccess

Trans Union
PO Box 2000
Chester, PA 19022
(800)916-8800
www.transunion.com

Please feel free to contact us at (25-8131 extension 32980, should you have any questions.

Sincerely,

Consumer Relations

Important Disclosure Information

> Please understand this is a comm   ion from a debt collector. This is an attempt to collect a debt. Any information obtained will be   or that purpose.

Calls to and/or from this company   monitored or recorded.

FIGURE 22

Violations are Worth $1,0

It's time to make collec   agencies and credit bureaus pay for their neg   nce and outright disregard of the law. Revie   e lists below. Think about if or how often you'   een subjected to these violations. Consider takin   gal action against any credit bureau or collectio   ency that has violated your rights. If there are r   nsequences for their actions, their violations w   continue. They all set aside money to pay suits.

YOU CAN SUE A CREDIT BUR   F:

- They refuse to corr   disputed information after being unable to v   y it with the furnisher.

- They reinsert a remo   item from your credit report without notify   you within five business days of reinserti

- They fail to respond   our written disputes within thirty days.

Collection agencies have made a business decision that it's more financially beneficial to break the laws and pay fines than to obey the law. They've set aside funds to pay the few consumers that are in the know. This decision has been made based on the fact that most consumers are unaware of their rights. Collectors and credit bureaus hate dealing with knowledgeable consumers. Collectors are never allowed to misrepresent what they can or can't do and what they will or won't do. With that in mind, here's a rundown of some of their more common violations.

YOU CAN SUE A COLLECTION AGENCY IF:

- They misrepresent themselves or the debt.

- They don't identify themselves as a collection agency. For instance, "This is Joe call me at (800) 555-1212"; that's a violation.

- They don't identify you as the person they are looking for, prior to discussing a debt.

- They fail to report a disputed debt, as disputed, to the credit bureaus.

- They do not validate your debt, yet continue to call, send letters, or try to sue you.

- You have sent them a cease and desist letter or verbally instructed them not to call and they still call. (I recommend against ever sending that letter. Even the messages they leave often violate the FCRA and are actionable.)

- You ask for validation of your debt prior to it being reported. They haven't validated it yet and report it to any credit reporting agency.

- They cash or threaten to cash a post-dated check before the date on the check.

- They take or threaten to take, any personal property without a judgment. A vehicle you have a loan on is not your property. It's the lender's until you pay it off.

- They call you after 9:00 at night or before 8:00 in the morning in your time zone.

- They call you at your place of employment knowing or having reason to know that your employer prohibits employees from receiving calls. For instance, you or a co-worker at the switchboard told them employees can't get calls.

- They tell friends, neighbors, relatives, or colleagues about your debt.

- They harass or abuse you.

- They threaten to garnish your wages or have you arrested, when in fact they can't.

- They say this will be reported to the credit bureau and they do not report to bureaus.

- They even suggest that you'll be sued, and they do not as a normal course of business sue anyone, ever. Or for instance, the balance is $500, and they never sue on balances under $1,000. Or they never take anyone to court.

- They report your credit history inaccurately and after being advised, fail to correct it.

- They pull a credit report without a legally permissible purpose.

- They "re-age" your account by updating the date of last activity (DOLA) on your credit report. This is a technique often used by debt buyers to keep the debt they've purchased on your credit report longer.

What Collectors Can't Say, and What They Must Say

When leaving a message, a collector must identify the call as being from a debt collector. Yet, they can't say the name of the person they are attempting to contact after identifying themselves as debt collectors. Here are examples of what they can and can't do.

The message they leave should be similar to the following. It fulfills both legal requirements of identifying themselves as a debt collector yet doesn't reveal the name of the person who is the debtor. This is known in the collection industry as the Zortman message. It was named after the person who sued for an improper collection message. That suit led to the following wording being used by most reputable collection agencies.

"Hello, my name is Jim Jones. I am calling from (collection company's name). This is an attempt to collect a debt. Please call me at (800) 555-1212 extension XYZ."

In the above message, they have satisfied the legal requirement of identifying themselves as debt collectors. Once they have taken care of the legal requirement to ID themselves as a collector, they're not allowed to divulge the name of the person they're attempting to contact. If someone returns a call based on that message, the collector must positively ID the caller as the person they are attempting to contact, prior to acknowledging the call is regarding a past due bill.

A COLLECTOR MUST:

Positively identify the person on the phone, as the debtor. They can't simply ask, "Is this John Smith" and have them say, "Yes this is," and consider that sufficient identification. Along with identifying someone by their name, they must use a secondary identifier such as the last four digits of their Social Security number, middle name, the street address, or even a zip code.

When confirming the identity of the person on the other end of the phone, a collector can't provide the consumer with the data the collector has on file, to which the consumer could simply answer "yes." The collector must have the consumer independently provide the requested information, and it must be identical to the collector's information on file.

After the positive ID verification, the collector must recite what is known as the "Mini-Miranda." It will be similar to the following: "My name is Jack Jones. I'm calling from A collection agency. This is an attempt to collect a debt. Any information obtained may be used for that purpose." In most cases, they will add, "This call may be monitored or recorded for quality assurance." After the positive identification of the debt and recital of the Mini-Miranda, then and only then is the collector legally allowed to discuss the bill. The reason they mention recording the call is, in some states, all parties to a conversation must be notified a call is recorded. To be on the safe side, they usually say it on every call. Even though legally the Mini-Miranda is only required during the first contact, most collectors will recite it before every conversation.

Although it's not being used too often anymore, you may hear the following known as the Foti message, also named because of a court case. The Foti message is, "This message is for Joe Smith, if you are not Joe Smith please hang up or disconnect. If you are Joe Smith, I will pause three seconds to allow you to listen to this message in private." There must be a three second pause before the message continues. After the pause, they leave the Mini-Miranda which is as follows: "My name is Jack Jones. I'm calling from ABC collection agency. This is an attempt to collect a debt. Any information obtained may be used for that purpose. Please call me at [contact number]."

Foti seems to have fallen out of favor because it identifies something about the debt, namely the person who owes it. Some courts have ruled that the Foti message could lead to someone, other than the intended consumer, listening to the message and that would be considered third-party disclosure, a violation of the FDCPA, whereas Zortman, since it doesn't ID the debtor is not a violation since it doesn't identify the person trying to be reached. If you get any collection messages, don't delete the message. If you receive a collection call, immediately contact a consumer rights attorney to see if the collector has broken the law. A consumers' rights attorney should not charge you to listen to these messages or to represent you. If they want any money to represent you or even filing fees,

call another attorney! Their fee will come from the defendant, not you.

Most of these violations carry a $1,000 fine. If a creditor, credit bureau, or collection agency has violated one or more of your rights, it's worth considering a lawsuit. Make sure you speak with an attorney who deals with FDCPA, FCRA, and TCPA laws.. You do not want, for instance, a real estate or criminal attorney representing you. It would be like speaking with your dentist about a heart problem. Just like doctors, lawyers specialize.

Under the FDCPA, a communication from the original creditor (OC) is not the same as a communication from a collector. The OC is not governed by the same laws as a collection agency. Since May 2016, the Consumer Financial Protection Bureau has been trying to encourage Congress to pass a law holding original creditors to the same standards as collectors. Often, state FDCPAs require the OCs and collection agencies to abide by the same rules; nothing from the fed yet.

DETAILS ON VIOLATIONS OF 15USC 1692 (AKA THE FAIR DEBT COLLECTION PRACTICES ACT):

Section 807 of the Fair Debt Collection Practices Act prohibits a debt collector from using any "false, deceptive, or misleading representation or means in connection with the collection of any debt." It provides sixteen examples of false or misleading representations. I list twenty-one of the common violations, but there are many more; most are subject to a court's interpretation of the law. Your attorney may come up with a new interpretation that will add to an already enormous list of violations. That's why you show everything to an attorney.

Prohibited actions are not limited to the twenty-one listed below. These are just a few examples of actions that violate this provision. In addition, section 807(10), which prohibits the "use of any false representation or deceptive means," by a debt collector, is particularly broad and encompasses virtually every violation, including those not covered by the other subsections of the law.

Some of the following violations of law overlap.

The Fair Debt Collection Practices Act (FDCPA) prohibits:

CREATING A FALSE SENSE OF URGENCY

The FDCPA prohibits the use of any document designed to falsely imply that it's issued from a state or federal source, or "which creates a false impression as to its source or urgency."

A collection agency sent me a letter. The words "Restricted" and "Priority" appeared on the envelope inside a green square. It looked like the letter had been sent certified mail. This was an obvious attempt to create a false sense of urgency, which is illegal under the FDCPA. I sued. I won $1,000 and the negative item was deleted from my credit report. There's a picture of the envelope (Figure 36) in the appendix.

CERTAIN SYMBOLS ON A COLLECTION LETTER OR ENVELOPE

A debt collector may not use a symbol on any correspondence that makes them appear to be a government official: for example, a collection letter depicting a police badge, a judge, or the scales of justice violates this section.

Section 807(2) of the FDCPA prohibits falsely representing either "(A) the character, amount, or legal status of any debt."

THE LEGAL STATUS OF THE DEBT

A debt collector may not falsely imply that legal action has begun or will be taken if they haven't already or do not intend to take legal action.

THE AMOUNT OF THE DEBT

A debt collector can't tell you a balance is higher than what you really owe. Many collectors inflate balances and then tell you they will settle for less. The alleged settlement offer is 100 percent of the true balance. In addition, they will claim there is interest accruing when it isn't. In most cases, unless they already have a judgment, or it was stated in the original contract, interest can't be charged.

They can't tell you "It must be paid today" or by a specific date. In most cases, they can't offer you a settlement and make arbitrary conditions for the settlement.

Many collectors work on salary plus commission. Since their commissions are determined by their monthly collection totals, collectors will almost always tell you the money must be paid on or before the end of the month. It is more than likely that any settlement that's offered will have an arbitrary month-end deadline and arbitrary amount. I owned a collection agency. I know how the system works. Most settlements will be honored the following month. By the way, ask the collector if the settlement they are offering is the best settlement available. As in any other negotiation, the first offer

is rarely the best offer. All collection agencies will have settlement authority that's been set up internally if they own the debt or by the client if they don't. If they own the debt, the deadline is arbitrarily set by the collection agency to meet monthly goals. Since an arbitrary date that a payment is due would create a false sense of urgency, it's deceptive and therefore illegal.

NONEXISTENT JUDGMENTS AND THE NONEXISTENT "PRE-LEGAL DEPARTMENT"

The first letter you receive from a collection agency informs you of your right to have the collector validate your debt. Usually, at the bottom of the letter, it'll say something like, "You have 30-days to dispute this bill or any part of the bill or we will assume the bill is valid." Then it will go on to include the words "copy of a judgment," even when there isn't judgment. It's just one of those quirks in the law. Don't panic. If they had a judgment, you would have been served a summons and wouldn't be looking at a letter asking if you wanted to dispute the debt.

A debt collector can't send a collection letter from a "Pre-Legal Department," unless they have a Pre-Legal Department. That wording could be deceptive, as it insinuates that legal action is pending when it really isn't.

A DEBT COLLECTOR CAN'T MISLEAD YOU

A debt collector may not state that he will take any action unless he intends to take the action or ordinarily takes the action under similar circumstances. They can't say things like "legal action," "garnishment," "attach wages or bank account," or "lien" unless they do those things. They can't insinuate they'll sue, or specifically threaten to sue you, for an amount that's lower than the minimum threshold that they would normally litigate. For instance, they can't communicate that they are going to sue you for a $500 balance when they will never actually sue on balances under $1,000 or they don't sue at all. Record everything!

THREAT OF CRIMINAL ACTION

A debt collector may not say they may report a "bounced" check or anything else to the police unless they intend to take that action.

THREAT OF ATTACHMENT

A debt collector may not threaten to attach a consumer's tax refund when he has no authority to do so or they don't intend to do so. Record everything!

ILLEGALITY OF THREATENING [... S]PEAK WITH A THIRD PARTY

A collector can't threaten [to c]ontact your employer. If you are in the military, th[ey] can't tell you they will contact your commanding [offic]er. Both these actions are illegal.

Collectors have been [kn]own to call human resources departments as[king] if there are any garnishments on your salary, [say]ing that HR will contact you saying, "Someone [cal]led asking if there are any garnishments agains[t yo]u." Even though the collection agency never ga[rnis]hees salaries, the collector hopes that this wil[l mo]tivate you to pay the bill to avoid a salary attac[hme]nt. A call to your HR department may be illega[l. If] it happens discuss it with a consumers' rights a[ttor]ney.

A garnishee is a legal r[eme]dy that allows money to be deducted from your [wag]es and in most cases, requires a judgment.

REFERRAL TO CREDITOR

A debt collector may not [fals]ely state that the consumer's account will be re[ferr]ed back to the original creditor (OC), who will ta[ke le]gal action.

FALSE ALLEGATION OF FRAUD

A debt collector may no[t ac]cuse the consumer of fraud.

MISREPRESENTATION OF LA[W]

A debt collector may n[ot te]ll the consumer that he has committed a crim[e by] issuing a check that bounced. The statute [agai]nst bounced checks applies only where there [is a] "scheme" or intent to defraud. If a debt collecto[r st]arts quoting law using words like "Legally" or "[the] law says" this may not only be a violation of the [FD]CPA but also an illegal practice of law.

DISPUTED DEBTS

If a debt collector know[s th]at a debt is disputed, and reports it to a credit [bur]eau, the collector must make sure it's reported a[s dis]puted.

FALSE REPRESENTATIONS A[ND D]ECEPTIVE MEANS TO LOCATE A CONSUMER OR C[OLLE]CT A DEBT

The FDCPA prohibits the [us]e of any false representation or deceptive mean[s to] attempt to collect any debt. The collector cann[ot at]tempt to mislead or lie to you. They also canno[t m]islead anyone else, to obtain information about [you]: for instance, information about where you w[ork o]r a phone number. In the olden days, collectors would call neighbors, relatives, or friends using all kinds of misleading representations to elicit information about debtors. They would call misrepresenting themselves as anything from the IRS to law enforcement to lottery officials or an old school friend and even radio stations offering prizes.

COMMUNICATION FORMAT

This provision expands on the rules about documents noted above under "Create a False Sense of Urgency." A debt collector may not communicate in any way including but not limited to phone, email, text, or envelope that misrepresents the nature, purpose, or urgency of the message. Any communication violates the FDCPA if it's deceptive or conveys to the consumer a false sense of urgency.

FALSE STATEMENT OR IMPLICATION THAT A SUIT IS PENDING

A debt collector may not falsely state or even imply that:

- A consumer is required to assign their wages to a creditor when they aren't.

- The debt collector has advised the creditor to sue.

- Adverse credit information has been entered on the consumer's credit record when it has not.

- The entire amount is due when it's not.

- They cannot tell you they can't accept partial payments when in fact they can.

- The collector cannot imply or state that there is a deadline for a settlement or payment when there isn't.

- The law says they CANNOT mislead, lie, or curse at you. Misleading you or lying would be deceptive acts and they are prohibited.

- Foul language or profanity would be barred inasmuch as that would be considered harassment.

Record everything!

SIMULATED LEGAL PROCESS

A debt collector may not send written communications that deceptively resemble legal process forms. He may not send any form or a collection letter that appears to be a summons when it isn't. However, one legal phrase (such as "notice of legal action" or "show just cause why") alone may not result in a violation of this section unless it contributes to an erroneous impression that a document is a legal form.

PERMISSIBLE BUSINESS NAME

A collection agency may not use a name that misrepresents its identity or deceives the consumer. A collector must use its full business name, the name under which it usually transacts business or a commonly used acronym. This does not mean a company like Allied Interstate is misrepresenting itself. Although it may sound like a trucking company, it's the name they're registered under as a collection agency. In fact, most collection agency names sound nothing like debt collectors. That's because, if they put their name on the outside of an envelope, they don't want a third party to identify the correspondence as being from a collection agency. A name that can be seen on the envelope that IDs the letter inside as being from a collection agency, for example, "Joe Collector Inc.," violates the third-party disclosure prohibition under FDCPA.

A WINDOWED ENVELOPE

A windowed envelope, which allows a third party to manipulate the window to see that the mail is from a debt collector, violates the third-party disclosure prohibition under FDCPA. Have a consumers' rights attorney examine all your debt collection mail, both letters and envelopes.

CREDITOR MISREPRESENTATION OF IDENTITY

A creditor may not use any name that would falsely imply that a third party is involved in the collection. The in-house collection unit of "United Corporation" may use the name "United Corp Collection Division," but not a totally different name like "Pay or Die Collection Agency" or some other unrelated name. A collection agency cannot use a name on the outside of an envelope that would allow a third party to recognize it as a collector. They could not use "ABC Collection Division," or "XYZ Collection Agency," but must use something like "ABC Corporation."

DISGUISED LEGAL PROCESS (SUMMONS)

A debt collector may not deceive a consumer into not responding to a summons by concealing the importance of the papers, thereby subjecting the consumer to a default judgment.

Chapter 19

HOW TO START A LAWSUIT ON YOUR OWN: FILING A COMPLAINT THEN SERVING THE SUMMONS

People often ask me: "Can I sue collection agencies and the credit bureaus on my own or do I need an attorney?" The answer is you can sue on your own. The first time I did it I had to feel my way around the paperwork and the court system. After that I realized how easy it was. Once you get a feel for the procedure and paperwork it's not that hard.

BUT...

This is important! Judges have the final say in their courtroom. Their ruling in a small claims case is final most of the time. In many states no one, defendant or plaintiff, has the right to appeal. In some states only the defendant has the right to appeal. In federal and state courts either party can appeal. The majority of these cases will be settled before a judge ever sees them. If you fill out the paperwork properly and state your case clearly, these cases are usually settled withing thirty to sixty days from the date the defendant is served.

Also, something to keep in mind is judges in Small Claims Courts seldom see these types of consumers' rights cases. The cases they normally see are, "Joe didn't pay me I want my money." You know, the ones Judge Judy and other TV judges preside over.

I had judges tell me I couldn't file these cases in Small Claims Court because they were based on a violation of the Fair Debt Collection Practices Act or the Fair Credit Reporting Act, both of which are federal laws. But they were wrong.

Small Claims Court, also known as Justice Courts in some parts of the country, are designed for people to be able to file lawsuits on their own. It's where the average person can represent themselves and get justice!

The Fair Debt Collection Practices Act allows a private right of action, meaning you as an individual have the right to sue. The following is the sentence as it appears in the FDCPA that allows you to sue in Small Claims Court: "An action to enforce any liability created under this title may be brought in any appropriate United States district court without regard to the amount in controversy, or in any other court of competent jurisdiction."

The phrase, "or in any other court of competent jurisdiction" is the one that a judge in Mesa, Arizona, cited as the key to allowing me to sue in Small Claims Court.

Below is the letter from the judge telling me I was right, and my case could go forward in Small Claims Court.

111

Here's the entire section of the FDCPA that says you can sue in any court that has jurisdiction.

§ 618. Jurisdiction of courts; limitation of actions [15USC § 1681i] An action to enforce any liability created under this title may be brought in any appropriate United States district court without regard to the amount in controversy, or in any other court of competent jurisdiction, within two years from the date on which the liability arises, except that where a defendant has materially and willfully misrepresented any information required under this title to be disclosed to an individual and the information so misrepresented is material to the establishment of the defendant's liability to that individual under this title, the action may be brought at any time within two years after discovery by the individual of the misrepresentation.

15 U.S. Code § 1681p - Jurisdiction of courts; limitation of action

An action to enforce any liability created under this subchapter may be brought in any appropriate United States district court, without regard to the amount in controversy, or in any other court of competent jurisdiction, not later than the earlier of—

(1) 2 years after the date of discovery by the plaintiff of the violation that is the basis for such liability; or

(2) 5 years after the date on which the violation that is the basis for such liability occurs.

Suing for violations of your consumer protection rights is all about:

- Filling out forms

- Knowing which law and what part of a consumer protection law they've violated (See the Cheat Sheet in the appendix for common FDCPA violations)

- Having the evidence, for instance, a recorded conversation, left message, or letter that proves they violated a law.

That's why you keep everything you've sent them, everything they've sent you, and you record all your calls. You'll probably never need most of the documentation, but better to have it and not need it than to need it and not have it.

In the appendix, you can see my paperwork for a few suits I personally filed. The courts don't care about penmanship or the wording, as long as it's on the right form, you clearly state your case, show them what law was violated, and they can read it.

In most cases the defendant, a collection agency or credit bureau, won't go to court; it's expensive and time-consuming. It's easier for them to pay you just to go away. They view settling these as a cost of doing business. They'll usually contact you through email prior to the court date offering to settle the case. The settlement is an offer. You don't have to accept it. Like every negotiator, they'll try to lowball you. Just as an example, they'll say $250 and you say $2,000. They go to $500, you go to $1,500, and you wind up settling for maybe $750 or $1,000. But keep in mind, they're negotiating because it's less expensive than going to court. If you set your sights too high, they might figure it's less expensive to take their chances with a judge.

For the average FDCPA or FCRA violation, settling for anywhere from $500 to $1,000 is reasonable. I've settled some for more and some for a lot more for clients. Technically, according to the FDCPA and FCRA, the maximum for one of these violations is $1,000. But that's only if the case is decided by a judge. If you settle prior to going in front of a judge or jury, anything you and the defendant agree to is the limit.

If you're suing solely for removal of a negative item from your credit report and don't care about the money, tell the defendant you'd settle for the removal of the derogatory listing from your credit report. If you're suing the owner of the account, make sure any settlement includes barring them from selling the account.

If you get wet feet and panic, you can always withdraw the suit. Withdrawing the complaint won't get you any money or resolve any issues, but you can still contact an attorney to represent you concerning the case.

Winning a lawsuit isn't just about money, although the money is nice! Critical elements of any lawsuit that you win or settle should include the removal of any negative listing on your credit report. Keep in mind, information furnishers, whether it's the collection agency or the original creditor, can only remove what they reported. If the original creditor outsourced the collection of the debt and the original creditor is the one that shows up on your credit report, the collection agency can't remove what the creditor reported. If the defendant is the owner of the debt, the settlement should also include wording that ensures that they don't sell the debt.

I have found that courts vary slightly in their procedures for filing suit. Google your state and county along with the words "Small Claims Court." Make sure you go to a dot gov website (as in .gov). In many counties you can fill out the forms, file them, and pay the fee online.

Depending on local COVID-19 restrictions, you may or may not be able to file a lawsuit in person. If you can and decide to file your suit in person, the following describes generally what will happen.

Tell the clerk that you want to file a small claims suit. They'll give you what's usually called a summons and complaint to serve on the defendant. You can usually serve the summons using certified mail. The summons tells the defendant they're being sued and gives them an opportunity to answer the suit and a deadline for doing so. The complaint is the reason that you're suing them.

You can fill out the form immediately or take it with you. You might not want to fill it out under pressure, right there at the courthouse. You might want to take it and fill it in the comfort of your home, with all the documentation you've compiled at your disposal.

Make sure to fill the form out completely. Include your phone number where it's asked for; you want the defendant to be able to contact you to make settlement offers in exchange for you dropping the suit. I've had settlement offers come by phone, in the mail, and at the courthouse during mediation.

On the form, you are the plaintiff; the party you are suing is the defendant. Fill in the Complaint section explaining why you're filing the suit. In the complaint, you're telling how the defendant did that violated the law. The complaint should be a short explanation as to why you're suing. That's where your diary and the cheat sheet in the appendix for common FDCPA violations come into play. Refer to them while you're filling out the complaint.

You have very limited space on a complaint form. Explain what happened in a few words. Be concise. The complaint is a short statement of what law they broke and a very short explanation of how they broke it. For example, I received a phone call, they violated, Section 15USC 1692(e) False representation of the amount of debt. Don't go into detail. Details would come later if this ever went to trial.

Bring the Summons and Complaint back to court and pay the fee.

The clerk will give you a copy of the Summons and Complaint to serve the company itself or their statutory agent. You will have been assigned a case number.

The summons is a stamped document showing the court accepted your filing, the date of filing the case number plus your complaint. The complaint explains why you are suing, noting the law you claim was violated and anything you want to add to show what they did. Make it complete but short and sweet. This is a complaint, not a trial. You just want a sentence, two or three at most, showing what they did that violated the law. That said, if you need more space for your complaint, you can usually add an additional page if needed.

Remember, this is just the basis for your suit. You don't need to go into specific detail like, "They called me, I said and then he said, then I said, and they said." All you need is something similar to this: "In violation of FDCPA Section 1692e(11) Section 807, on August 1, 2020 a collector called from the ABC Collection agency and they didn't recite the Mini-Miranda." Describe what happened but make it as short as possible to get the general idea across.

In most states you can mail the summons certified mail return receipt requested to the registered agent. The agent is the entity hired by a business to receive legal documents. To find the agent, Google your state name, "Division of Corporations-resident agents." Type in the name of the company you're suing and mail the summons to the agent. If you need help with any of this, my contact info is at the beginning and end of the book.

Chapter 20

REPOSSESSIONS AND SOME OTHER THINGS TO CONSIDER

When you finance or lease any motorized vehicle, including motorcycles, personal watercrafts, and ATVs, the loans are secured by the vehicle as collateral. This means until you've completed all the loan payments or fulfilled your leasing obligation, the creditor or lessor holds specific rights to your vehicle. If you default on your contractual agreement, they have the right to take back the vehicle. In fact, even being a day late could give the lender a reason to legally repossess the collateral. It's important to know what your contract says about default and your state laws governing repossession.

Imagine being on a date, returning to the parking lot after that overpriced movie, and finding your car has been taken by the repo man. If you haven't lived up to your contractual agreement, in any way shape or form, the lender or leasing company probably has the right to repossess the vehicle.

In most states, they can do it legally, without warning and without any court action. They must, however, conduct the repo itself without breaching the peace. Breaching the peace according to *Black Law Dictionary* is "A violation of the public tranquility and order." That means you can go out and yell, scream, or lay down in front of the vehicle they're trying to repossess, and by law, they must stop the repo. Now I don't necessarily advise laying down in front of a vehicle (especially if you don't have witnesses); it's an exaggeration to make a point. But then again, I can't tell you what to do or not to do. If there is a repo of my collateral in progress, personally, I would contact the police immediately and get out there and cause a commotion. Contrary to what's portrayed on so-called reality TV shows like *Operation Repo, Lizard Lick Towing*, if you cause a breach of the peace, they must leave.

If you're present when they're hooking up the vehicle, you or someone else should video everything. Let them know that you are recording it and that you're aware that they must repossess "without breaching the peace." Keep in mind that repo guys have been known to run people over to get the car. But also keep in mind that the wacky crap repo guys pulled was much more common in the days prior to everyone having a cellphone to record all the action. No one likes video evidence of them breaking the law!

It is worth emphasizing again the importance of reading your contract. Understand what constitutes a default in your individual situation. The loan contract must disclose the lender's repossession policy and your rights. If your state has specific vehicle repo laws, they should be outlined in the contract too.

What If You Can No Longer Pay for the Vehicle?

If lowering the payments would help, your first step should be to contact the creditor to see if you can refinance to lower the payments. This should be done sooner rather than later. The minute you realize there is going to be a problem, make the call.

Be careful. You're on a slippery slope!

Record the conversation. They will ask all kinds of personal and financial questions. You may be giving them location information they'll use to repo the vehicle. If they do repo the vehicle and there's a deficiency balance, you may also be giving them information that they can use to locate attachable assets to collect what wasn't covered by selling the collateral. The information you may be providing may lead to money being taken from your wages or a bank account, post-repossession. If you have decided to do a voluntary repo and decided to turn in the car anyway, if it will help, then, by all means, try to refinance first. But again, be careful. Remember, at this point, the lender is not your friend. If they don't refinance, they will undoubtedly use the information you supply to collect any balance that's due.

If you ever made a payment using any type of bank account, they know where you bank. If they repo your car . . . switch banks. But don't just switch to any bank. Google "Banks that don't use ChexSystems." ChexSystems is a database used by most banks. The only data ChexSystems collects is negative transactions on your checking account for the past five years and inquiries from member banks.

If you never overdrew your account or bounced a check, ChexSystems may seem harmless enough. The danger is, ChexSystems also has the inquiries from all member banks. If you move your checking account to a member bank, the inquiry will show up. Any collector pulling a ChexSystems report will see the inquiry and assume you opened an account at the inquiring financial institution. Now they have the info regarding your new account. The next thing you know, there's a judgment against you and they're taking money from that checking account. Always be very, very careful about giving lenders information that they don't already have.

Many of us are faced with temporary financial challenges like medical bills or unemployment and need to find an interim solution. Call your creditor. But as I outlined above, be cautious. Try to work out a new payment schedule by taking on payments to the end of your contract or rewriting it altogether. If successful, be sure to obtain the new agreement in writing. As usual, record the conversation.

If the creditor or leaseholder refuses to work with you, and repossession is likely, you may decide that a "voluntary" repossession is right for your situation. Giving the vehicle back voluntarily will reduce your creditor's expenses for repossession fees and therefore ultimately reduce what you owe. But you will still be responsible for paying any deficiency on your loan or lease. The late payments and the repossession will be reflected on your credit report. No matter what they tell you, a voluntary repo will damage your credit just as badly as any other repossession. Don't let them tell you any differently. The only advantage to a voluntary repo is you avoid the repo fee; an ordinary repo usually runs about $300.

The Repossession Process

This is important. There's a relatively new repo technique.

New technology has allowed the lender to repo your car without having to hunt you down and find their collateral. In some cases, they have installed a remote ignition kill switch. It allows the repossessor to keep you from starting the vehicle. If they installed a remote kill switch, they have more than likely installed GPS tracking too. There's not much point in disabling your vehicle if they don't know where they can come pick it up. They will normally only put these devices on vehicles financed by high-risk borrowers, and they must tell you that the devices are installed. You must sign a document saying you've been told about the device and receive a copy of the notification. Some lenders only install the GPS tracker without the kill switch and will send a repo guy to stealthily snatch your vehicle.

A typical repossession will progress through the following steps:

You might be notified in writing by your creditor or lessor that your payment is late. Believe it or not, they are not required to send late notices unless it's called for in your contract or by state law.

You might receive a second notice, phone call, or even a text, alerting you to the fact that you have an overdue payment. In any communication, they may or may not notify you that if you don't pay they will repossess the vehicle. This requirement depends on your contract and state laws.

WHAT HAPPENS DURING AND AFTER THE REPOSSESSION?
If you default on your loan, laws in most states allow the lender or leasing company to repossess collateral. However, some state laws place specific limitations on the ways collateral can be repossessed and sold. Review your state laws by Googling your state name along with "Repossession Laws." If any laws are broken, you could be entitled to monetary damages from the repossessor, creditor, or leasing company.

If a "breach of the peace" occurs, you may be entitled to compensation, including getting the vehicle back and cash. For your state's laws just Google the state you live in and "Repossession Laws." Violations include but are not limited to:

- Public disturbance
- Injury to a person
- Damage to property
- Moving any personal property, for instance, a car blocking your car to get at your car

- Entering fenced, gated, or private property that's visibly posted as private (courts have ruled both ways legal and illegal if there's no posting)
- Entering a closed garage

If they repossess your vehicle, they have three options: sell it at an auction, sell it at a private sale, or keep it. If they keep it, they can't come after you for any money. It's considered satisfaction in full on your debt. If they have an auction, you are required by law to be notified of where and when. The law typically provides a time requirement that the sale of the repossessed vehicle be conducted in a "commercially reasonable manner." All that really means is they're required to have an advertised auction. The auction price, with rare exception, covers only a portion of the debt. You are left owing the balance. The lender or any collection agency who will try to recover that amount will refer to it as a deficiency balance.

Review state laws regarding limitations on deficiency balances after a foreclosure.

Generally, at auction, the selling price for the vehicle must be in line with the book value or the established market value of a comparable vehicle. The reality is the price will usually be at the low end of the wholesale price for the vehicle or less. The method of selling the car must be conducted in a commercially reasonable manner, according to standard custom, for the appropriate market. Depending on your individual state law. Failure to sell your vehicle in a commercially reasonable manner and get a fair and honest market price may provide grounds for a lawsuit against your creditor for damages.

State laws require creditors to let you know what's happening to the vehicle and that you have a right to recover the vehicle. When and where will the auction be held? They may allow you to participate in the auction. If you buy back the vehicle, you're going to pay your the storage, repo, and auctioneer's fees immediately. If there's a deficiency balance (an amount due above the auction price), the lender might allow you to make payments. If the creditor doesn't supply this info, state law may allow you to recover damages.

Personal property in your vehicle is not the property of the repo guy, creditor, or leasing company. In fact, they must inventory and list all the possessions in the vehicle. They're required to ensure that nothing in the vehicle nor the vehicle itself is damaged or removed. Depending on state law, you may have a right to monetary compensation for missing or damaged articles of personal property resulting from the repo or storage process. Generally, personal property can be described as "freestanding" items that are left in the car: the ones that aren't physically attached. For instance, a built-in GPS or DVD/CD player or even that customized sound system isn't yours anymore. If you would have to use tools to remove it, it's not personal property. It's part of the vehicle and goes with the car. Those wheels you paid $1,000 for and the sound system you paid $2,000 for aren't your property. They're part of the car!

If your vehicle is in jeopardy of being repossessed, think about what you can remove and sell to possibly pay off the loan.

HOW MUCH YOU OWE AFTER YOUR CAR WAS REPOSSESSED AND SOLD

THE "DEFICIENCY BALANCE" AND WHAT YOU CAN DO ABOUT IT

But . . . it's not over yet. Your car was repossessed. It sold for pennies on the dollar. You bought a clunker but at least it gets you to work. You figure the nightmare is over. But wait, it gets worse! Now you're in front of a judge being sued for the deficiency balance. How can this possibly be right? They got the car back, what more do they want?!

Often, when your car is repossessed, the creditor sells it for less than the amount remaining on your loan. When this happens, they come after you for the rest of the money; it's called the deficiency balance.

Creditors can and will come after consumers for the balances that are left after they auction off loan collateral. This is referred to as a deficiency balance. To determine the deficiency balance, add the repo fee, auction fee, and storage fee to the remaining loan balance after the money received at the auction is applied. If allowed by state law or the loan contract, they may continue to charge interest on the deficiency balance but normally can't charge interest on anything except the loan balance. They can't charge interest on fees.

If you are sued for an auto deficiency, you'll get a summons. With the summons, there's a form entitled, "The Answer." You will want to raise every defense, no matter how insane it might sound on that form. Use any grounds for disputing the lawsuit such as a failure to follow the proper procedure for serving the summons, improper notification of the auction, they didn't get enough money for the car, or there was damage to the car that occurred after the repossession. Dispute everything. Be creative! Who knows what documents they have or don't have. Keep in mind, in many states, for some legal proceedings, they can simply publish the summons in a newspaper or stick it on the door of your last known address.

Make sure you show up for court dates or the judge can rule against you, awarding the plaintiff a judgment by default.

You can find out the proper procedure for serving a summons by calling or going to your local court, online, or from your state attorney general.

The local court should have on file an "affidavit of service." Process servers are required to file paperwork outlining the manner, date, and location of service. If the summons was personally delivered, it describes the recipient of the summons. Process servers have been known to file affidavits without serving anyone. It's called "sewer service," a term meaning they took the summons and never actually served it but filed a bogus affidavit with the court saying they did.

Examine the affidavit of service. Are they claiming they served you and describing an entirely different person? For example, if they say they served you and the affidavit describes you as 5'3", 400 pounds with brown hair and brown eyes when you are in fact 6'1", 180 pounds with red hair and blue eyes, there's a problem for the plaintiff and the process server. You can have the judgment vacated based on improper service. Each state has slightly different rules for serving summonses. You may need to do some research. Call your courthouse. They will answer procedural questions or direct you to where you can find the answers, but they can't and won't give legal advice.

AVOIDING (OR AT LEAST DELAYING) THE REPO MAN
Beware of posting information on social media like Facebook! Repo guys, collection agencies, and skip tracers look at Facebook all the time and many will "friend" you to get info. Be careful. Like your mother always told you, "Don't talk to strangers."

I was asked by a subscriber what she should do. She was in default and her business was not going to pick up for about three months.

I advised her that she basically had three alternatives: negotiate with the creditor, pay up, or hide the vehicle. If it's a run of the mill, see-it-snatch-it repo,

repossessors make $250–$300 to grab the collateral. If the collateral isn't recovered in two or three days by their primary repo guy, the lender will send out an "all-points bulletin" similar to the police. This means any repo guy that sees it and picks it up gets paid. The lender has nothing to lose. They only pay if the collateral is picked up, not for the attempt. The longer the car is out there, unrecovered, the higher the repo fee becomes.

Repo guys will usually come when most people are asleep, in the still of the night or very early in the morning. They want to avoid any confrontation that would cause a breach of the peace. If they try the normal repo tactics and are unsuccessful because you have blocked the vehicle with another vehicle or the vehicle is garaged (which I recommend), they will sit down the block somewhere on a stakeout. They'll follow you until you leave the car, and they can easily tow the vacated vehicle. They can do their dirty work and be gone in two or three minutes.

The longer the vehicle is out for repo, the higher the "bounty" on the vehicle becomes. If they're forced to resort to extraordinary tactics, like following you, they usually will get $500–$600 a pop and often more. Depending on the value of the collateral, the extraordinary means they're required to employ, and time involved, I've seen repo fees go into the thousands. Whatever the lender pays for the repo is added on to what you ultimately owe. Watch in your mirror to see if you are being followed.

They'll sell the vehicle at an auction. You will not only owe the balance on the loan but additional charges for the repossession, auction, and storage fees. Repossessed vehicles, at auction, usually sell for about 75 percent of the wholesale value. Auctions aren't usually open to the public; check your state's law. If the auction is public, and you have the cash available, you can go and bid on and buy the vehicle. You'll still owe the deficiency balance, but at least you can be sure the car didn't sell for a song, and you'll have transportation. If someone else wins the bid, you still owe the deficiency balance and have nothing to show for it.

There Are State Laws for Repossession

Most states don't have any licensing requirements specifically for auto repossessors. Most states license auto repossessors through other governing bodies. For instance, they might be licensed through a state's private investigation licensing boards, towing regulators, the att[...]ey general's office, c[...]-lection agency licensing [...]rtments, or even st[...]e banking regulators.

If your vehicle is rep[...]ssed, check the int[...]-net to see if the repo a[...]y needed some fo[...]n of "licensing" in your st[...] If they did need to [...]e licensed and weren't at [...] time of the repo, y[...] should sue.

Can They Sue Me for a B[...]ce Left After a Foreclosure?

In many states, after a [...]closure, if the ho[...]e was a single-family, owne[...]ccupied residence, y[...]u cannot be sued for a de[...]ncy judgment on [...]e mortgage. Google "Defici[...]y judgments after fo[...]-closure" for info on whi[...]tates can sue you [...]r deficiencies and which on[...]an't.

A collection agency came after me for $61,000 on a foreclosure deficiency balance. I sent Capital a letter, asking for the original contract that created the debt. I also asked how they arrived at the balance they claimed I owed. They never replied or stopped collection efforts as required by the Fair Debt Collection Practices Act (FDCPA). I sued without an attorney in the small claims division of an Arizona Justice Court. Prior to the court date they settled. They knew they had violated the FDCPA; it was less expensive for them to settle than to try to defend a case where they knew they were wrong. They removed the negative item from my credit report, wiped out the debt, and sent me $800. I knew my rights.

Figure 23 shows the copy of the letter from Capital Management offering the settlement. Figure 24 is a copy of the suit I filed. And finally, Figure 25 is the 1099 they sent showing that they paid me $800.

726 E[...] Street, Suite 700
Buffal[...] York 14210
ADDR[...]RVICE REQUESTED

CAPITAL MANAGEMENT SERVICES, LP
726 Exchange Street - Suite 700, Buffalo, NY 14210
Office Hours: M-Th 8 a.m. - 11 p.m. ET
Fri 8 a.m. - 10 p.m., Sat 8 a.m. - 4 p.m. ET
Sun 9 a.m. - 1 p.m. ET
Toll Free: 1-866-899-1978, Fax: (716) 852-1620

#BWN[...]*******AUTO**3-DIGIT 852[...]8 P1
#0450[...]#
Richa[...]sfield
PO B[...]
Mesu[...]74-0652

Previous Creditor: HomeEq Servicing Corp.
Current Creditor: LVNV Funding LLC
Account #: 53742341
Balance: $61053.09

PLEASE DETACH A[...] RETURN TOP PORTION WITH PAYMENT

December 19, 2008

Dear Ric[...] Mansfield:

This con[...]as been engaged by Resurgent Ca[...]al Services, LP, the servicer of the account, to resolve your delinque[...] of $61053.09. Please make your [...]ck or money order payable to Capital Management Services, LP. and send[...] above address.

Unless y[...]y this office within 30 days after [...]eiving this notice that you dispute the validity of this debt or any portion[...] this office will assume this debt [...]alid. If you notify this office in writing within 30 days from receiving[...]otice that you dispute the validit[...] this debt or any portion thereof, this office will obtain verificat[...]he debt or obtain a copy of a jud[...]nt and mail you a copy of such verification or judgment. If you request[...]ce in writing within 30 days afte[...]ceiving this notice this office will provide you with the name and address[...]riginal creditor, if different than [...] current creditor.

Capital[...]ement Services, LP is authorized [...]ccept less than the full balance due as settlement of the above account[...]ttlement amount of $9,157.96, [...]ch represents 15% of the amount presently owed, is due in our office n[...]han forty-five (45) days after rec[...]ng this notice. We are not obligated to renew this offer.

For you[...]nience, this settlement may be m[...]online at: www.cms-trans.com. For other payment options, please c[...]apital Management Services, L[...]t 726 Exchange Street, Suite 700, Buffalo, NY 14210 or call 1-866-8[...]8 Mon. through Thurs. 8 am to [...]m ET, Fri. 8 am to 10 pm ET, Sat. 8 am to 4 pm ET, or Sun. 9 am to [...]

Please s[...]rtant privacy information inclu[...]with this notice.

Should[...]h to discuss the manner in which [...]ur account has been handled, please call Capital Management Service[...]ompliance Department at 1-800-[...]9-2687.

This is[...]npt to collect a debt; any inform[...]n obtained will be used for that purpose. This communication is from a[...]llector.

FIGURE 23

I sued. I settled. They removed the negative item from my credit report, agreed not to re-sell the debt, and I was paid $800. Just because I knew my rights, I wound up getting rid of a potential $61,000 debt, the negative item on my credit report, and made $800.

Notice I didn't use any long legal explanation in my suit and it's handwritten—you don't have to be fancy. These courts are set up for an individual to represent themselves. This was one of the first suits I personally filed.

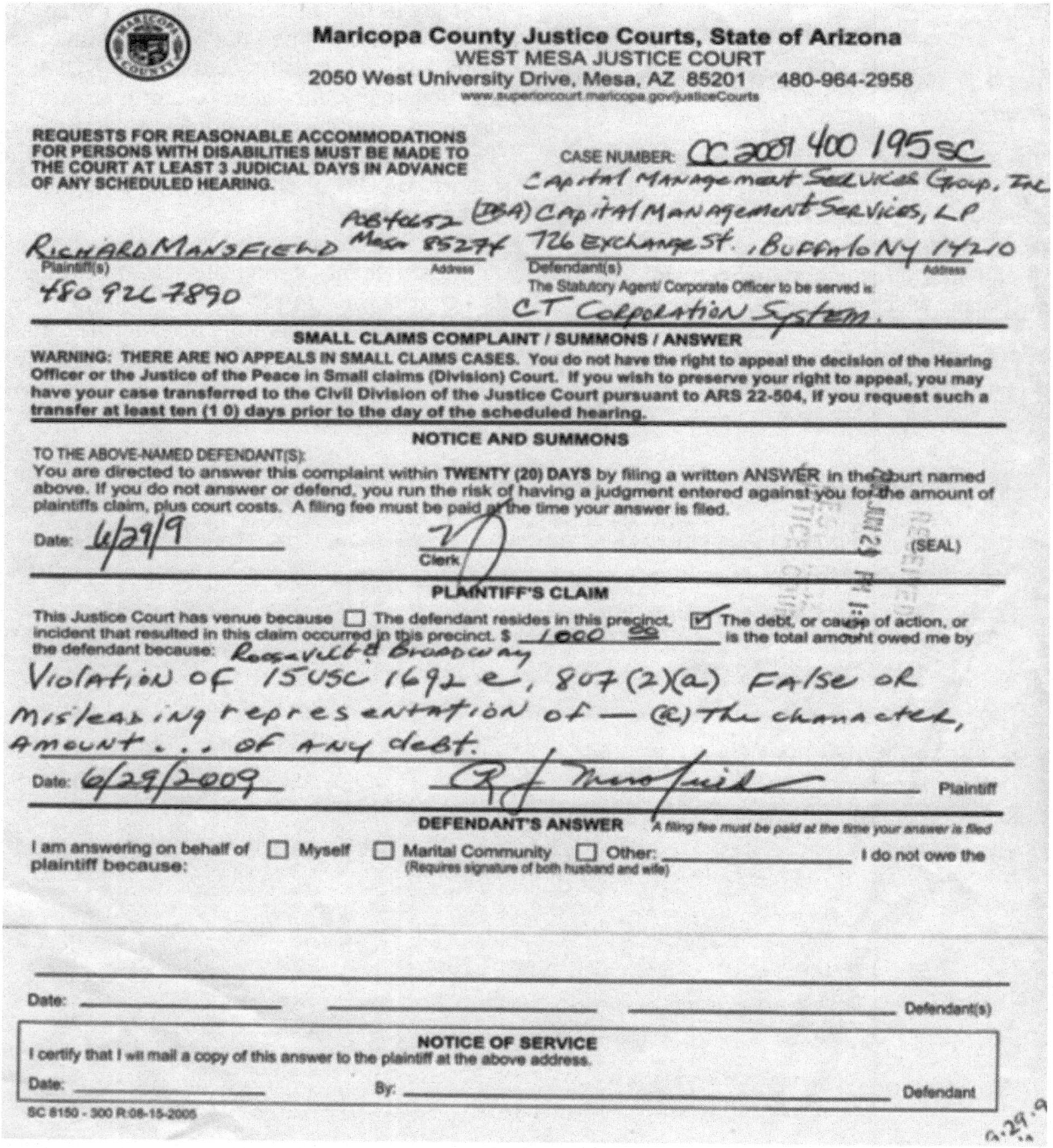

Maricopa County Justice Courts, State of Arizona
WEST MESA JUSTICE COURT
2050 West University Drive, Mesa, AZ 85201 480-964-2958
www.superiorcourt.maricopa.gov/justiceCourts

REQUESTS FOR REASONABLE ACCOMMODATIONS FOR PERSONS WITH DISABILITIES MUST BE MADE TO THE COURT AT LEAST 3 JUDICIAL DAYS IN ADVANCE OF ANY SCHEDULED HEARING.

CASE NUMBER: CC2009 400 195SC

Capital Management Services Group, Inc (DBA) Capital Management Services, LP 726 Exchange St., Buffalo NY 14210
Defendant(s) Address

Richard Mansfield PO Box 6652 Mesa 85274
Plaintiff(s) Address
480 926 7890

The Statutory Agent/ Corporate Officer to be served is: CT Corporation System.

SMALL CLAIMS COMPLAINT / SUMMONS / ANSWER

WARNING: THERE ARE NO APPEALS IN SMALL CLAIMS CASES. You do not have the right to appeal the decision of the Hearing Officer or the Justice of the Peace in Small claims (Division) Court. If you wish to preserve your right to appeal, you may have your case transferred to the Civil Division of the Justice Court pursuant to ARS 22-504, if you request such a transfer at least ten (1 0) days prior to the day of the scheduled hearing.

NOTICE AND SUMMONS

TO THE ABOVE-NAMED DEFENDANT(S):
You are directed to answer this complaint within TWENTY (20) DAYS by filing a written ANSWER in the court named above. If you do not answer or defend, you run the risk of having a judgment entered against you for the amount of plaintiffs claim, plus court costs. A filing fee must be paid at the time your answer is filed.

Date: 6/29/9 Clerk (SEAL)

PLAINTIFF'S CLAIM

This Justice Court has venue because ☐ The defendant resides in this precinct. ☑ The debt, or cause of action, or incident that resulted in this claim occurred in this precinct. $ 1000.00 is the total amount owed me by the defendant because: Roosevelt & Broadway

Violation of 15 USC 1692 e, 807(2)(a) False or misleading representation of — (a) the character, amount ... of any debt.

Date: 6/29/2009 Plaintiff

DEFENDANT'S ANSWER — A filing fee must be paid at the time your answer is filed

I am answering on behalf of ☐ Myself ☐ Marital Community (Requires signature of both husband and wife) ☐ Other: ______ I do not owe the plaintiff because:

Date: ______ Defendant(s)

NOTICE OF SERVICE
I certify that I will mail a copy of this answer to the plaintiff at the above address.
Date: ______ By: ______ Defendant

SC 8150 - 300 R:08-15-2005

FIGURE 24

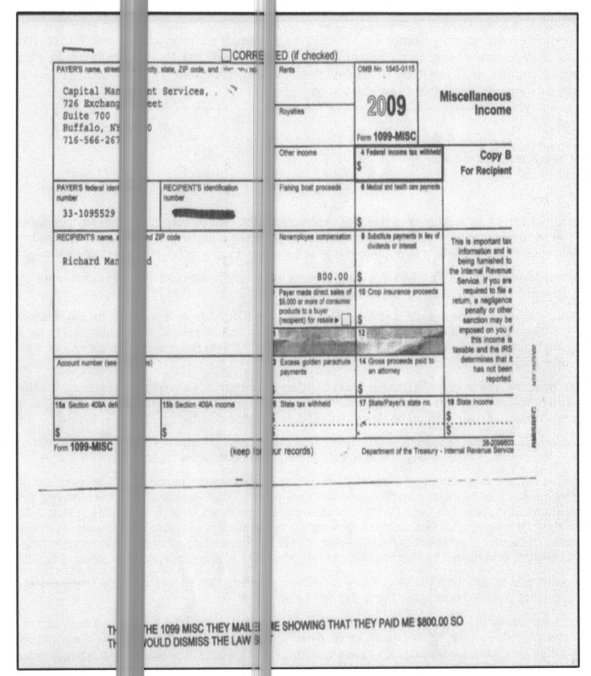

FIGURE 25

Dispute Immediately, as [Soon] as You Get a Letter or Call

Figure 26 is an opinion [lett]er from John F. Le[Fe]vre, an attorney for the [Fede]ral Trade Commiss[i]on (FTC). In it Mr. LeFev[re sa]ys, "the reality is [th]at debt collectors use the [repo]rting mechanism [as] a tool to persuade consum[ers t]o pay, just like dur[ni]ng letters and telephone cal[ls]."

Mr. LeFevre outlines [the] reasons that I ad[vi]se everybody to dispute e[very]thing, as soon as [y]ou become aware that a debt has been placed with a collection agency. All collection activity is barred by the FDCPA while an account is within the thirty-day validation period and you've disputed the debt. I'm going to repeat that: "And you've disputed the debt!"

The FDCPA Section 1692g (b) mandates that all collection activity ceases as soon as a validation request is received. Call the collector immediately and record the conversation. Ask them if they reported the account. If it hasn't been, according to the FDCPA, they are not allowed to report until the dispute is resolved. Often, they cannot sufficiently resolve your dispute and because they can't validate the debt, they cannot report the debt. If the collection agency has already reported, they must note it as being disputed, but the negative notation will remain. It's always easier to stop them from reporting than to get them to remove an item they've already reported.

12-23-1997
Robert G. Cass Compliance Counsel
2448 E. 81st Street, Suite 5500
Tulsa, OK 74137-4248

Dear Mr. Cass:

Mr. Medine asked me to reply to your letter of October 28, 1997, concerning the circumstances under which a debt collector may report a "charged-off debt" to a consumer reporting agency under the enclosed Fair Debt Collection Practices Act. In that letter, you pose four questions, which I set out below with our answers.

"Is it permissible under the FDCPA for a debt collector to report charged-off debts to a consumer reporting agency during the term of the thirty-day validation period detailed in Section 1692g?"

Yes. As stated in the Commission's Staff Commentary on the FDCPA, a debt collector may accurately report a debt to a consumer reporting agency within the thirty-day validation period. We do not regard the action of reporting a debt to a consumer reporting agency as inconsistent with the consumer's dispute or verification rights under § 1692g.

"Is it permissible under the FDCPA for a debt collector to report, or continue to report, a consumer's charged-off debt to a consumer reporting agency after the debt collector has received, but not responded to, a consumer's written dispute during the thirty-day validation period detailed in § 1692g?"

As you know, Section 1692g(b) requires the debt collector to cease collection of the debt at issue if a written dispute is received within the thirty-day validation period until verification is obtained.

Because we believe that reporting a charged-off debt to a consumer reporting agency, particularly at this stage of the collection process, constitutes "collection activity" on the part of the collector, our answer to your question is No. Although the FDCPA is unclear on this point, we believe the reality is that debt collectors use the reporting mechanism as a tool to persuade consumers to pay, just like dunning letters and telephone calls. Of course, if a dispute is received after a debt has been reported to a consumer reporting agency, the debt collector is obligated by Section 1692e (8) to inform the consumer reporting agency of the dispute.

"Is it permissible under the FDCPA to cease collection of a debt rather than respond to a written dispute from a consumer received during the thirty-day validation period?"

Yes. There is nothing in the FDCPA that requires a debt collector to continue collecting a debt after a written dispute is received. Further, there is nothing in the FDCPA that requires a response to a written dispute if the debt collector chooses to abandon its collection effort with respect to the debt at issue. See *Smith v. Transworld Systems, Inc.*, 953 F.2d 1025, 1032 (6th Cir. 1992).

"Would the following action by a debt collector constitute continued collection activity under § 1692g(b): reporting a charged-off consumer debt to a consumer reporting agency as disputed in accordance with § 1692e (8), when the debt collector became aware of the dispute when the consumer sent a written dispute to the debt collector during the thirty-day validation period, and no verification of the debt has been provided by the debt collector?"

Yes. As stated in our answer to Question II, we view reporting to a consumer reporting agency as a collection activity prohibited by § 1692g(b) after a written dispute is received and no verification has been provided. Again, however, a debt collector must report a dispute received after a debt has been reported under § 1692e (8).

I hope this is responsive to your request.

Sincerely, John F. LeFevre Attorney

FIGURE 26

Examples for most o[f the] letters you'll n[ee]d
are in the appendix. Mos[t are] legal precedent t[h]at
reminds the recipient o[f th]eir legal obligati[on]s.
These are the letters an[d te]chniques that wor[k]ed
for me.

Validation Letter to the C[redi]t Bureau

Keep disputing negative [lis]tings with the cr[ed]it
bureaus. When you hit on [the] right dispute, the [lis]t-
ing will be completely re[mo]ved from your re[por]t.
For instance, if you disp[ute] the date the acc[ou]nt
was opened, and the cre[dit b]ureaus can't verify [th]e
opening date, they dele[te t]he entire listing. [Yo]u
will need to change the [reas]on for the reinves[tig]a-
tion, so the credit bureau[s wil]l have something [ne]w
to investigate. Here aga[in i]s a list of a few th[in]gs
that you can dispute. A[nyth]ing they report, [yo]u
can dispute. Note that in [the] Fair Credit Repor[tin]g
Act, even your first disp[ute] is legally termed [a] a
"reinvestigation."

- Not my account

- Not late that month

- Wrong amount

- Wrong account numb[er]

- Wrong original credit[or]

- Wrong charge-off date

- Wrong date of last act[ivity]

- Wrong balance

- Wrong credit limit

- Wrong status (there [are] about twenty of t[he]se
  and you can dispute e[ver]y one)

- Wrong high credit.

The first time you cha[n]ge a listing, you m[ig]ht
say the account is "not [lat]e." The second [tim]e,
you could say "never lat[e." T]he third time, "w[ro]ng
balance," fourth time "[wron]g credit limit." [Ke]ep
going: this may turn into [a n]umbers game. Bu[rea]us
receive thousands of lett[ers d]aily. Understaffin[g an]d
human error work in y[our f]avor. According t[o t]he
FCRA the bureaus have [thirt]y days to reply to [a dis]-
pute. Day one starts the [day] they receive you[r dis]-
pute. The content of the [lette]r is usually forw[ard]ed
to India, the Philippine[s, o]r one of three S[ou]th
American countries. Th[e le]tters are review[ed] by

someone whose first language isn't English. They
take your dispute, determine what three letter code
best describes the gist of your complaint and send
that to the information furnisher in an email. The
understaffed information furnisher reviews your
dispute, in most cases solely based on the code
they received and determines how to respond to the
bureau. The bureau then responds to you. Is this
system flawed? Does this work in your favor? Yes
and yes!

> **LOANS APPROVED WITHOUT A SIGNATURE.
> APPLICATIONS ONLINE OR OVER THE PHONE DON'T
> REQUIRE A SIGNATURE**

The "Account Stated" Doctrine

Lawmakers intentionally word laws to confuse non-
lawyers, so that if you want to know what a specific
law means you pay an attorney to interpret it. So,
I'll give you the legalese, but I'll explain it in plain
English too.

Legally, an account stated is "an agreement based
upon prior transactions between the parties with
respect to the items composing the account, and the
balance due, if any, in favor of one of the parties."

In English that means, when you apply for credit
online or over the phone, creditors rarely require a
signed application. That's when the account stated
doctrine comes into play.

Here's more of the legalese. "To create an
account stated, the agreement must amount to
a recognition of a debt by a party, with a promise,
express or implied, to pay the debt." This can be
established by the creditor through regular mail or
by emailing the debtor a statement regarding the
account and the amount owed. The consumer is
required to examine the statement, and they admit
that it's correct by either not disputing it or making
a payment. This, in most cases, establishes a binding contractual relationship known as an account
stated. Once an account stated is established, it acts
as an admission by both parties that the amount
indicated is due.

In plain English, an account stated is established
when a consumer fails to object to a bill from a creditor within a reasonable time, usually within thirty
days after the first sent billing. What it boils down
to is, if you made payments or didn't dispute the
debt, you have acknowledged that it's your account.
If you have an account that you applied for online

and never made a payment, you have a case that the debt isn't yours.

If an account shows up as open or past due, I would dispute it with the CRAs first indicating "I never made a payment. This isn't mine." If they send you a letter saying they "verified" the account as yours, I would then call the original creditor or collection agency making the same argument, that I never had that account, and I never made a payment acknowledging the account.

If they refuse to resolve the situation, request a copy of the payment history along with copies of the payment instruments themselves: for example, the checks or money orders. If there was never a payment made, this should go away. On the other hand, if payments were made and the address they have on record is your physical address or a correct email address, it's difficult to claim your ID was stolen and it's not your account. ID thieves don't normally make payments on fraudulent or stolen accounts and don't receive correspondence sent directly to you. That said, it's not impossible that someone in your household opened the account with your info, intercepted bills addressed to you, and made payments too! I had a situation similar to this with an Arizona utility company where payments were actually made for five years on an account that wasn't mine.

If you claim an account that payments were made on isn't yours, the creditor's first question will be,

"If you didn't make the payments, who did?" My response to that is, "According to the Fair and Accurate Credit Transaction Act, it's not my job to provide the name of an identity thief. It's your job to prove what you're reporting is accurate."

That's exactly what happened to me with a utility company and an apartment complex. A family member rented an apartment in my name and turned on the utilities without my knowledge. They paid for nearly five years. Since the utility bill and rent were paid on time, nothing showed up on my credit report. After they stopped paying, two collection agencies listed derogatory items: one was the utility bill and the other one for the unpaid rent. I disputed both and neither information furnisher could prove the debt was mine. I sued when they refused to remove the items from my report. They settled the suits for a total of $8,000 and both items were deleted. The entire scenario for that fraudulent APS utility bill is outlined around the middle of chapter 6. If you didn't read it and are interested, you can go there and read it now.

It's very important to note that you only retain your right to sue the original creditor, regarding the accuracy of a reported item, AFTER you have first sent a dispute and received a reply from the credit bureau.

Chapter 21

COLLECTION AGENCIES

Dispute Letter to a Collection Agency / Prove It / Remove It

Figure 27 is the letter I sent Midland Credit Management and Figure 28 is their reply. They removed the account from all three bureaus.

FIGURE 27

May 2, 2011

Midland Credit Mgmt. Inc. #3730XXXX
Original Creditor: HSBC Bank Nevada NA

To Whom It May Concern:

This letter is sent regarding TransUnion credit report. I am requesting that you provide validation of this debt per FDCPA § 1692 g(B) Collector must cease collection efforts until the debt is validated (Credit Reporting is an attempt to collect a debt). True validation should not be simply verifying the original creditor, my name, and Social Security number. Validation must have the requisites to enable it to be recognized and enforced by law. To this end, I am asking for a copy of the original contract you alleged that I signed, the related payment history to include an accounting of all charges added to the original balance and the contractual authority referenced that allows these added charges.

Validation must also include copies of all payments made and an accounting of how these payments were applied to include but not limited how much went to the principal, late charges or other fees. If you cannot provide the requested validation, I demand that ALL credit bureau notations regarding this account be removed. This would include but not be limited Experian, Equifax, and TransUnion.

If you do not comply with this request by June 10, 2011, I will immediately file a complaint with the Federal Trade Commission and the appropriate State Attorneys General's offices. Civil claims will be pursued.

Sincerely,

R J Mansfield
PO Box 40652
Mesa, AZ 85274
SSN-xxx-xxx-xxx

FIGURE 28

CHARGE-OFF COLLECTION AGENCY, ALSO KNOWN AS PRIMARY COLLECTION AGENCY

Many lenders have made a business decision that it's financially beneficial to outsource pre–charge-off collection accounts.

Depending on the lender, accounts are usually placed with a pre–charge-off agency when they're three or four payments in arrears.

The delinquent status on pre–charge-offs is reported to the credit bureaus, but the fact they've been placed with an agency isn't. If the account is paid up to date, settled, or paid in full, it's returned to the lender. If a borrower doesn't make any payments or makes sporadic payments and the consumer becomes six payments past due, it's usually returned to the original creditor (OC) and charged off. It's then sent to what's referred to in the industry as a third-party collection agency and reported as being with a collection agency. The collection agency notation is worse for your credit score than simply being past due.

Some pre–charge-off collection agencies are authorized to offer settlements. If they can offer a settlement, it's usually around 80 to 90 percent of the balance. Settlements have a negative impact on your credit score and are noted as "settled for less than full balance," but the notation of settled is better than having unpaid, past due accounts on your report.

There are occasions where a collection agency will not offer you the best settlement that's authorized by the original creditor. If you decide to go the settlement route, always ask if this is the best settlement available. ALWAYS RECORD CONVERSATIONS!

Once they tell you it is the best settlement they are authorized to offer, call the original creditor to make sure it is the best settlement available. Keep in mind that the original creditor might not discuss anything with you and simply refer you back to the collection agency. But, if you find out that they were authorized to settle for less than what you agreed to, and they told you that was the best they could do, that's deceptive. You have a basis for a lawsuit.

THIRD-PARTY COLLECTION AGENCY

These agencies usually handle accounts that have been charged off by the lender. They usually remain with the third-party agency for sixty to ninety days. If they are not settled or paid in full, or you have an ongoing payment arrangement that you are not faithfully keeping, they're forwarded to a different third-party agency.

You cannot pay an account up to date once it's charged off. If charged off the entire balance is contractually due, and there is no such thing as current or up to date for credit reporting purposes. Once an account is charged off, even if you make an arrangement with the collector and keep to it, the account is not current and will not show up on your credit report as current.

Depending on the original creditor's internal policies, accounts may go to from one to four different collection agencies before your account is "pooled" together by the OC, with other similarly delinquent accounts, and is sold to a debt purchaser.

Third-party collectors usually have settlement authority of anywhere from 70 percent to 90 percent of the total balance, depending on how far past due the account is and how many other agencies have tried to collect it.

DEBT PURCHASERS

Debt purchasers can be many different types of companies: from attorneys to collection agencies to individuals who purchase debt on their own to collect. Some states require licenses to collect and some don't. As of the publishing of the book, some of the states that do not require licenses are Georgia, Iowa, Kansas, Kentucky, Mississippi, Missouri, Montana, New York (New York City does require licensing), Oklahoma, Pennsylvania, South Carolina, Vermont, and Virginia. The licensing requirement is dictated by where you live not where the collection agency is calling from. Some local governments like New York City and Chicago have their own licensing requirements. Licensing requirements seem to be changing by the minute. If you're interested, Google, "States that require collection agency licensing." If you live in a metropolitan area Google your city or better yet, call your state attorney general's office to find out if collectors are required to be licensed.

I know there are urban legends about being able to settle accounts with debt buyers for five to ten cents on the dollar. Those occasions are extremely rare so they're not worth thinking about. Purchased debts are usually settled for 25 percent to 75 percent or more. A smart collector will offer you a settlement higher than the minimum they can actually accept. They want your money. The more they get you to pay, the more the collection agency and the individual collectors can make. Negotiate!

QUESTIONS TO ASK THE COLLECTOR

RECORD ALL CONVERSATIONS and NEVER ADMIT YOU OWE THE BILL.

- Are you guys licensed to collect in (whatever state you live in)?
- Are you collecting for the original creditor or do you own the account?
- What was the date of last payment?
- Has this account been reported to a credit bureau?
- Do you report to any credit bureau?
- Has the statute of limitations (SOL) expired? (Expired SOLs are also known as time-barred debts.)
- If I do at some point realize this is my debt, is there a settlement available?
- Is that the best you can do on a settlement?
- Can the settlement be made in payments?
- Ask for a copy of the contract you allegedly signed.
- If they said they don't have a signed contract, ask, Then how can you prove this is my account? (Remember the "Account stated" doctrine mentioned previously, a few pages back. If you applied for and completed this loan online, they don't need a signed contract.)
- What will happen if I can't pay, will you sue me? (If they say that they will sue, and you find out that they never sue anyone, you can sue them. The basis for your suit would be "false and misleading representation and harassment." You'd wind up with $1,000 in your pocket, the balance would be wiped out, and the item removed from your credit report.)

The questions you ask don't need to have any specific intent behind them: for instance, asking about a settlement when you have no intent on paying the account. Ask any question you can think of. The more they talk, the greater the chance that they will violate the law.

Under the FDCPA a collector cannot mislead you. If the debt is beyond the statute of limitations, and the collector threatened to sue or told you the debt isn't time-barred, they have violated the FDCPA. Make sure you've recorded the conversation and immediately contact a consumers' rights attorney in your state.

STATUTE OF LIMITATIONS (COLLECTING VAMPIRE OR ZOMBIE DEBT)

Most states and the federal government are in the process of attempting to pass laws that will prohibit lawsuits from being initiated on debts where the statute of limitations (SOL) has expired. Legally, these are referred to as "time-barred" debts. As of October 2021 the expiration of the SOL does not mean that a creditor cannot file a lawsuit.

The SOL applies exclusively to the ability of a creditor to win a judgment. It doesn't mean they must stop calling and sending letters or in any way stop trying to collect the debt.

What the expiration of the SOL does mean is, that if a suit is filed, you have an affirmative defense against the lawsuit. You should show up for the court date or in the written answer to the summons, advise the judge that the SOL has passed. I'd go in person. Yes, even when you are in the right, being in court is uncomfortable, but I don't trust anything to get done right unless I do it myself. The judge should dismiss the suit based on the expiration of the SOL. If you don't inform the court that the SOL is expired, the creditor / collection agency will likely be granted a judgment by default. The plaintiff is then entitled to go forward with enforcing the judgment. Enforcement could include but not be limited to wage garnishment, placing a lien on your property, and taking money from your bank accounts. NEVER ignore a summons. If you do, the judge has no alternative but to consider everything the plaintiff alleges as true and you will probably lose. The judge is there to look at both sides of every case. If they only hear the "other" side, you, in all likelihood, will lose.

In most states, the statute of limitations begins running from the date the last payment, of any amount, was made on the account. This means that if you paid just one cent to a collector or anyone else who owned the account yesterday, the statute of limitations for that debt could have been reset to that date.

As I am typing this, there are legislators bringing up this exact question as to possibly changing the law, so as not to allow suit to be brought at all, on out of statute debt. It absolutely makes sense to stop this predatory practice. As it stands now, a consumer could have a judgment against them and possibly their wages and bank accounts attached when all they had to do was tell the court the SOL expired. While the FTC has issued an opinion that they think collecting on out of statute debt is unethical, they didn't go so far as stating that it was illegal.

Be careful not to restart the statute of limitations. Anytime you do just about anything with an account, the statute of limitations is restarted. In many states, making a payment, making a promise of payment, entering a payment agreement, even just acknowledging that the debt is yours may restart the statute of limitations. When the SOL clock restarts, it restarts at zero, no matter how much time had elapsed before the act that restarted it. Oh, and here's another one. If you file for bankruptcy and include an account on your list of creditors, if you didn't finalize the bankruptcy and it was dismissed or withdrawn, just the act of listing it may restart the statute. All debts listed in a Chapter 7 that are discharged are wiped out. There's no worry about discharged debt coming back to haunt you.

In the past, I listed the statute of limitations for each type of account by state. Unfortunately, they are being changed so often that I stopped that listing. It seemed by the time I re-listed the new info they changed it. To find accurate data on the statutes in each state, Google your state and "Statute of Limitations on Debt."

WRITTEN CONTRACT VS. PROMISSORY NOTE

The question always comes up: What's the difference between a "Written Contract" and a "Promissory Note"? In a written contract both parties sign and agree to fulfill an obligation; there may or may not be money involved. A promissory note only needs the signature of the borrower, and it's an agreement between a lender of money and a borrower. It usually spells out payment amounts, due dates, interest rate, and has a termination date.

Each state has its own statute of limitations on debt. It's the amount of time they can win, not start, but win, a lawsuit against you. The statute of limitations varies depending on the type of debt you have—credit card, oral, written, or promissory note—and is usually between three and six years but is as high as ten or fifteen years in some states. Before you respond to a debt collection call or letter, research the statute of limitations for your state. There could be serious consequences to what you do next. Be careful not to restart the SOL.

RESTARTING THE STATUTE OF LIMITATIONS

If you pay one cent on an overdue debt, in most states, under most circumstances, you have "reset" the statute of limitations. If the statute of limitations on a debt was due to expire in thirty days, and you send the collection agency even a penny, you've reset the clock . . . to five years, maybe ten, whatever the statute of limitations is in your state.

That's why I recommend NEVER making payments or even arrangements on charged-off accounts. If you think you want to settle a debt or pay it in full, make sure you're financially able to do it in one shot. Once your account has been charged off, there's no advantage to making payments unless they are going to sue you if you don't. Please resist the temptation to send in a check for $1 as revenge or just to "tick them off." That one dollar or one cent can reset the statute of limitations.

Making any payment, making a promise of payment, or entering into a payment agreement can restart the statute of limitations on your account. When the clock restarts, it restarts at zero, no matter how much time had elapsed before the activity. If you file for bankruptcy and then decide you don't want to go through with it, simply listing a debt, on your schedule of debt, can restart the clock for the statute of limitations.

STATUTE OF LIMITATIONS AFTER THEY HAVE A JUDGMENT

After a creditor wins a lawsuit and is awarded a judgment, there's a time limit for collecting that judgment. However, many states allow judgments to be renewed one or more times, which could substantially extend the enforceability of the judgment. This can potentially result in a permanent legal obligation until it's paid. The statute of limitations for starting a suit and the statute for collecting after a judgment is obtained are two entirely different things. Be careful.

DO YOU STILL OWE THE DEBT AFTER THE STATUTE OF LIMITATIONS HAS EXPIRED?

Yes. The only thing that erases your obligation to pay a debt is a cancellation from the creditor, discharge in bankruptcy, or actual payment of the debt. However, the creditor or collector no longer has the ability to use the courts to force you to pay. They can still repo your car or take any other collateral that was used for that specific loan.

Chapter 22

DIFFERENT TYPES OF COLLECTION AGENCIES (CAs), DIFFERENT TYPES OF SETTLEMENTS, HOW AND WHEN TO NEGOTIATE A SETTLEMENT

Types of Collection Agencies and How Much They'll Settle For

PRE–CHARGE-OFF

The Original Creditor still owns the account. If you pay the account up to date, it will be returned to the creditor. If you don't pay the past due amount, the account will be charged off and sent to a Primary Collection Agency. Pre–charge-off agencies never sue. But ask them anyway. If they say they sue or threaten to sue but as a business practice they never sue anyone, then that's just a threat: Sue them.

PRIMARY

The account has been charged off, placed with a collection agency (CA) for the first time after charge-off. The original creditor still owns the debt. They rarely sue. Ask them if they sue. If they say they sue or threaten to sue but as a business practice they never sue anyone, then that's just a threat: Sue them.

THIRD-PARTY

All agencies after the Primary Agency are called "Third-Party." They very rarely sue. Ask them if they sue. If they say they sue or threaten to sue but as a business practice they never sue anyone, then that's just a threat: Sue them.

DEBT BUYER

If, after placed with one, two, or more collection agencies, the OC may sell the account to a debt buyer. They sometimes will sue. Ask them if they sue. If they say they sue or threaten to sue but as a business practice they never sue anyone, then that's just a threat: Sue them.

LAW FIRM

Law firms are often debt buyers. They are the most likely to sue to collect the debt. If you speak with them, never answer questions regarding your financial situation, employment, or address. They will try to befriend you. They will appear to make arrangements with you to pay your account, when in reality, they're "fishing" for information that will help them find assets, locate collateral, obtain a judgment, and collect the account. They're NOT your friend. They are looking for ways to collect money or recover collateral. You are not legally required to divulge information. If you supply any information, they will use the information to locate you, your job, bank accounts, or their collateral, then sue you and enforce a judgment.

If you decide to pay the bill, always tell any collector that you're broke and that if you had access to the amount of money they wanted, you wouldn't be in this situation. Even if you do have the money, always tell them you are borrowing it from a friend or relative. You can use that later as a negotiating point, telling the collector that the "friend" or "relative" could only lend you "X" number of dollars to settle the account and you can't come up with any more money.

Knowing the type of collection agency you're dealing with does two things; it lets you know the likelihood that they will sue, and it'll also give you an idea as to the percentage of the balance you can pay to settle the account . . . if you decide to settle. Plus, you want to remember, legally they can't tell you they sue to collect if they, in fact, don't sue. With that in mind, you can simply ask them if they'll sue you if you don't pay voluntarily. As usual, record all conversations.

Pre–charge-off settlements are usually from 80 percent of the balance to no settlement. Debt buyers are the most likely to give great deals, from 25 to 50 percent, depending on how long they've owned the debt. Debt buyers will be tough negotiators if they recently bought the account. Law firms are working for creditors or own the debt. Their settlement strategies depend exclusively on what assets they can find, things like do you own property, do you have a job they can garnishee, or have they found your bank account.

Most agencies will run a credit report to see if you have access to borrowing funds. If your other credit isn't a disaster, they will usually play hardball and try to get you to borrow the money from a bank or try to get you to pay them off by transferring the debt to credit card.

You'll get better settlement offers if your credit is poor or you tell them that you will try to borrow the money from a friend or relative. Remember, this entire process is a negotiation at this point and depends on who can "sell" their idea better. Can they convince you that you MUST pay the balance TODAY, or can you convince them that you are broke and the best you can do is come up with a portion of the balance?

NEVER make payments. There is no advantage to making payments at this point. If you decide you want to go the settled or paid in full route, wait until you have the money on hand. If you make payments or even just agree to a payment plan verbally, it may restart the statute of limitations from ground zero.

All collection agencies, even those that buy debt, operate on the same basic bonus timetable. You will usually get a better settlement at the end of the month. Bonuses for the individual collectors, the managers, and the entire office, close out on the last day of the month. With that in mind, you're in a better position to negotiate on the second to last day of the month. They are either trying to make their goal which nets them a bonus or exceed their goals, so they get a percentage of the overage.

The reason you don't call on the last day of the month is that you will never know exactly what time on that last day they will consider the month "closed." Depending on what time of day they "close out" you may be calling when they are working on the following month, putting you in a bad negotiating position.

Start the settlement negotiation about a week prior to month end. This is how the settlement conversation will go.

They will usually ask for a postdated check or debit card. Tell them you don't want to give out information on your bank account until you're sure the money is available.

Call on the second to last day of the month, tell them you couldn't come up with the entire amount of the settlement, and offer them less. Tell them you tried to borrow money from a friend, and between what they'd lend you and what you have, you could come up with "X" amount. Remember, this is a negotiation. You're both bending the truth to get the advantage! Ninety percent of the time you will get a better deal. It may only be less than the original settlement by $50 or $100, but it's better off in your pocket than theirs! If the collector refuses to lower the settlement, ask to speak with a supervisor: They can override the collector's decision. The supervisors have goals to meet too. RECORD THE CONVERSATION.

Never make the first offer in any negotiation. Always ask if they can settle the account and how much they will take. A good collector will never give you their best settlement offer first. Once they give you a dollar amount, that's just a starting point.

Never give the collector your best offer first. Lowball your first offer. Discuss the dollar amount of the settlement first. AFTER you agree on an amount, tell them you need to make payments on any settlement and keep in your negotiating toolkit the actual dollar amount you are willing to settle for as a one-shot payment. For example, they would rather settle for a one-shot of $1,000 than $1,500 in five monthly payments. This, of course, is just an example. Each situation is different, but this will give you an idea of how it works.

APPENDIX

More PROOF: What, How, and Why I Did It

Figure 29 is a copy of a page on my credit report. As you can see it's dated September 9, 2013. It shows a negative item from a collection agency, Collections Service Bur, who is actually Collection Service Bureau. It's reported in the amount of $1,010 and indicates the original creditor is Progressive Medical Associates. The purpose of showing you this is that on the next three pages I will show you how simple it is to get medical items removed as a result of the procedure I followed. Oh, and by the way, not only did I get this item removed, I made $1,001 while getting it deleted. Figure 30 is a copy of the check.

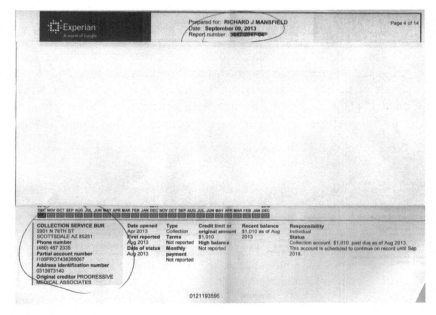

FIGURE 29

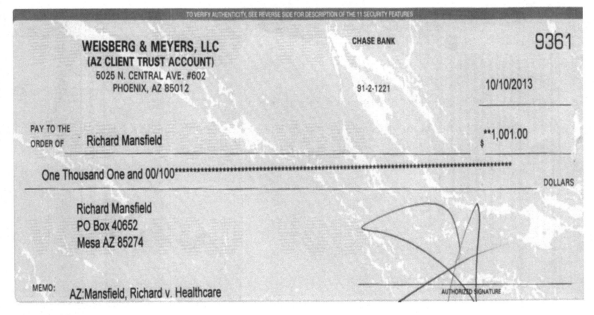

FIGURE 30

Figure 31 is a copy of the dispute letter I sent to Experian.

It's the exact letter I give you as a template in the appendix for medical disputes.

September 10, 2013

Creditor: Collection Service Bur
Progressive Medical Associates
Balance: $1,010.00

Credit Bureau Rep:

The above captioned medical bill is not mine. Please verify it with the reporting entity Collection Service Bur/ Progressive Medical Associates.

Simply verifying that someone used my name, Social Security number and or address is insufficient to confirm that I am the person in question and owes this alleged debt. When the reinvestigation reveals that the information is inaccurate or cannot be verified, the CRA must promptly delete the information and notify me that they deleted it.

15 USC § 1681i (a). A failure to conduct a reasonable reinvestigation violates the Fair Credit Reporting Act (FCRA). *Cushman v. TransUnion*, 115 F .3d 220, 223-224 (3d Cir. 1997). The burden to conduct the reinvestigation is on the credit reporting agency. It cannot be shifted back to the consumer. In plain English, that means you shouldn't be asking me for documentation to prove my dispute. I am not required to do your job. The law says you must reinvestigate and that if you can't prove it you are required to remove it.

Proof is not "simply parroting" erroneous information. I demand a document or photograph showing I am the person that owes this bill.

Do not tell me I am required to fill out a police report since the FCRA does not require the consumer to do that.

The legal obligation and requirement of a CRA to reinvestigate includes but is not limited to verifying the accuracy and dependability of the original source of the reported information. Since the information is blatantly incorrect, I am by way of this letter advising you that the information supplier is unreliable. Your duty often includes going beyond the original source. If the CRA is required to go beyond the original source depends on a number of factors, including but not limited to:

Did the consumer notify the CRA that the original source may be or is unreliable?

Should the CRA know that the information reporter, the original source is unreliable?

As part of any reinvestigation, a CRA must provide the original source of the derogatory item with notification of exactly what the consumer is disputing along with any relevant documentation submitted by the consumer as per 15 USC § 1681i(a)(2). The Third Circuit Court of Appeals confirmed that a reasonable reinvestigation "must mean more than simply . . . making a cursory investigation."

A provision of the FACTA regulations is the notice of negative information provision, covered in section 623(A) (7).

I have never received a billing or notification that this was or was going to be reported to a CRA. FACTA (Fair and Accurate Credit Transactions Act) requires creditors to give you a "warning" notice.

I look forward to your immediate cooperation.

(Your name printed)
(Signature)
(Social Security Number)
For Identification purposes, I am enclosing copies of:
My Social Security Card
My Driver's License *(or other government issued picture ID)*

FIGURE 31

Figure 32 is the Experian reply to my letter challenging the item reported by "Collections Service Bur." You can see toward the middle of their letter, under the heading Credit Items and Outcome, it says, "Deleted."

The Credit Service Bureau item was deleted, and I made $1,001 because they continued to call on a debt that they couldn't prove was mine. The so-called experts advise consumers to tell collectors to stop calling. I never want them to stop calling. The more they call, the better the chances they'll violate your rights. Once they violate your rights, contact a consumers' rights attorney in your area.

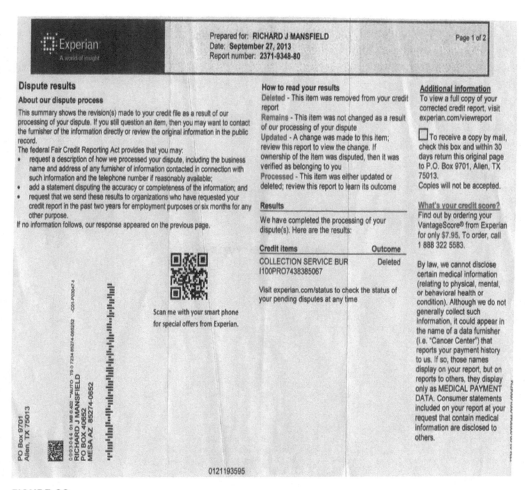

FIGURE 32

Here's another one I put in the win column. Figure 33 is a letter I received from a collection agency, Capital Management Services.

I pulled my credit reports and they had not reported my account as yet. I sent the letter shown in Figure 34 asking for a breakdown of what they claimed I owed and reminding them that they couldn't report the debt to the credit bureau until it was "validated." Plus, the loan in question was an in-person transaction with a signed contract. Keep in mind, I know all about this loan. As required by the FDCPA and FCRA, I'm forcing them to produce documentation to prove I owe it! I asked for a copy of the contract. Remember, there's a difference between asking for a signed contract if one exists and asking for one if you applied online. Online transactions don't have traditional signed contracts. If you didn't read it toward the end of Chapter 20, I explain how unsigned contracts are valid under the "account stated" doctrine. According to the FCRA and FDCPA, once I notified the collector that I wanted validation of the debt, they have two options; reply to the request or stop all collection activity. Not only didn't they reply they reported the account to Experian! Credit reporting is legally an attempt to collect a debt and a big no-no since they didn't reply to my request for validation.

726 Exchange Street, Suite 700
Buffalo, New York 14210

ADDRESS SERVICE REQUESTED

CAPITAL MANAGEMENT SERVICES, LP
726 Exchange Street - Suite 700, Buffalo, NY 14210
Office Hours: M-Th 8 a.m. - 11 p.m. ET
Fri 8 a.m. - 10 p.m., Sat 8 a.m. - 4 p.m. ET
Sun 9 a.m. - 1 p.m. ET
Toll Free: 1-866-899-1978, Fax: (716) 852-1620

#BWNJTHB ********AUTO**3-DIGIT 852 T228 P1
#0450700612#

Richard J Mansfield
PO Box 40652
Mesa, AZ 85274-0652

Previous Creditor: HomeEq Servicing Corp.
Current Creditor: LVNV Funding LLC
Account #: 53742341
Balance: $61053.09

PLEASE DETACH AND RETURN TOP PORTION WITH PAYMENT

December 19, 2008

Dear Richard J Mansfield:

This company has been engaged by Resurgent Capital Services, LP, the servicer of the account, to resolve your delinquent debt of $61053.09. Please make your check or money order payable to Capital Management Services, LP. and send to the above address.

Unless you notify this office within 30 days after receiving this notice that you dispute the validity of this debt or any portion thereof, this office will assume this debt is valid. If you notify this office in writing within 30 days from receiving this notice that you dispute the validity of this debt or any portion thereof, this office will obtain verification of the debt or obtain a copy of a judgment and mail you a copy of such verification or judgment. If you request this office in writing within 30 days after receiving this notice this office will provide you with the name and address of the original creditor, if different than the current creditor.

Capital Management Services, LP is authorized to accept less than the full balance due as settlement of the above account. The settlement amount of $9,157.96, which represents 15% of the amount presently owed, is due in our office no later than forty-five (45) days after receiving this notice. We are not obligated to renew this offer.

For your convenience, this settlement may be made online at: www.cms-trans.com. For other payment options, please contact Capital Management Services, LP. at 726 Exchange Street, Suite 700, Buffalo, NY 14210 or call 1-866-899-1978 Mon. through Thurs. 8 am to 11 pm ET, Fri. 8 am to 10 pm ET, Sat. 8 am to 4 pm ET, or Sun. 9 am to 1 pm ET.

Please see important privacy information included with this notice.

Should you wish to discuss the manner in which your account has been handled, please call Capital Management Services, LP. Compliance Department at 1-800-519-2687.

This is an attempt to collect a debt; any information obtained will be used for that purpose. This communication is from a debt collector.

FIGURE 33

I sued in Small Claims Court. They wrote me and asked me to call them. They offered $400. I countered with $1,200. We settled on $800, with the conditions that they would wire the money to me to be received the next day, that they would not resell the debt, and upon receipt, I would dismiss the suit. Figure 35 is the release I filed.

12-28-2008

Dear Debt Collector,

Please provide a copy of the original debt contract, showing my signature.
Also provide the debt calculations for the amount that you claim I owe ($61053.09). Under the FCRA, I believe this should not be reported to any CBR until the debt is validated. My phone number is 719-422-1093. Please only contact me in writing

Rich Mansfield
PO Box 40652
Mesa, AZ 85274
Acct# 53742341

FIGURE 34

Maricopa County Justice Courts, State of Arizona
WEST MESA JUSTICE COURT   2050 West University Dr., Mesa, AZ 85201   480-964-2958

CASE NUMBER: CC 2009-400195

RICHARD MANSFIELD
PO B 40652
MESA AZ 85274

_____ Plaintiff(s) Name / Address / Phone

Capital Mgmt Services Group Inc
Capital Mgmt Services LP
726 Exchange St.
Buffalo NY 14210

_____ Defendant(s) Name / Address / Phone

_____ Attorney for Plaintiff(s) Name / Address / Phone

_____ Attorney for Defendant(s) Name / Address / Phone

☑ NOTICE OF VOLUNTARY DISMISSAL   ☐ STIPULATED DISMISSAL   ☐ SATISFACTION OF JUDGMENT
CHECK ONE OF THE ABOVE

PLEASE TAKE NOTICE THAT:

☑ I am the Plaintiff. No answer or other defensive pleading has been filed in this case (if the defendant has filed an answer, a dismissal must be agreed to by both parties) and I voluntarily dismiss my complaint.

☐ The plaintiff and defendant agree to dismiss this case (signed by both parties below).

☐ This dismissal is:
  ☐ With prejudice (case cannot be refiled at a later date).
  ☐ Without prejudice (case may be refiled at a later date).

☐ I am the judgment creditor in this action. I have received payment in full of the judgment entered herein. The judgment has been satisfied.

Date: 7-29-2009

_____ Plaintiff / Judgment Creditor

Date: _____

_____ Defendant

I CERTIFY that I mailed / delivered a copy of this NOTICE of DISMISSAL / SATISFACTION OF JUDGMENT to:

☐ Plaintiff at the above address or   ☐ Plaintiff's attorney   ☑ Defendant at the above address or   ☐ Defendant's attorney

Date: 7-29-2009   By: _____   ☑ Plaintiff ☐ Defendant

FIGURE 35

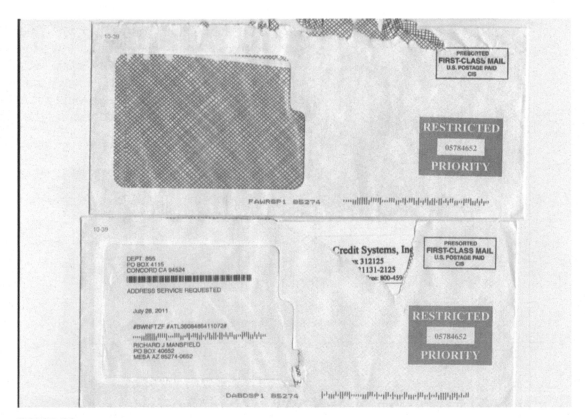

FIGURE 36

Here's the basis for another suit I filed.

It is deceptive to have an image on an envelope that would lead the consumer to believe that the letter is urgent when it is not. In Figure 36, the image says, "Restricted Priority" and it is in the same green color as certified mail and has what appears to be a certified mail number. This was sent regular mail and is deceptive, in violation of the FDCPA section 807(10)(2): "A debt collector may not communicate by a format or envelope that misrepresent the nature, purpose or urgency of the message. It is a violation to send any communication that represents a false sense of urgency." The intent is clearly to misrepresent this communication, as a certified letter, and as such, a sense that this letter is urgent is a violation.

Figure 37 shows the complaint I personally filed in Small Claims/Justice Court against National Credit Systems. Indicated under "Plaintiffs Claim," I told the court what I claimed that they violated. They violated Section 808 (1 & 2), section 809 (6), and 807 (10) of the FDCPA. State the violation(s) as briefly as you can. There's no need to go into detail unless you go to trial. I never saw the inside of a courtroom on any of my suits. You more than likely won't either.

Maricopa County Justice Courts, Arizona

West Mesa Justice Court   2050 W. University Dr., Mesa, AZ 85201   480-964-2958

FIGURE 37

Next is a judge, notifying me that I can't file this suit against National Credit Systems in small claims court, that this is a federal case, and that he has no jurisdiction. The judge told me I had to show him the legal basis for and cite the legal authority that allows me to file the complaint in Small Claims Court. Figure 38 is a copy of the letter I sent. Figure 39 is the judge's letter.

Maricopa County Justice Courts, Arizona

West Mesa Justice Court   2050 W. University Dr., Mesa, AZ 85201   480-964-2958

CASE NUMBER CC2011163515SC

R MANSFIELD
P O Box 40652
Mesa, Az 85274

NATIONAL CREDIT SYSTEMS

ORDER

THIS COURT HAS REVIEWED PLAINTIFF'S SMALL CLAIMS COMPLAINT. THIS COMPLAINT INDICATES "VIOLATIONS FDCPA SECTIONS 806(1)&(2), SECTION 807(10) SECTION 809(6)".

IF THE ABOVE SECTIONS ARE VIOLATIONS OF U S GOVERNMENT FEDERAL RULES, THIS COURT DOES NOT HAVE JURISDICTION.

PLAINTIFF HAS TO 5:00 P.M., SEPTEMBER 11, 2011, TO FURNISH A LEGAL BASIS WHICH ESTABLISHES THE PLAINTIFF'S AUTHORITY TO FILE SUCH A COMPLAINT IN THIS COURT.   THIS LEGAL BASIS MUST BE IN WRITING AND CITE TO THE PERTINENT LEGAL AUTHORITIES.

IF THIS DOCUMENTATION IS NOT RECEIVED PRIOR TO THE DATE AND TIME STATED, IN THIS ORDER, THIS COURT, THEREAFTER, WILL DISMISS THIS COMPLAINT.

Date 8/19/11   Justice of the Peace

I CERTIFY that I delivered / mailed a copy of this ORDER to:
☑ Plaintiff at the above address   ☐ Plaintiff's attorney   ☐ Defendant at the above address   ☐ Defendant's attorney

Date 9.6.11   By   Clerk

CV 8150-138 R 6/2/08

FIGURE 39

CC2011163515 SC

Date/ September, 19 2011

Per the Court's request I submit the following for consideration.

The Fair Debt Collection Practices Act, 15 USC 1692K, 813(d), captioned below, states the action created by this title may be brought .."in any court of competent jurisdiction".

(d) An action to enforce any liability created by this title may be brought in any appropriate United States district court without regard to the amount in controversy, or in any other court of competent jurisdiction, within one year from the date on which the violation occurs.

This being a civil action, within one year of the violation, for an amount under the upper statutory limit set by the State of Arizona, I believe allows it to be heard in Justice Court..

Additionally please note that a previous case was brought before this Court at this venue involving an FDCPA claim, CC2009-400195. Neither the Court nor the Defendant brought up the question of jurisdiction.

Thanking you in advance for your valuable time and consideration,

R. Mansfield

RECEIVED
2011 SEP 20 AM 9:35

FIGURE 38

The judge agrees that he does have jurisdiction (see Figure 40), hears the case, I win $1,000, and nothing is reported to the credit bureau. Once again this was my delinquent account, but they broke the law trying to collect it.

Maricopa County Justice Courts, Arizona

West Mesa Justice Court 2050 W. University Dr., Mesa, AZ 85201 480-964-2958

CASE NUMBER CC2011163515SC

R MANSFIELD
P O Box 40652
Mesa, Az 85274
Plaintiff(s) Name / Address / Phone

NATIONAL CREDIT SYSTEMS
Defendant(s) Name / Address / Phone

Attorney for Plaintiff(s) Name / Address / Phone

Attorney for Defendant(s) Name / Address / Phone

ORDER

THE COURT HAS REVIEWED PLAINTIFF'S EXPLANATION FOR THE COURT'S REQUEST OF AUGUST 19, 2011 REGARDING LEGAL BASIS FOR FILING IN THIS COURT.

BASED ON THE EXPLANATION, CITING IN PART, "OR IN ANY OTHER COURT OF COMPETENT JURISDICTION", THE COURT PERSONNEL WILL CONTINUE TO TREAT THIS COMPLAINT UNDER THE RULES OF SMALL CLAIMS PROCEDURES.

Date: 9/27/11 Justice of the Peace

COURT SEAL

I CERTIFY that I delivered / mailed a copy of this ORDER to:

☑ Plaintiff at the above address ☐ Plaintiff's attorney ☐ Defendant at the above address ☐ Defendant's attorney

Date: 9.27.11 By Clerk

CV 8150-136 R: 8/2/06

FIGURE 40

Here's another win. The date on this letter (Figure 41) and the date the settlement must be in by are the same—impossible to comply with unless I paid a fee for a check by phone or sent something like a Western Union or MoneyGram. It's a violation of the FDCPA for them to require me to do anything that will incur a charge for me that isn't called for in the original contract.

Alpha Recovery Corp.
5660 Greenwood Plaza Blvd, Suite 101
Greenwood Village, CO 80111
Toll Free 877-359-8714

12/31/2012

393013
Richard J Mansfield
PO BOX 40652,
MESA, AZ 852740652

RE:		
	Creditor:	JEFFERSON CAPITAL SYSTEMS, LLC.
	Acct Number:	393013
	Original Creditor:	JUNIPER MASTERCARD
	Original Creditor Account No.:	5140218028115879
	Current Balance Claimed Due:	$3,056.07

Dear Richard Mansfield,

Our client, JEFFERSON CAPITAL SYSTEMS, LLC., has authorized this office to offer you an opportunity to pay less than the amount due to satisfy your delinquent account. This settlement, as offered shall be in the total amount of $1,410.00.

This settlement offer will expire unless we receive your payment of $1,410.00 due in our office on or before 12/31/2012. In the event that you are unable to make the settlement payment within the time frame indicated, call our office prior to the deadline date. It may be possible to extend the deadline under certain circumstances. If you fail to comply with the above terms this office will, without further notice, declare the entire balance due immediately and proceed accordingly. Upon clearance of funds, this account will be considered satisfied.

If you have any questions relative to the above referenced settlement, please do not hesitate to contact our office toll free at 877-359-8714, Monday through Friday 8:00am-5:00pm Mountain time. Please refer to the account number indicated above.

Alpha Recovery Corp.

This is an attempt to collect a debt. Any information obtained will be used for that purpose.

This is a communication from a debt collector.

***A $9.95 convenience fee will be charged on all credit/debit cards and ACH transactions except in CO, CT, ID, MA, MN, WA, or WI.*

FIGURE 41

The email I sent to my attorney (Figure 42) explains this FDCPA violation in more detail.

pets1951@msn.com
Outlook.com Active View
1 attachment (412.6 KB)
Download MANSFIELD, RICHARD J.pdf (402.6 KB)
MANSFIELD, RICHARD J.pdf
View online
Download as zip
Mr Panvini:

This settlement letter is deceptive. It gives a settlement expiration date as the date it was emailed. It says "In the event you are unable to make the settlement payment within the time frame indicated to call our offive PRIOR to the deadline date." A condition which is obviously impossible to meet. Also they indicated, verbally, that the only way to accomplish the sif was to do it with a check by phone for which they would charge a $9.95 fee (also indicated at the bottom of the email). I asked if that could be waved and they sd no. I believe recent rulings have deemed a fee for payment a violation of the FDCPA. They also indicated in the email that if I had any questions regarding the settlement I could call Mon-Fri at a toll free number. Considering the time restraint on the sif that would be useless. The "least sophisticated debtor" would be very confused by this letter and the options given that are actually unavailable

Actionable?

Rick Mansfield

FIGURE 42

I sued Alpha Collections and won $1,000. Figure 43 is a copy of the check.

Thompson Consumer Law Group, PLLC
IOLTA Account
5235 E. Southern Ave. D106-618
Mesa, AZ 85206

Chase Bank

009008

4/22/2014

PAY TO THE ORDER OF Mansfield, Richard $ **1,000.00

One Thousand and 00/100*** DOLLARS

Richard Mansfield
P. O. Box 40652
Mesa AZ 85274

Memo
AZ:Mansfield, Richard v. Alpha D130242C11(AZ

AUTHORIZED SIGNATURE

⑈009008⑈ [redacted]

Thompson Consumer Law Group, PLLC 009008

Mansfield, Richard 4/22/2014

Date	Type	Reference	Original Amt.	Balance Due	Discount	Payment
3/3/2014	Bill	AZ:Mansfield, Richar	1,000.00	1,000.00		1,000.00
					Check Amount	1,000.00

AZ IOLTA AZ:Mansfield, Richard v. Alpha D130242C11(AZ 1,000.00

FIGURE 43

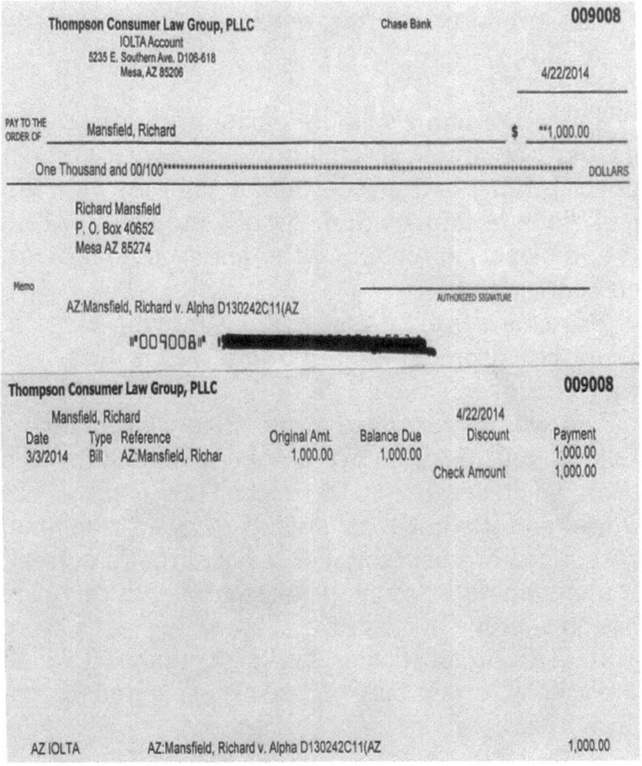

Judgments are easy to remove! There's a copy of the letter I used in the appendix (page 154).

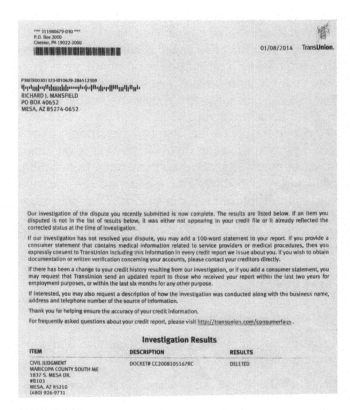

*** 311980679-030 ***
P.O. Box 2000
Chester, PA 19022-2000

01/08/2014 TransUnion.

P38ITX00301323-I010629-284512309
RICHARD J. MANSFIELD
PO BOX 40652
MESA, AZ 85274-0652

Our investigation of the dispute you recently submitted is now complete. The results are listed below. If an item you disputed is not in the list of results below, it was either not appearing in your credit file or it already reflected the corrected status at the time of investigation.

If our investigation has not resolved your dispute, you may add a 100-word statement to your report. If you provide a consumer statement that contains medical information related to service providers or medical procedures, then you expressly consent to TransUnion including this information in every credit report we issue about you. If you wish to obtain documentation or written verification concerning your accounts, please contact your creditors directly.

If there has been a change to your credit history resulting from our investigation, or if you add a consumer statement, you may request that TransUnion send an updated report to those who received your report within the last two years for employment purposes, or within the last six months for any other purpose.

If interested, you may also request a description of how the investigation was conducted along with the business name, address and telephone number of the source of information.

Thank you for helping ensure the accuracy of your credit information.

For frequently asked questions about your credit report, please visit http://transunion.com/consumerfaqs .

Investigation Results

ITEM	DESCRIPTION	RESULTS
CIVIL JUDGMENT MARICOPA COUNTY SOUTH ME 1837 S. MESA DR. #B103 MESA, AZ 85210 (480) 926-9731	DOCKET# CC2008105167RC	DELETED

FIGURE 44

EQUIFAX
CREDIT FILE : February 19, 2014
Confirmation # 4043041376

005392
001592558-5392
Richard J Mansfield
PO Box 40652
Mesa, AZ 85274-0652

P. O. Box 105518
Atlanta, GA 30348

Dear Richard J Mansfield:

Below are the results of your reinvestigation request and, as applicable, any revisions to your credit file. If you have additional questions regarding the reinvestigated items, please contact the source of that information directly. You may also contact Equifax regarding the specific information contained within this letter or report within the next 60 days by visiting us at www.investigate.equifax.com or by calling a Customer Representative at (888) 425-7961 from 9:00am to 5:00pm Monday-Friday in your time zone.

For an added convenience, use one of the below options to start an investigation or check the status of your dispute.

Please note, when you provide documents, including a letter, to Equifax as part of your dispute, the documents may be submitted to one or more companies whose information are the subject of your dispute.

Visit us at **www.equifax.com/CreditReportAssistance** or Call us at 866-349-5186.

Thank you for giving Equifax the opportunity to serve you.

The Results Of Our Reinvestigation

Public Record Information (This section includes public record items obtained from local, state and federal courts.)

>>> ***We have reviewed the judgement information. Case or ID # - CC2008105167RC The results are:*** This item has been deleted from the credit file. If you have additional questions about this item please contact: ***South Mesa Gilbert Justice, 1837 S Mesa Dr, Mesa AZ 85210-6219***

Notice to Consumers

You may request a description of the procedure used to determine the accuracy and completeness of the information, including the business name and address of the furnisher of information contacted, and if reasonably available the telephone number.

If the reinvestigation does not resolve your dispute, you have the right to add a statement to your credit file disputing the accuracy or completeness of the information; the statement should be brief and may be limited to not more than one hundred words (two hundred words for Maine residents) explaining the nature of your dispute.

If the reinvestigation results in the deletion of disputed information, or you submit a statement in accordance with the preceding paragraph, you have the right to request that we send your revised credit file to any company specifically designated by you that received your credit report in the past six months (twelve months for California, Colorado, Maryland, New Jersey and New York residents) for any purpose or in the past two years for employment purposes.

(Continued On Next Page) Page 1 of 2 4043041376ICR-001592558-5392 - 6820 - AS

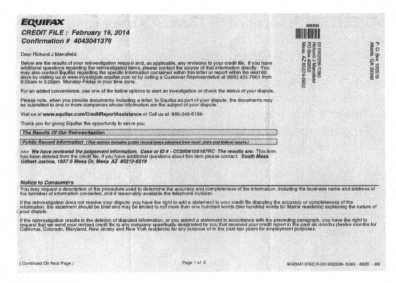

FIGURE 45

Figures 44 and 45 show another judgment deleted!

Big Brother Is Watching—Three Credit Bureaus You Know, and Forty You Probably Never Heard Of

Forty-three agencies have information about you. Forty of them you've probably never heard of.

Credit bureaus (also called credit reporting agencies, or CRAs) have information about you, from how you pay your bills and rent to the medications you use and possibly even your gambling habits. Big brother is watching you!

Prior to the pandemic, you had a legal right to one free copy of your credit report from each of the three major bureaus, Equifax, Experian, and TransUnion, once every 365 days. Post-pandemic the bureaus started offering free reports weekly. That was originally to end in April of 2021 but has continued indefinitely. You can go to www.annualcreditreport.com/index.action to see what the current situation is. You can also obtain a free copy from the three major CRAs free for the following reasons:

- You are unemployed and looking for work.

- You are receiving public assistance like food stamps or an EBT card.

- You believe you are a victim of identity theft.

You also have a legal right to a free copy of a credit report from a credit reporting agency if adverse action was taken against you because of information supplied by them, for instance:

- You have been denied credit.

- You were approved for credit, but your interest rate was not the best rate available. This includes credit cards and any type of loan including mortgages, auto loans, personal loans, and lines of credit.

- You have been denied a job or promotion because of their credit report.

- Your insurance rates went up because of a credit report.

- You were required to make a larger down payment, for instance on an auto loan or mortgage.

- You're renting a house, apartment, or commercial property and they required a larger security deposit.

There are numerous personal information databases. I compiled a list here along with a short description of what they do, a contact number, and website information. As of October 2021 all the information including the phone numbers are correct.

Bureaus seem to enjoy being moving targets. Don't be surprised if you go to a web address and they've moved!

You will be surprised at who has what information on you. Until I started doing research for this book, I didn't realize all the information that was out there, and it's not that difficult to get for anyone, authorized or unauthorized. Make sure it's correct. It's incredible what long-reaching effects this data has on your life.

In most circumstances, the lesser known "behind the scenes" credit bureaus are also required to supply a free report.

THE BIG THREE

Equifax Credit Information Services, Inc.
P.O. Box 740256
Atlanta, GA 30374-0256
www.Equifax.com
(800) 685-1111: free credit report

Experian
P.O. Box 4500
Allen, TX 75013
www.Experian.com
(888) 397-3742: free credit report

TransUnion
P.O. Box 2000
Chester, PA 19016-2000
www.TransUnion.com
(800) 916-8800: free credit report

THE OTHERS

Innovis is rarely used for credit decisions. It is used for consumer mailing lists and skip tracing (for instance, collection agencies and repossessors trying to locate consumers). You have a right to a free copy of what they have on file for you, just like any other credit reporting agency.

Innovis
250 East Broad St.
Columbus, OH 43215
www.Innovis.com
(800) 540-2505

Certegy Check Services collects check writing histories and provides check screening services primarily for retailers and gaming establishments who accept checks as payment in their stores. The company will provide one free report every twelve months. Certegy is affiliated with Fidelity National Information Services, Inc. (FNIS).

Certegy Check Services Inc.
P.O. Box 30296
Tampa, FL 33630-3296
www.AskCertegy.com
(866) 543-6315

ChexSystems provides account verification services to its members, which consist primarily of financial institutions. It collects data on checking account applications, openings, and closures, including reasons for account closure. When you apply for a new checking account, many banks and credit unions will refer to this database before they approve the account.

The company will provide one free report every twelve months. ChexSystems is affiliated with Fidelity National Information Services, Inc. (FNIS).

ChexSystems, Inc.
Attn: Consumer Relations
7805 Hudson Rd., Ste. 100
Woodbury, MA 55125
www.ConsumerDebit.com
(800) 428-9623

Early Warning Services assists financial institutions and other financial entities in detecting and preventing fraud associated with bank accounts and payment transactions. They collect data on checking account applications, openings, and closures and may be checked by banks and credit unions before they approve a new account. The company will provide one free report every twelve months.

Early Warning Services
16552 North 90th St., Ste. 100
Scottsdale, AZ 85260
www.earlywarning.com/consumer-information.html
(800) 325-7775

TeleCheck collects check writing history. They provide information on check fraud and conduct check verifications for retailers who accept checks as payment in their stores. The company will provide one free report every twelve months. TeleCheck is a wholly owned subsidiary of First Data Corporation.

TeleCheck
Attention: Consumer Resolutions-FA
P.O. Box 4514
Houston, TX 77210-4514
www.firstdata.com/telecheck/telecheck-consumer-contacts.html
(800) 366-2425

Clarity Services provides information on payday loans, financial services, check cashing services, and auto loans.

Clarity Services
P.O. Box 5717
Clearwater, FL 33758
www.clarityservices.com/support/file-disclosure/
(866) 390-3118

DataX provides information on credit histories of subprime consumers. Request a free annual report.

Data X Ltd.
Attn: Customer Service
325 E. Warm Springs Rd., Ste. 202
Las Vegas, NV 89119
www.DataXltd.com
(702) 853-6964; (800) 295-4790

FactorTrust provides lending data and bankruptcy information to payday lenders. The company will provide one free credit report every twelve months.

FactorTrust
P.O. Box 3653
Alpharetta, GA 30023
http://ws.factortrust.com/consumer-inquiry/
(866) 910-8497

MicroBilt tracks consumer information about payday loans and provides information to payday and title loan lenders. The company will provide one free credit report every twelve months.

Microbilt
Attn: Compliance Department
P.O. Box 440693
Kennesaw, GA 30160
www.MicroBilt.com
(800) 884-4747 (Option 5)

Teletrack collects consumer information about and provides data to payday lenders, rent-to-own businesses, furniture stores that offer financing, auto finance companies, high-risk consumer finance businesses, non-prime mortgage businesses, non-prime credit card issuers, credit unions, and cable/telecom companies. Teletrack is affiliated with CoreLogic.

CoreLogic Teletrack
P.O. Box 509124
San Diego, CA 92150
Attention: Consumer Disputes
www.corelogic.com/about-us/contact-us.aspx
(Request Form)

Insurance Information Exchange provides motor vehicle records, including traffic violations, upon request with a permissible purpose.

iiX
1716 Briarcrest Dr., Ste. 200
Bryan, TX 77802
www.IIX.com
(866) 560-7015 (verify this number as it changes regularly)

Insurance Services Office (ISO) (A Plus Property Reports) collects insurance claims and loss information associated with homes or commercial buildings.

A-PLUS Consumer Inquiry Center
(ISO)
545 Washington Blvd., FL 22
Jersey City, NJ 07310-1686
www.ISO.com
(800) 709-8842

C.L.U.E. Inc. (C.L.U.E. Personal Property Report) collects information on insurance coverage and losses associated with individuals and their personal property. The company will provide one free report every twelve months. C.L.U.E Inc. is affiliated with LexisNexis Risk Solutions Bureau LLC.

C.L.U.E. Inc. Consumer Center
P.O. Box 105295
Atlanta, GA 30348-5295
https://personalreports.lexisnexis.com/access_your_full_file_disclosure.jsp
(866) 312-8076

C.L.U.E. Inc. (C.L.U.E. Auto Report) provides information about individuals' automobile insurance coverage and losses. The company will provide one free report every twelve months. C.L.U.E Inc. is affiliated with LexisNexis Risk Solutions Bureau LLC.

C.L.U.E. Inc. Consumer Center
P.O. Box 105295
Atlanta, GA 30348-5295
https://personalreports.lexisnexis.com/fact_act_disclosure.jsp
(866) 312-8076

CreditIQ Credit Report by CoreLogic Credco collects property ownership and mortgage obligation records; property legal filings and tax payment status; rental applications and collection accounts; and consumer bankruptcies, liens, judgments, and child support obligations. The company will provide one free report every twelve months.

CoreLogic Credco
P.O. Box 509124
San Diego, CA 92150
www.Credco.com
(800) 637-2422 (Consumer Assistance for Your Free Credit Report)
(877) 532-8778 (CoreLogic Credco Consumer File inquiries)

L2C provides credit reports comprised of data from a variety of purchased and publicly available sources.

L2C, Inc.
P.O. Box 550089
Atlanta, GA 30355
www.transunion.com/L2C
(866) 268-7156

LexisNexis Risk Solutions Bureau LLC probably has more diverse information on you than anyone. When you dispute a public record—for instance, a bankruptcy, tax lien or judgment—the three major bureaus may use these guys to verify the info. You can access your Consumer Disclosure Report for free once every twelve months. If your insurance company has sent you an adverse action letter there's information on the website so you can get information related to that letter.

LexisNexis Risk Solutions Bureau
RiskView Consumer Inquiry Department
P.O. Box 105108
Atlanta, GA 30348-5108
https://personalreports.lexisnexis.com/access_your_personal_information.jsp
(866) 312-8076

Pay Rent Build Credit (PRBC)/MicroBilt provides credit information, bill payment information, employment information, bank account data, property records, court judgments, address and phone information. The company will provide one free credit report every twelve months.

Pay Rent Build Credit
(PRBC)/MicroBilt
Attn: Compliance Department
P.O. Box 440693
Kennesaw, GA 30160
www.microbilt.com
(800) 884-4747 (Option 5)

National Consumer Telecom and Utilities Exchange collects information on new connect requests, account and payment histories, defaults, and fraudulent accounts associated with telecommunications, pay TV, and utility (electric, gas and water) services. The company will provide one free report every twelve months.

Exchange Service Center Disclosure
P.O. Box 105161
Atlanta, GA 30348
www.NCTUE.com
(866) 343-2821

Certegy Gaming Services provides gaming establishments with real-time data and analytics to help its clients make decisions on extending marker credit and check cashing. The company will provide one free report every twelve months. Certegy is affiliated with Fidelity National Information Services, Inc. (FNIS).

Certegy Gaming Services, Inc.
Attn: Gaming Bureau
P.O. Box 30296
Tampa, FL 33630-3296
www.creditreportproblems.com/certegy-gaming-services/
www.askcertegy.com
(866) 543-6315

Contemporary Information Corp. conducts background tenant screening services.

Contemporary Information Corp.
42913 Capital Dr., Unit 101
Lancaster, CA 93535
www.CICreports.com
(800) 288-4757 (Option 5)

CoreLogic SafeRent collects information for tenant and employment screening, including landlord-tenant actions and court judgments. The company will provide one free report every twelve months.

CoreLogic SafeRent Consumer Relations
P.O. Box 509124
San Diego, CA 92150
www.residentscreening.net/rsn/login.aspx (go to Request Form)
(888) 333-2413

First Advantage Resident History Report conducts background screening services. The company will provide one free report every twelve months.

First Advantage Consumer Center
P.O. Box 105292
Atlanta, GA 30348
www.FADV.com
(800) 845-6004

Leasing Desk (Real Page) Provides data for tenant screening. The company will provide one free report every twelve months.

Leasing Desk Consumer Relations
4000 International Pkwy.
Carrollton, TX 75007
www.RealPage.com
(866) 934-1124

Tenant Data Services provides information on rental performance history (damages, unauthorized pets, lease violations, skips, etc.).

Personal Report Request
Tenant Data Services, Inc.
P.O. Box 5404
Lincoln, NE 68505-0404
www.TenantData.com
(800) 228-1837 (Option 6)

MIB, Inc. collects information about medical conditions and hazardous avocations from insurance applications with the consumer's authorization. You will not have a MIB consumer report unless you applied for individually underwritten life or health insurance at a MIB member insurance company within the past seven years. The company will provide one free credit report every twelve months.

MIB, Inc.
50 Braintree Hill Park, Ste. 400
Braintree, MA 02184
www.MIB.com
(866) 692-6901

Milliman IntelliScript collects information on prescription drug purchase histories. You may have a prescription report about you if you authorized the release of your medical records to an insurance company and that company submitted a request to Milliman; otherwise there should not be a history. Note that many employment reporting companies won't have information on you unless you authorized your employer or a potential new employer to obtain a report.

Milliman IntelliScript
15800 Bluemound Rd., Ste. 100
Brookfield, WI 53005
www.RxHistories.com
(877) 211-4816

Accurate Background conducts background screening services.

Accurate Background, Inc.
6 Orchard, Ste. 200
Lake Forest, CA 92630
www.AccurateBackground.com
(800) 784-3911

American DataBank conducts background screening services.

American DataBank
110 Sixteenth St., 8th Floor
Denver, CO 80202
www.AmericanDataBank.com
(800) 200-0853

EmployeeScreenIQ, also known as Sterling, provides pre-employment screening services.

EmployeeScreenIQ
P.O. Box 22627
Cleveland, OH 44122
www.EmployeeScreen.com
(800) 235-3954 (Option 5)

First Advantage conducts background screening services. The company will provide one free report every twelve months.

First Advantage Consumer Center
P.O. Box 105292
Atlanta, GA 30348
www.FADV.com
(800) 845-6004

HireRight conducts employment background screening services. The company will provide one free report every twelve months.

HireRight
P.O. Box 33181
Tulsa, OK 74153
www.HireRight.com
(800) 381-0645

Infocubic provides pre-employment screening services.

Infocubic
9250 E. Costilla Ave., Ste. 525
Greenwood Village, CO 80112
www.InfoCubic.com (Request report form)
(877) 360-4636

Pre-employ.com provides employment background, investigative, consumer reports.

Pre-employ.com
Attn: Compliance Department
P.O. Box 491570
Redding, CA 96049-1570
www.Pre-Employ.com (Request report form)
(800) 300-1821 (ext. 199)

Professional Screening & Information, Inc. provides pre-employment screening services.

PSI, Inc.
P.O. Box 644
Rome, GA 30162
www.PSIBackgroundCheck.com (Request report form)
(877) 235-7574

Sterling Infosystems, Inc. conducts employment background screening services. The company will provide one free report every twelve months.

Sterling Infosystems, Inc.
ATTN: Consumer Reports
6111 Oak Tree Blvd.
Independence, OH 44131
www.sterlingInfoSystems.com (Request report form)
(877) 424-2457

Trak-1 Technology, also known as People Facts, conducts background screening services.

Trak-1 Technology
Consumer Report Request
7131 Riverside Pkwy.
Tulsa, OK 74136
www.Trak-1.com
(918) 779-7000

Verifications Inc. conducts background screening services. The company will provide one free report every twelve months.

Verifications Inc.
Attention: Applicant Services
1425 Mickelson Drive
Watertown, SD 57201
www.verifications.com/credit-reports/
Possibly out of business. I couldn't find a phone number.

The Work Number provides employment and income verification, including data collected from large private-sector payroll processors. This is information supplied by your current and/or previous employer. Using IRS forms 4506T or 4506T-EZ signed by the taxpayer, a lender that needs proof of income can get it immediately from the IRS. Not all employers are members of this site. The company will provide one free report every twelve months. Equifax Workforce Solutions, also known as TALX Corporation, operates The Work Number. TALX is a wholly owned subsidiary of Equifax.

Annual Credit Report
P.O. Box 105281
Atlanta, GA 30348-5281
www.TheWorkNumber.com (Request form)
(866) 604-6570

Cheat Sheet for Common FDCPA Violations

§ 1692 e(1) Falsely stating or implying the debt collector is affiliated with the United States or any state, including the use of any badge, uniform, or facsimile
§ 1692 e(2) Falsely representing the character, amount, or legal status of the alleged debt
§ 1692 e(3) Falsely representing any individual is an attorney or that any communication is from an attorney
§ 1692 e(4) Falsely representing nonpayment of any debt will result in the arrest or imprisonment of any person or the seizure, garnishment, attachment
§ 1692 e(5) Threaten to take any action that cannot legally be taken or that is not intended to be taken
§ 1692 e(6) Falsely representing sale or transfer of any interest in the debt will cause the consumer to lose any claim or defense to payment of the debt

§ 1692 e(7) Falsely representing that a consumer committed any crime or other conduct in order to disgrace the consumer

§ 1692 e(8) Threatens or communicates false credit information, including the failure to communicate that a debt is disputed

§ 1692 e(9) Falsely representing that any documents are authorized, issued, or approved by any court, official, or agency of the United States or any state

§ 1692 e(10) Any false representation or deceptive means to collect a debt or obtain information about a consumer

§ 1692 e(11) Communication fail to contain the mini-Miranda warning: "This is an attempt to collect a debt . . . communication is from a debt collector."

§ 1692 e(12) Falsely representing a debt has been turned over to innocent purchasers for value

§ 1692 e(13) Falsely representing documents are legal process when they are not

§ 1692 e(14) Using any name other than the true name of the debt collector's business

§ 1692 e(15) Falsely representing documents are not legal process forms or do not require action by the consumer if they do

§ 1692 e(16) False representation or implication the debt collector operates or is employed by a consumer reporting agency

UNFAIR PRACTICES

§ 1692 f Any unfair or unconscionable means to collect or attempt to collect the alleged debt

§ 1692 f(1) Attempting to collect any amount not authorized by the agreement creating the debt or permitted by law

§ 1692 f(2) Soliciting postdated check by more than 5 days without 3 business days written notice of intent to deposit

§ 1692 f(3) Accepting or soliciting postdated check for purpose of threatening criminal prosecution

§ 1692 f(4) Depositing or threatening to deposit a post-dated check prior to actual date on the check

§ 1692 f(5) Caused any charges to be made to the consumer, e.g., collect telephone calls

§ 1692 f(6) Taken or threatened to unlawfully repossess or disable the consumer's property

§ 1692 f(7) Communicated with the consumer by postcard

§ 1692 f(8) A collector cannot use any language or symbol on the envelope that indicates the communication concerns debt collection

MULTIPLE DEBTS

§ 1692 h Collector must apply payments on multiple debts in order specified by consumer and cannot apply payments to disputed debts

THIRTY-DAY VALIDATION NOTICE

§ 1692 g Failure to send the consumer a 30-day validation notice within five days of the initial communication

§ 1692 g(a)(1) Must state the Amount of Debt

§ 1692 g(a)(2) Must state the Name of Creditor to Whom Debt Owed

§ 1692 g(a)(3) Must state you have the Right to Dispute within 30 Days

§ 1692 g(a)(4) Must state you have the Right to Have Verification/Judgment Mailed to Consumer

§ 1692 g(a)(5) Must state that they Will Provide Name and Address of original Creditor if Different from Current Creditor

§ 1692 g(B) Collector must cease collection efforts until debt is validated (Credit Reporting is an attempt to collect a debt)

LEGAL ACTION

§ 1692 i(a)(2) Brought any legal action in a location other than where contract signed or where the consumer resides.

DECEPTIVE FORMS BY CREDITOR

§ 1692 j It is unlawful to design, compile, and furnish any form knowing that such form would be used to create the false belief in a consumer that a person other than the creditor of such consumer is participating in the collection of or in an attempt to collect a debt such consumer allegedly owes such creditor, when in fact such person is not so participating.

Instructions for Using the Letters

There are a few things I have already mentioned that you should review before you start using these templates. Always keep copies of the letters you send or receive. Always send letters certified mail and get a return receipt. Always record credit/debt-related conversations both incoming and outgoing.

Anything sent or received that's debt related, you must keep records, keep all documentation . . . you get the idea.

The letters I provide as examples have instructions included in parentheses ( ) and/or are *italicized* within the parentheses and in the instructions above the letters. Make sure the instructions are NOT in your final letter. Read the letter before you send it to make sure it says what you want it to say. When appropriate use the plural or singular of the word you're typing like "account" or "accounts" or "item" and "items." Use the legal references in the letters, word for word. These are the cases I've cited in my letters and they work. If you feel comfortable doing it, feel free to get creative with anything other than the case citations.

Here are a few ideas regarding what you can dispute to get rid of negative items that are correctly reported. Keep in mind that this is sometimes a numbers game. There is a human element in every credit bureau's dispute verification process. Mistakes happen. Often, information furnishers don't reply to the disputes that have been forwarded to them within the thirty-day window. A reply within thirtydays is required by the FCRA and/or the FDCPA. This delay results in removal of the unverified data.

- Identity mistakes such as an incorrect name, phone number, or address (none of these effect your credit scores).

- Mixed files—This can happen if you and another individual have the same or similar names. Your credit report could have account information belonging to someone else.

- An account incorrectly listed because of identity theft

- Closed account being reported as open

- An open account reported as closed

- You are reported as the account owner when you are in fact an Authorized User.

- A delinquent debt that you paid off and shows as unpaid

- Any delinquent account where the original date of delinquency is more than seven years old

- Accounts listed multiple times with the same or different creditor

- Wrong balances
- Wrong credit limits
- Wrong account number
- The date of my last payment is incorrect.
- You listed a payment I never made.

Be creative. Anything, and I mean *anything*, they report you can dispute. There are laws that require collectors to tell the truth. There is no law that says consumers can't bend the truth!

Never dispute anything online through the online service provided by the bureaus. Yes, it's convenient, and they intentionally make it easy to dispute online because if you do, you're giving up very important rights like the right to sue. Always send dispute letters certified mail with a return receipt requested. This is proof of your mailing and confirmation of the date they received your letter.

The date on your return receipt will start the clock ticking for the time within which they must respond to your dispute or remove it. The legal requirement for that response time is that they must mail it to you within thirty days. In consideration of how slow regular mail is, I wait forty days to take my next step.

That next step is either another letter, calling the CRA, or contacting a consumers' rights attorney. If you make phone calls, make sure to record the calls. If you decide to sue, you need proof. Make sure you confirm the date of your recording by casually asking the credit bureau representative, "What's today's date?" They will say the date and now you have a confirmed recorded date for your call. Having a dated timeline of events is critical in lawsuits.

The FDCPA and FCRA only protect consumers and not businesses. If you have a business account you did NOT personally guarantee, that's both good and bad. The good news is that it cannot legally show up on your credit report. You simply notify the CRAs that it's a business account and it will be removed, or if they don't, sue the credit bureau and the information furnisher. The bad news is that you have no consumer protection or rights under the FCRA and FDCPA. For instance, they can discuss the account with employees or business associates, and even neighbors. They can call and leave messages without identifying themselves. There are zero consumer protections in play on business debts.

When a consumer disputes the completeness or accuracy of any information contained in their credit report, the consumer reporting agency (CRA) must conduct a "reinvestigation." The word *reinvestigation* is the term used in the law that the average person would actually call an investigation. To my simple way of thinking, a reinvestigation would indicate that they investigated it already and are reviewing it again, but that's how the law reads; it says *reinvestigation*.

If the reinvestigation reveals that the information is inaccurate or cannot be verified, the CRA must promptly delete the information and notify you that they deleted it. 15 USC § 1681i (a) says "A failure to conduct a reasonable reinvestigation violates the Fair Credit Reporting Act (FCRA). *Cushman v. TransUnion*, 115 F .3d 220, 223-224 (3d Cir. 1997)." The burden to conduct the reinvestigation is on the credit reporting agency. It cannot be shifted back to the consumer. In plain English, that means they shouldn't be asking you for documentation to prove your dispute. You aren't required to do their job. The law says the bureaus must reinvestigate and that if they can't prove it they are required to remove it.

The legal obligation and requirement of a CRA to reinvestigate includes but is not limited to verifying the accuracy and dependability of the original source of the reported information. This duty often includes going beyond the original source. If the CRA is required to go beyond the original source depends on a number of factors, including but not limited to:

Did the consumer notify the CRA that the original source may be or is unreliable?

Should the CRA know that the information reporter, the original source, is unreliable?

NOTICE OF NEGATIVE INFORMATION

A provision of the FACTA regulations is the notice of negative information provision, covered in section 623(A) (7).

FACTA (Fair and Accurate Credit Transactions Act) now requires creditors to give you a "warning" notice. The notice might alert you that a payment you thought was made was never received or that someone opened an account in your name, or you flat out just didn't make a payment. You may have to look closely to even see this new notice. It is not necessarily a separate notice. They sometimes will include it with other mailings they send you.

This started in December 2004. All financial institutions that extend credit are required to send you a notice before or no later than thirty days after negative information is furnished to a credit bureau. Negative information includes late payments, partial payments, over your credit limit, or any type of default on the account.

If they send this notice, make the payment and or dispute it immediately. The only time you will get this notice is the first time you were ever past due on the account.

They are not required to give this notice EVERY TIME they report a negative. It's a one-time notice. You are only entitled to the notice the FIRST time they report. They can notify you before or within thirty days after the first late payment is reported. The financial institution can continue to report negative information about the same account without notice of further reporting.

DATE OF FIRST DELINQUENCY (DOFD)

This is a very important date. This date starts the seven-year time frame that a negative is legally allowed to be reported. The date of first delinquency is the date you first became past due and never caught up to date. If you are past due and then pay the account up to date, the clock for the date of first delinquency restarts if you ever became past due again and never bring the account up to date. There is a detailed explanation of the DoFD at the end of chapter 10. If you're interested and didn't read it, go take a look.

DO NOT confuse how long a negative item can remain on your credit report with the statute of limitations (SOL). They are two separate issues. The statute of limitations varies from state to state and varies based on the type of debt: credit card, verbal, contractual, etc. The SOL only governs the amount of time that they can collect an account by suing you. Keep in mind they can still sue you, but you can go to court and point out to the judge that the account is beyond the SOL. It's called an affirmative defense and the judge will dismiss the case. You must show up if you get a summons or you lose. Put the name of the state you're in now and Google it along with "statute of limitations on debt." You'll see a breakdown on how long the SOL lasts on different types of debts.

You may not find a letter that says everything, word for word, for your situation. Feel free to change the language in these letters to accomplish your goal. Just make sure that if I refer to a legal document, for example when I say, "Legally it is known as 15USC §1681i" or "§611 (5)(a)" or anything that seems like legal speak, always include those terms or phrases word for word. It lets them know that you know what you're talking about.

Read your letters before mailing them. Do not just copy the form letters. If you do you may not be successful in getting your goals accomplished. These are sample letter templates and are meant to give a form to follow with cited references. Although you may feel more comfortable using these letters word for word, I gave them to you as an example.

Use them as a guide to express what you want to be done. Don't worry about writing a perfect letter. They will know what you are saying as long as you include the cited references. The collection agencies and credit bureaus are much more likely to do what you demand in your letter if it looks like you know what you're talking about. They get thousands of dispute letters every day and that volume works in your favor. They are unable to investigate each one as specifically required by law.

Dispute Letter to Be Sent to Credit Bureaus

This following letter is the general dispute letter. Always send this letter first. This is the letter that says, "Not my account." If you receive a negative reply to this letter, send it again, changing the "not my account" to one of the other dispute reasons that are listed in the book. You can dispute anything they report: balance, account number, date of last activity, date of first delinquency, type of account, etc.

You can't use the same reason for a dispute for an account with the same bureau. For instance, you can't say that's not my Amex card to Experian twice. But you can use that not my account letter and send it to each bureau that lists the Amex account you're disputing.

Send every letter certified, return receipt requested, so you have documentation for the date the letter was received. The date they sign the return receipt is the date that starts the thirty-day clock ticking for their response.

If you don't have the actual Social Security card apply for a new one now.

They are legally allowed to refuse to investigate or reinvestigate disputes they think are credit repair company–generated or not written by the consumer.

Since you control when the letters are sent and how fast you follow up on the replies, your credit improves much more quickly than using a traditional credit repair company. Traditional credit repair organizations have no incentive to do anything quickly. They make money by charging monthly. They drag their feet to increase their revenue.

Date:

(Insert name of the credit bureau)

Credit Bureau Rep:

It has come to my attention that there are errors on my credit report. Case law, in *Cushman v. TransUnion*, courts ruled that information may not simply be "parroted" and that a "reasonable investigation" must take place upon receipt of a consumer complaint. According to the FCRA, when a credit reporting agency receives a dispute the CRA must prove it or remove it. I am demanding that proof be provided that these accounts are in fact mine or removed.

Simply verifying that names, addresses and or Social Security numbers match is insufficient. That's what fraud is, using information belonging to someone else to obtain credit. DO NOT tell me I need to file a police report as there is no requirement to do so under the Fair Credit Reporting Act. It's your obligation under the FDCPA to prove it or remove it.

In *Hinkle v. Midland Credit Management, Inc.*, the courts said, during a dispute and subsequent reinvestigation, with the original creditor, collector, or a credit bureau, that the original creditor or collector, must provide "account-level documentation." That means an original contract or similar proof, not just a printout of the payments that were made.

I am also notifying you that pursuant to 15 USC § 1681(a) that you should be aware the information furnishers have lost numerous suits and are unreliable.

I will await the appropriate time as prescribed by law at which time I will proceed to protect my good name and avail myself of any and all legal rights including but not limited to legal action.

The following is a list of the accounts that are not mine. (*I listed four spaces below. Use as many or as you need*)

(Insert Creditor here and account number exactly as it appears on your credit report)
(Insert Creditor here and account number exactly as it appears on your credit report)
(Insert Creditor here and account number exactly as it appears on your credit report)
(Etc. as needed)

Sincerely,
(Signature)
(Your name printed)
(Your mailing address)
(Social Security Number)
For Identification purposes, I am enclosing copies of:
My Social Security Card
My Driver's License *(or other government issued picture ID)*

Follow-Up Dispute Letter to the Credit Bureau

This is the letter to use as a follow-up to any letter in which the credit bureau claims that they verified that your account is correct as reported or similar wording. Never use the same reason for the dispute that you previously have used. The names of the creditor/ information furnishers and the reason for the disputes that I used here are examples. Use the creditors that appear on your credit report and use any dispute reason that you have not previously used.

Date:

(Insert name of the credit bureau)

Creditor: *(Insert name of information furnisher here)*

Credit Bureau Rep:

It has come to my attention that there are errors on my credit report. The following accounts are not mine. Case law, in *Cushman v. TransUnion*, the courts ruled that information may not simply be "parroted" and that a "reasonable investigation" must take place upon receipt of a consumer complaint. According to the FCRA, when a CRA receives a dispute the CRA must prove it or remove it. I demand that proof be provided that this account is in fact mine or that it be removed.

I will await the appropriate time as prescribed by law at which time I will proceed to protect my good name and avail myself of any and all legal rights.

The following is a list of the accounts, which are disputed for the following reasons:

(List Creditor/Information Furnisher
and then
Dispute Reason
for example Wrong Balance, Wrong Account Number, Wrong Date of Last Payment.)

Sincerely,
(Signature)
(Your name printed)
(Social Security Number)
For Identification purposes, I am enclosing copies of My Social Security Card
My Driver's License *(or other government issued picture ID)*

Incorrect Address Removal

Use this template if you want an address removed.
They usually will do this automatically upon request if
you use this format.

Date:

(Insert Credit Bureau Name)

Representative,

I recently reviewed my credit report. You have addresses linked to me that I have never lived at nor owned. The Fair Credit Reporting Act states that information contained on my credit report must be accurate, complete and verifiable. I am not sure where you would have compiled these address records for me, but they are inaccurate. Please remove the following incorrect addresses from my credit report:

(List address(es))

I look forward to your immediate cooperation.

Sincerely,
(Signature)
(Your name printed)
(Social Security Number)
For Identification purposes
I am enclosing copies of My Social Security Card (If you don't have the actual card, apply for a new one)
My Driver's License *(or other government issued picture ID)*

(NOTE: Do NOT include ID that has an address that you are claiming never to have lived at.)

Authorized User Removal

Send this if you are an authorized user and the account is delinquent. DO NOT send this if the account is current. If you are a co-signer this will not work. Co-signers are equally responsible for payment on accounts they co-signed.

ALL mailings must be sent certified return receipt requested so you have proof. Instead of requesting a green card receipt you can save about $1.65 by going online at USPS.com and requesting an electronic receipt, which will be emailed to you.

Date
(Name of Credit Bureau)
Re: *(Creditor)*
(Account Number)

Sir/ Madam,

I recently reviewed a copy of my credit report. There is a negative item listed by *(insert the name of the creditor here)*. I am now and always have been simply an authorized user on that account and NOT financially responsible. Accordingly, and as required under the Fair Credit Reporting Act I am notifying you that I want this item removed immediately.

Your refusal to do so will force me to exercise my rights under the FCRA and file suit. I will wait 30 days from the date you signed for this mailing for your notification of the deletion. After the statutory 30 days have passed, I will file suit along with notifying the Consumer Financial Protection Bureau and the FTC of your FCRA violation.

I look forward to your immediate cooperation.

Sincerely,
(Signature)
(Your name printed)
(Social Security Number)
For Identification purposes, I am enclosing copies of My Social Security Card (If you don't have the actual card, apply for a new one)
My Driver's License *(or other government issued picture ID)*

Date

(Insert the name of the Judgment Creditor or Tax Lien etc. holder here)

Bureau Representative:

I recently viewed a copy of my credit report maintained by your company. There is a glaring error that I demand be corrected. The balance on my (Insert account) is incorrect. I am aware that according to the FCRA you are required to verify the information or remove it. In *Cushman v. TransUnion*, it was established that verification cannot be accomplished when "the consumer reporting agency knows or should know that the original source is unreliable." With this letter, I am notifying you that the source of said information is in fact unreliable.

Accurate verification on your part cannot reasonably be concluded through a source such as the Court, Recorder's Office or County Clerk as their information is stale and rarely if ever, updated. Valid verification would be contacting the Original Creditor in this case (Insert for instance name of taxing authority like the IRS, bankruptcy court or the judgment creditor etc.). According to the FCRA, it is not my obligation to prove that I don't owe the balance that you report, it is your obligation to verify a correct amount and report every detail of the account accurately.

As we both know, you have no way of verifying a (insert here whatever you are disputing) since your third-party vendor never contacts the original creditor but simply parrots old, inaccurate documentation in violation of *Cushman v. TransUnion*.

I demand that you report the current balance not the original balance or remove this item from my credit report. I will pursue all legal remedies to clear my good name and restore my credit. I will wait 30 days from the date your representative signed for my certified mailing and then contact an attorney to start suit for your blatant, willful violation of the FCRA.

Sincerely,
(Signature)
(Your name printed)
(Social Security Number)
For Identification purposes, I am enclosing copies of:
My Social Security Card (If you don't have the actual card, apply for a new one)
My Driver's License *(or other government issued picture ID)*

ChexSystems

If a financial institution tells you that you are unable to open an account due to a ChexSystems report write this letter to ChexSystems or Google "Second Chance Checking Account Banks" and apply at one of those banks / credit unions.

ChexSystems is a pain in the butt to deal with and probably not worth the effort when you can just go to another financial institution.

Date:
ChexSystems, Inc.
7805 Hudson Road, Suite 100
Woodbury, MN 55125

To Whom It May Concern:

I have reviewed a copy of my ChexSystems report.

There is negative information reported by (Insert the name of the information furnisher) included in the file ChexSystems maintains under Social Security number *(Insert your SSN)*

I never had a banking relationship with this bank.

Please validate this information with (Insert the name of the information furnisher) and provide me with copies of any documentation associated with this account bearing my signature. In the absence of any such documentation bearing my signature, I demand that this information is immediately deleted from the file you maintain under my Social Security number.

I look forward to your immediate cooperation.

Sincerely,
(Signature)
(Your name printed)
(Social Security Number)
For Identification purposes, I am enclosing copies of:
My Social Security Card (If you don't have the actual card, apply for a new one)
My Driver's License *(or other government issued picture ID)*

Removal Foreclosure and Short Sale (First Letter)

The dispute process is no different for foreclosures and short sales debt than any other debt. You can dispute anything that is reported. Start with not my account and move on to wrong account number, wrong balance, etc. Anything they report you can dispute.

Date:

(Insert Creditor Name)
(Insert Account Number as Shown on Credit Report)

Dear *(Insert Name of the Credit Bureau)* Representative:

I recently viewed a copy of my credit report. There is a derogatory item from (Insert Name of Creditor). It shows a (insert "foreclosure" or "short sale" etc.) on a property at an address of (Insert address). I never lived at nor owned property at that address. Please remove this immediately.

I am applying for a job in 60–90 days and do not want erroneous information on my credit report that may be reviewed by my potential employer. If your erroneous reporting causes my potential employer to decline my application for employment, I will exercise all my rights under the FCRA. This will include contacting a consumers' rights attorney to initiate litigation. I will wait 30 days from the date you signed for this certified mailing for your notification of the removal of this error.

Sincerely,
(Signature)
(Your name printed)
(Social Security Number)
For Identification purposes, I am enclosing copies of:
My Social Security Card (If you don't have the actual card, apply for a new one)
My Driver's License *(or other government issued picture ID)*

Date:

(Insert Creditor Name)
(Insert Account Number as Shown on Credit Report)

Dear (Insert Name of the Credit Bureau) Representative:

I recently reviewed a copy of my credit report. There is a derogatory item from (Insert Name of Creditor). It shows a (insert "foreclosure" or "short sale") on a property at an address of (insert address). I never lived at nor owned property at that address. This is to inform you that the furnisher of this information is unreliable. I demand that this captioned item be removed immediately. Due to the sensitive nature of the position I am being considered for, the HR Department advised me that derogatory items such as this one will receive close scrutiny and may be a reason for not being hired. They advised me to clear this up immediately. I do not want erroneous information on my credit report when it is accessed by my potential employer. Your erroneous reporting will result in my potential employer declining my application for employment. I will at that time exercise all my rights under the FCRA. This will include contacting a consumers' rights attorney to initiate litigation. I will wait 40 days from the date you signed for this certified mailing for your notification of the removal of this error.

Please reinvestigate this error and remove it immediately.

Sincerely,
(Signature)
(Your name printed)
(Social Security Number)
For Identification purposes, I am enclosing copies of:
My Social Security Card (If you don't have the actual card, apply for a new one)
My Driver's License *(or other government issued picture ID)*

Date:
Creditor(s):
Account number(s):

Representative,

The Fair Credit Reporting Act and The Fair and Accurate Credit Transaction Act require that all information on my credit report be accurate. I am hereby notifying you that there (is/are) account(s) that have been fraudulently opened in my name. I have no idea who may have done this. I demand that these fraudulent accounts be deleted immediately, or I will hire a consumers' rights attorney to clear my good name and to sue you for statutory damages.

Do not tell me to file a police report as I am aware that the FCRA does not require me to do so. The FCRA dictates that you remove unverifiable information.

I will wait 30 days as required by law for your notification that these have been deleted.

I look forward to your immediate cooperation.

Sincerely,
(Signature)
(Your name printed)
(Social Security Number)
For Identification purposes, I am enclosing copies of:
My Social Security Card
My Driver's License *(or other government issued picture ID)*

Fraudulent Account Removal with the Original Creditor

Use this letter only if you filed a police report.

Date:
Creditor:
Account number:

Representative,

The Fair Credit Reporting Act and Fair and Accurate Credit Transaction Act require that all information on my credit report be accurate. I reviewed my credit report and I am hereby notifying you that there is an account with your organization that has been fraudulently opened in my name. I have no idea who may have done this and have filed a police report that I have enclosed. I demand that these fraudulent accounts be deleted immediately or I will hire a consumers' rights attorney to clear my good name and to sue you for statutory damages.

I will wait 30 days as required by law for your acknowledgment that these have been deleted at which time I will pursue legal options for removal and monetary damages.

I look forward to your immediate cooperation.

Sincerely,
(Signature)
(Your name printed)
(Social Security Number)
For Identification purposes, I am enclosing copies of:
My Social Security Card
My Driver's License *(or other government issued picture ID)*

Public Records Judgment / Tax Lien / Bankruptcy

Do NOT send this to the IRS, Recorder, or Court. This is to be sent to the credit bureau regarding a judgment, tax lien, or bankruptcy.

Date

(Lien or Judgment creditor's name)
(Account number as noted on your credit report)
Credit Bureau Employee:

I recently viewed a copy of my credit report maintained by your company. There is a glaring error that I demand be corrected. The balance on my *(insert judgment creditor, or tax lien, naming the taxing authority/ lien holder, for instance, the IRS or the State of Arizona, New York State etc. whatever state is appropriate)* is incorrect.

I am aware that per the FCRA/ FACTA you are required to verify the information or remove it. In *Cushman v. TransUnion*, it was established that verification cannot be accomplished when "the consumer reporting agency knows or should know that the original source is unreliable." With this letter, I am notifying you that the source of this information is unreliable.

Accurate verification on your part cannot reasonably be verified through a source such as the Court, Recorder's Office County Clerk or PACER as their information is stale and rarely updated. Valid verification would be contacting the Original Creditor in this case *(insert for instance name of taxing authority like the IRS or the judgment creditor)*. I am informing you that the balance you are reporting is inaccurate.

I am aware through conversations with (Insert the same as above, for instance, name of taxing authority like the IRS or the judgment creditor) that they are never contacted by (Insert name of the credit bureau. Equifax, Experian, TransUnion) or your vendor.

Per the FCRA/FACTA, it is not my obligation to prove that I don't owe the balance that you report. It is your obligation to verify a correct amount. Your third-party vendor never contacts the original creditor but simply parrots old, inaccurate outdated documentation. I demand that you remove this item from your records, or I will pursue all legal remedies to clear my good name and restore my credit. I will wait 40 days from the date that your organization signed for my certified mail for the error to be remedied. If said error remains unresolved, I will contact an attorney to start suit for your blatant and willful violation of law.

Sincerely,
(Signature)
(Your name printed)
(Social Security Number)
For Identification purposes, enclosed are copies of: My Social Security Card or driver's license

Medical Billing Dispute to Be Sent to the Hospital or Doctor

The dispute process is no different for a medical debt than any other loan. You can dispute anything that is reported. Start with "Not my account" and move on to wrong account number, wrong balance, etc. Anything they report you can dispute.

Date:

Creditor: *(as shown on Credit Report)*
Balance: *(as shown on Credit Report)*

Sir/Madam,

The above captioned medical bill is not mine. Simply verifying that someone used my name, Social Security number and/or address is insufficient to confirm that I am the person in question and owe this debt.

The court has ruled in *Hinkle v. Midland Credit Management, Inc.* that during a dispute and subsequent investigation, with the original creditor, collector or a credit bureau, that the original creditor or collector, must provide "account-level documentation." That means an original contract or similar proof. To this end, I am demanding an itemized bill to include but not limited to:

The diagnosis and procedure(s) performed that I am being billed for.
Dates of said procedure(s).
Cost and itemization of any medication you may have provided.
Cost and itemization of any medical devices you may have provided.
Office visits.
Consultation.
Hospital visits.
Miscellany.
Itemization of any insurance coverage.

As I am not the person who owes this bill, I am aware that providing the information requested may lead to third-party disclosure; a HIPAA violation. That's your problem, not mine. Do not tell me to file a police report since neither the Fair Credit Reporting Act nor the Fair Collection Practices Act requires the consumer to do so.

In addition, a provision of the FACTA is the notice of negative information provision, covered in section 623(A) (7). It requires notification prior to or within 30 days after a derogatory item is reported to a credit reporting agency. I have never received notification that this had been or was going to be reported to a CRA. FACTA (Fair and Accurate Credit Transactions Act) requires creditors, including doctors and hospitals, to give the consumer a "warning" notice, so the matter can be addressed before a negative item such as this is reported in error.

I also am requesting a copy or outline of your in-house procedures that enable you to avoid the problems that lead to the improper identification of patients and the subsequent misreporting to the credit bureaus.

In lieu of supplying the information required, you can simply cease all collection activity, including but not limited to removing all references to this bill you erroneously claim is mine from all credit reports. Along with cessation of collection activity, I require a commitment not to sell this account that you have erroneously linked to me. If this is not done within 30 days of the receipt of this letter, I will proceed to exercise all my legal rights, including litigation, to protect my good name.

I look forward to your immediate cooperation.

Sincerely,
(Signature)
(Your name printed)
(Social Security Number)
For Identification purposes, I am enclosing copies of:
My Social Security Card
My Driver's License *(or other government issued picture ID)*

Medical Billing Dispute to Be Sent to the Credit Bureau or Collection Agency

The dispute process is no different for a medical debt than any other loan. You can dispute anything that is reported. Start with "Not my account" and move on to wrong account number, wrong balance, etc. Anything they report you can dispute.

Date:

Creditor: *(as shown on Credit Report)*
Balance: *(as shown on Credit Report)*

To Whom It May Concern:

The above captioned medical bill is not mine. Please verify it with the reporting entity *(insert name as shown on credit bureau)*. Simply verifying that someone used my name, Social Security number and/or address is insufficient to confirm that I am the person in question who owes this alleged debt.

The court has ruled in *Hinkle v. Midland Credit Management, Inc.* that during a dispute and subsequent reinvestigation, with the original creditor, collector, or a credit bureau, that the original creditor or collector must provide "account-level documentation." That means an original contract or similar proof, not just a printout of the payments that were made.

15 USC § 1681i(a). A failure to conduct a reasonable reinvestigation violates the Fair Credit Reporting Act (FCRA). *Cushman v. TransUnion*, 115 F .3d 220, 223-224 (3d Cir. 1997). The burden to conduct the reinvestigation is on the credit reporting agency. It cannot be shifted back to the consumer. In plain English, that means you shouldn't be asking me for documentation to prove my dispute. I am not required to do your job. The law says you must reinvestigate and that if you can't prove it you are required to remove it.

Proof is not "simply parroting" erroneous information. I demand a documentation, including a billing showing medication, including prescriptions and procedures performed.

Do not tell me I am required to fill out a police report since the FCRA does not require the consumer to do that.

The legal obligation and requirement of a CRA to reinvestigate includes but is not limited to verifying the accuracy and dependability of the original source of the reported information. Since the information is blatantly incorrect, I am by way of this letter advising you that the information supplier is unreliable. Your duty often includes going beyond the original source. If the CRA is required to go beyond the original source depends on a number of factors, including but not limited to:

Did the consumer notify the CRA that the original source may be or is unreliable?

Should the CRA know that the information reporter, the original source, is unreliable?

As part of any reinvestigation, a CRA must provide the original source of the derogatory item with notification of exactly what the consumer is disputing along with any relevant documentation submitted by the consumer as per 15 USC § 1681i(a)(2). The Third Circuit Court of Appeals confirmed that a reasonable reinvestigation must mean more than simply making a cursory investigation and parroting unsubstantiated data.

A provision of the FACTA regulations is the notice of negative information provision, covered in section 623(A) (7).

I have never received a billing or notification that this was or was going to be reported to a CRA. FACTA (Fair and Accurate Credit Transactions Act) requires creditors to give you a "warning" notice.

I look forward to your immediate cooperation.

Sincerely,
(Signature)
(Your name printed)
(Social Security Number)
For Identification purposes, I am enclosing copies of:
My Social Security Card
My Driver's License *(or other government issued picture ID)*

Original Creditor Billing Error

This is if there is a legitimate billing error with the
original credit card issuer.

Date:

Creditor(s):
Account number(s):

Representative,
I am writing to point out an error that appears on my billing statement (insert date here)

Merchant's name:
Amount in error:

The problem is as follows:

I understand that the law requires you to acknowledge receipt of this letter within 30 days unless you correct this billing error before then. Furthermore, I understand that within two billing cycles but in no event more than 90 days, you must correct the error or explain why you believe the amount to be correct.

I look forward to your immediate cooperation.

Sincerely,

(Signature)

(Your name printed)

(Social Security Number)

For Identification purposes, I am enclosing copies of:

My Social Security Card

My Driver's License *(or other government issued picture ID)*

Too Old to Be Reported: They Must Remove This

The law (FCRA) requires that most negative items be removed from your credit report after seven years from the date they were originally reported. That date cannot be changed by anyone under any circumstances, for instance, the purchase of the account by a debt purchaser / collection agency. The exception to the seven-year limit are unpaid tax liens, which can remain forever, paid tax liens seven years from paid date, and Chapter 7 bankruptcies, ten years. (See my letters on removing tax liens and bankruptcies.)

Date:

Creditor:
Account number:

Representative,

The above-captioned account must be removed from my credit report. The Fair Credit Reporting Act, Section 605(a)(5) of the FCRA specifically mandates the maximum reporting time for this type of account is 7 years.

I will await the mandatory 30 days from your receipt of this letter for your reply. I will after that consult with a consumers' rights attorney to start litigation to enforce my rights under the law.

I look forward to your immediate cooperation.

Sincerely,
(Signature)
(Your name printed)
(Social Security Number)
For Identification purposes, I am enclosing copies of:
My Social Security Card
My Driver's License *(or other government issued picture ID)*

Wrong Social Security Number or Commingling of
Your Accounts with Another Person

Date:
Your Name:
Your SSN:

Credit Bureau Rep,

There is a major error on my credit report. You have erroneously reported my Social Security number as _(XXX-XX-XXXX)_ and/or commingled my reports with same. This causes major problems when I apply for credit. I demand that you make the appropriate changes. I have enclosed the proper ID to identify myself.

The FCRA says that upon request that all creditors, employers, and others that have pulled my credit report in the past 2 years must be notified of the changes. This is that request. I would also demand notification as to who you have notified of said change(s).

I will wait 30 days as required by law from the date the mailing receipt was signed as the law requires. After which time I will contact a consumers' rights attorney to protect my rights along with notifying the CFPB of your blatant and willful violation of the Fair Credit Reporting Act.

I await your swift reply.

Sincerely,
(Signature)
(Your name printed)
(Social Security Number)
For Identification purposes, I am enclosing copies of: My Social Security Card
My Driver's License _(or other government issued picture ID)_

Student Loan Removal Letter

The dispute process is no different for a student loan than any other loan. You can dispute anything that is reported: not my account, wrong account number, wrong balance, etc. Anything they report you can dispute.

Date:

(Insert the name of whatever you are disputing)
(Insert identifying account number)

Dear *(Insert Name of the Credit Bureau)* Representative:

I recently viewed a copy of my credit report. It shows a student loan identified as *(Insert name of Dept. of Education, original creditor (OC), collection agency (CA) etc. Whatever it shows as the current information reporter)* I have never taken out a student loan through *(Insert name of the OC)*.

In *Hinkle v. Midland Credit Management, Inc.*, the Courts said, during a dispute and subsequent reinvestigation, with the original creditor, collector or a credit bureau, that the original creditor or collector, must provide "account-level documentation." That means an original contract or similar proof, not just a printout of the payments that were made.

Please reinvestigate this error and remove it immediately.

Sincerely,
(Signature)
(Your name printed)
(Social Security Number)
For Identification purposes, I am enclosing copies of:
My Social Security Card
My Driver's License *(or other government issued picture ID)*

Student Loan Removal Second Letter

If they do not remove the disputed student loan after your first letter, keep sending them until they give up. Remember the person who cares the most wins. It's just a job to the CRA rep. They will eventually give up or screw up. Time and persistence are on your side.

Date:
(Insert what you are disputing, high balance, days past due etc.)
(Account number of what you are disputing)

Credit Bureau Rep,

I contacted *(Whoever the information furnisher is)* and they do not have documentation to show that this is my account. I am notifying you that (Information Furnisher) is an unreliable source for purposes of credit reporting accuracy.

When the reinvestigation reveals that the information is inaccurate or cannot be verified you must promptly delete the information. Per 15USC § 1681i(a). Failure to conduct a reasonable reinvestigation violates the FCRA. *Cushman v. TransUnion Corp.*, 115 F.3d 220, 223–24 (3d Cir.1997). The burden to conduct the reinvestigation is on the credit reporting agency. It cannot be shifted back to the consumer. It's not up to me to get a police report or anything else they want me to do. It's your job to verify the accuracy of the information they have erroneously provided.

The legal requirement of a credit reporting agency's reinvestigation is to verify the accuracy of its original information. This duty may include going beyond the original source. One of the instances that trigger going beyond the original source is a notification that the information furnisher is unreliable. With this letter, I am notifying you that *(Information Furnisher)* is an unreliable source. Their accuracy has been disputed numerous times and found to be incorrect.

In *Hinkle v. Midland Credit Management, Inc.*, the Courts said, during a dispute and subsequent reinvestigation, with the original creditor, collector or a credit bureau, that the original creditor or collector, must provide "account-level documentation." That means an original contract or similar proof, not just a printout of the payments that were made.

The Third Circuit Court of Appeals confirmed that a reasonable reinvestigation "must mean more than simply making a cursory investigation into the reliability of information that is reported to potential creditors." *Cortez v. TransUnion, LLC*, 617 F.3d 688, 713 (3d Cir.2010) (citing Cushman, 115 F.3d at 225).

I demand that this information be deleted immediately,

Sincerely,
(Signature)
(Your name printed)
(Social Security Number)
For Identification purposes, I am enclosing copies of: My Social Security Card
My Driver's License *(or other government issued picture ID)*

Date:
Creditor:
Account number:

Collection Agency Representative,

I am requesting that you provide validation of this debt. True validation should not be simply verifying the original creditor, my name, and Social Security number. Validation must have the requisites to enable it to be recognized and enforced by law.

In *Hinkle v. Midland Credit Management, Inc.*, the Courts said, during a dispute and subsequent reinvestigation, with the original creditor, collector, or a credit bureau, that the original creditor or collector, must provide "account-level documentation." That means an original contract or similar proof, not just a printout of the payments that were made.

Provide me with the following:

A copy of the original contract you allege that I signed.

An accounting of how payments were applied.

The interest that was added along with any ancillary charges.

Identify the original creditor.

Prove the Statute of Limitations has not expired.

Provide verification or copy of a judgment if there is one.

Provide licensing information that allows you to collect in my state.

Per the FDCPA §1692g, all collection activity must cease until validation is supplied. Collection activity includes credit reporting. Per the FDCPA this should not be reported to any CRA until validation is provided.

If you do not comply with these requests by *(insert 30 days from the date of the letter)* I will immediately file a complaint with the CFPB, the FTC, and the State Attorney General. I will contact a consumers' rights attorney to pursue my rights for private action under the FDCPA and or the FCRA where appropriate.

Sincerely,
(Signature)
(Your name printed)
(Social Security Number)
For Identification purposes, I am enclosing copies of:
My Social Security Card
My Driver's License *(or other government issued picture ID)*

GET GOING. DON'T LET THESE BLOODSUCKERS RUIN YOUR LIFE!!!!!

Without having a conversation with everyone who reads this book and without knowing the specifics of your particular circumstances, I covered everything I possibly could. For most people, the information in the book will be enough. If you have a particularly difficult situation that's not covered, I offer FREE consultations. I also conduct private, personalized coaching. My coaching includes, among other services, speaking to collectors, creditors, and the credit bureaus on your behalf along with composing letters as needed.

For complete details on coaching and for a FREE consult, go to my website at www.rickmansfield .com/credit-repair-coaching. You can email me using the form at the bottom of the website page.

Tell me you bought the book. I'm more than willing to answer one or two questions for people who have purchased my book.